CONVERSATIONS WITH
JAZZ MUSICIANS

Forthcoming
CONVERSATIONS

Conversations With Writers I

Conversations With Writers II

Conversations with Jazz Musicians

Louis Bellson   **Barry Miles**

Leon Breeden   **Sy Oliver**

Dizzy Gillespie   **Charlie Spivak**

Eric Kloss   **Billy Taylor**

Jimmy McPartland   **Phil Woods**

Sol Yaged

A Bruccoli Clark Book

Gale Research Company
Book Tower   Detroit, Michigan 48226

Editorial Director: Matthew J. Bruccoli

Managing Editor: C. E. Frazer Clark, Jr.

Project Editor: Richard Layman

Editors
Margaret M. Duggan
Glenda G. Fedricci
Cara L. White

Transcriptions: Rhonda W. Rabon

All interviews by Zane Knauss.

Technical assistance by Ed Breland.

Library of Congress Cataloging in Publication Data

Main entry under title:

Conversations with jazz musicians.

    (Conversations with ; v. 2)
    "All interviews by Zane Knauss."
    "A Bruccoli Clark book."
    1. Jazz musicians--Interviews. I. Knauss, Zane.
II. Series.
ML395.C66   785.4'2'0922 [B]   77-13012
ISBN 0-8103-0944-0

CONTENTS

LOUIS BELLSON • 2

LEON BREEDEN • 32

DIZZY GILLESPIE • 62

ERIC KLOSS • 78

JIMMY MCPARTLAND • 98

BARRY MILES • 118

SY OLIVER • 150

CHARLIE SPIVAK • 178

BILLY TAYLOR • 202

PHIL WOODS • 226

SOL YAGED • 262

INTRODUCTION

Conversations with Jazz Musicians has been planned with three chief goals in mind: first, to provide a forum for the leading jazzmen by preserving their comments on their work and careers; second, to provide readers with insights into the profession of musicianship in our time; third, to present an accurate image of the musicians as individuals—to reveal their aspirations, their feelings about music, and their responses to the world they live in.

The interviewer for this series was selected for his knowledge of the material and for his interviewing experience. He was asked to submit cassette tapes of his interviews along with short biographical sketches of his subjects and short descriptions of the settings of the interviews. The tapes were transcribed and edited at the *CONVERSATIONS* editorial office. Transcriptions were then sent to both interviewer and his subjects for approval before final editing.

Recordings of these interviews are being preserved and will become part of a permanent archive of oral history.

CONVERSATIONS WITH JAZZ MUSICIANS

Louis Bellson was born and raised in Rock Falls, Illinois. Before his eighteenth birthday, he was playing with the Benny Goodman band. After the war, he joined the Tommy Dorsey band, and he played with Harry James before going with Duke Ellington. Now fifty-four, Bellson continues to display his technical facility as a drummer, along with his talent as a composer and arranger. He is married to entertainer Pearl Bailey and the two are frequent headliners in clubs and theatres. In recent years, he has been recording with Count Basie and with his own big band, which is headquartered in California.

Louis Bellson

Louis Bellson and Zane Knauss met for this conversation on Seabrook Island off the coast of South Carolina in June 1977. Bellson was to be featured with the North Texas State 1 O'Clock Band at the Spoleto Festival. The first half of the conversation took place on a Trailways bus, while Bellson was waiting his turn on the bandstand. The second half of the conversation took place in a handsome condominium, while Bellson cooled down after his whirlwind performance.

Conversations: You mentioned when we first met, just an hour or so ago here at Seabrook, that after you set up your drums you wondered why you ever got into music. It's such a complicated business. When you started playing drums in Illinois you didn't have so much paraphernalia, did you?

Bellson: That's right. That was in the days when my dad had the music store and I was using one bass drum, an ordinary set. It's very interesting that you ask me that question because there's an article in one of the drum magazines—they have quite a few of them now; I think it's called *The Different Drummer* or something like that—where Buddy Rich states that all a drummer really needs is a bass drum, a small tom-tom, a big tom-tom, a couple of cymbals, and high hats. That's very true; those are the basic instruments that a drummer needs. However today, you know, we're in such a highly intensified musical world that drummers are called upon to do the impossible. So you have to have the standard concert toms if you're going to be doing some recording work or some studio work; and if you're in a certain band that requires a lot of different sounds, then you need all these extra things. Like in my case, I've got roto-toms and two bass drums—

Conversations: Well, the two bass drums are your signature.

Bellson: Yeah, that's an identification with me, right.

Conversations: How did that get started? Did you just decide to impulsively add a drum, or what?

Bellson: It was very interesting the way that happened. I just mentioned Buddy Rich, and Buddy ties in with this. Buddy and I are two of the drummers of a certain era. We were tap dancers when we were little.

Conversations: You were a tap dancer?

Bellson: Yeah. Buddy was known as "Traps" when he was three or four years old, with his parents. And I did a lot of tap dancing as a kid, too, along with the drumming. That ties in beautifully with drumming. Some of the great tap dancers of the past could always sit behind a set of drums—the two of them are just related. And so when I was going to high school I did a lot of playing—they used to put me on stage before a pep meeting for a basketball game or a football game, and I would do a lot of things between the one bass drum and the high hat. So one day I thought it would be nice to have another bass drum over here and still utilize the high hat. So in art class I designed this double bass drum setup—I guess it was around 1937 or '38—and I got an A on it. Of course, it took me a long time to take that idea to the drum factory.

Conversations: And they finally bought the idea?

Bellson: They finally bought the idea. At first there was a lot of criticism, like anything new. And then, of course, as time went on the various drummers in the swing groups and rock groups saw the value and, of course, today it's like standard equipment.

Conversations: What kind of music were you listening to that encouraged you to be a drummer in your high school days in Illinois?

Bellson: Well, first of all, I was very lucky, because coming from a musical family—my dad had the music store, and four boys and four girls—we just lived and breathed music twenty-four hours a day.

Conversations: All of the children were musicians?

Bellson: All of us, yeah. All four boys and four girls. And so, as a result, I really got what you would call a good basic foundation in music, and I thank my dad for that, because he taught us how to listen to Stravinsky, to Ravel. Then he said, "Okay. Now you want to listen to something else? You want to listen to jazz? Okay, fine." And then he taught us how to listen to string quartets.

Conversations: But he didn't push it.

Bellson: No, he didn't push it. He said, "If you're interested in music, learn to listen to everything, because music covers a vast territory and there's a lot going on when you talk about music. By the time most of us were thirteen years old we were familiar with almost every aria from every opera. So I'm glad that he gave us that education, because today it makes me a much more well rounded musician, and I can appreciate things with that kind of foundation.

Conversations: Your perspective is stronger, isn't it?

Bellson: Yeah, it really is, because I can go to a place like Oklahoma and listen to a marvelous country and western group and appreciate it, if they play it well. Why not? It's music.

Conversations: Very few people take that attitude. Jazz sometimes is still the odd person out, isn't it?

Bellson: Yes, it is. I must say it's getting better over here in this country, because a lot of middle-aged or older people, and especially a lot of young people are beginning to recognize who Dizzy Gillespie is, who Count Basie is, who Duke was.

Conversations: It's sort of belated, though. Sort of tragic, isn't it?

Bellson: It is.

Conversations: Basie has had a stroke—he's fine now; Kenton now is very ill but recovering; Ellington is gone. What does this mean? That these people will be venerated and new people will step up to take their place? Do you think jazz now will really grow roots and move?

5

Louis Bellson

Bellson: Oh, I think it will. We're here listening to Leon Breeden and his wonderful North Texas State Band. When you think about it, twenty-five years ago, when I was going to high school, we didn't have anything like this. Oh, my Lord! You were lucky if you had a pro band playing what these college kids are playing. Really.

Conversations: Let's talk a little bit about some of the bands you've been with. You were with Tommy Dorsey in the forties, weren't you?

Bellson: Well, yeah, I started—first of all, I started in 1942 with Ted Fio Rito. Remember him? He came through my hometown.

Conversations: Wasn't exactly a jazz group, was it?

Bellson: No, no. But he always had a good band. Jimmy Zito was in that band. He always had some good players. I stayed with him for three months, and then I got my big break to join Benny Goodman's band. There I was sitting up in Benny's band in 1942, a seventeen-year-old kid. Gene Krupa had just left a couple of years before, so there I am playing "Sing, Sing, Sing" and all these marvelous things with all these great guys in the band.

Conversations: Was Wilson still in the band?

Bellson: Teddy had just left. Jess Stacy was playing piano. Hymie Shertzer was still playing lead alto.

Conversations: This is before Mel Powell, then.

Bellson: That's right. Then Mel joined the band shortly after that. So I had a chance to work with Mel.

Conversations: That was a break, and you were how old?

Bellson: I was only seventeen years old at the time. So that was my first really big-name band. And then, of course, right after that I had a little three-year period with Uncle Sam. But I was very fortunate to be able to play with a good musical group when I was in the service.

Conversations: In the Special Services?

Bellson: Yeah. 304th, Army Service Forces Band, Washington, D.C. And then when I came back out of the services in '46, I repeated myself and went back with Ted Fio Rito for three months, then went back with Benny for another year. Then from that point, it was Tommy Dorsey for three years.

Conversations: Charlie Spivak has suggested that Tommy was pretty tough sometimes.

Bellson: Yes.

Conversations: Did you find him to be difficult?

Bellson: Tommy was really tough, he was. But I understood why he was; he was a very demanding perfectionist. He wanted an A 1 performance at all times. He didn't care whether you had just finished a 500-mile trip on the bus and you hadn't eaten—that didn't enter into the picture. All he knew was you're on the bandstand; you've got your horn; there are people out there; and let's show them we have a great band. So with that kind of attitude, I could never really criticize that man for what he did, because his love for music made him just realize that that was it— performance, you know.

Conversations: What kind of job was it for you to succeed Buddy Rich in the Tommy Dorsey band? His personality was really associated with the group.

Bellson: Well, I had to do that quite often, because, see, Buddy and I are almost the same age—he's got me by about four years. He still thinks that I am the same age as him and I always put him on. I say, "No! I remember you when I was in knee pants." But he's a dear friend. We've been friends for thirty-five years. He's one of the all-time greats; he's a great player. But Buddy and I sort of grew up together. When I was with Benny's band, he was with Tommy's band. But later on, after I had worked with Tommy, and then I had joined Harry James's band, and then Ellington's band—

Conversations: And Buddy was with him, too—with James.

Bellson: Yeah, with James. Buddy went back to work with Tommy a couple of times and then I had to take his place, because he got sick a couple of times, and Tommy would call up and say, "Hey, come on down and help us out." So it was one of those things where I would fill in for Buddy. Then, of course, I

7

Louis Bellson

took over his band for him for a month about two years ago. He had a serious back operation.

Conversations: Are your styles similar?

Bellson: Well, yes and no. The yes part is that we feel rhythmically about the same, because we came up in the same era. But technically we may be the same, too—we're both known as technicians who can still play time in the band.

Conversations: Are you suggesting that the younger drummers can't?

Bellson: Well, no, there are some, though—there are some drummers, even from our era, who were known as great drummers but were not necessarily solo drummers, like Dave Tough, for example. To me he was a marvelous player. But you never let him play more than an eight-bar drum solo, because he wouldn't play it.

Conversations: He was with Dorsey, too, at one point.

Bellson: He was with Tommy, with Benny, Artie Shaw. Buddy was a great time player, and to me—I'm sure a lot of other drummers like Joe Jones and Buddy will agree—when you are a time player that's all you need to do. If you can play solos, great—that's secondary. But I'd hate to see a guy that can play great solos that can't play time in the band; then he's defeated his purpose, you know.

Conversations: He's just a showman.

Bellson: Right.

Conversations: This percussion group that you put together at one point with Persip and Philly Joe Jones and Buddy—you took it to Japan, didn't you?

Bellson: Well, that was George Wein that did that, you know.

Conversations: What did you do, the four of you? That's a lot of drums.

Bellson: First of all, we were accompanied by a wonderful small group. Blue Mitchell was playing trumpet, and Junior Cook was playing tenor, and wonderful Toshiko Akiyoshi—who has a great big band now with her husband, Lew Tabackin—she was playing piano, and she was playing great then. I must add—that big band that they have now is just beautiful. She's marvelous, and she writes just tremendously. But anyway Toshiko was playing piano, and the bass player was Gene Wright, or somebody like that. So what happened on a combination like that is Charlie Persip went out and played first with the quartet—or, no, the first thing on the program was all four of us came out and we made our initial showing. We played fours with the group.

Conversations: Lots of showmanship.

Bellson: Yeah, yeah. But it was laid out well so that each guy played a little bit and then a short solo. Then each guy did his half-hour segment with the group—like Charlie Persip did a half hour, then Philly Joe Jones. Then they reserved the second half for Buddy and myself. Then at the very end, all four of us came out and did our solo bits again. The Japanese are great music lovers and tremendous drum lovers. They just flipped; they just flipped.

Conversations: Tell me about your introduction to Duke Ellington. How did you happen to get into the band the first time? I know you were there several times.

Bellson: Yeah. Well, with Duke—see, I was with Harry James's band, and when I worked with Harry James's band, Juan Tizol was a member of that band and so was Willie Smith.

Conversations: Willie was playing alto.

Bellson: For those that don't know, Willie Smith was with Jimmie Lunceford for many, many years. And Juan had been with Ellington for many, many years. So we worked with Harry about a year. All of a sudden Duke, who knew Tizol very well, said, "Look, I need an alto saxophone player and I need a drummer. So how about you and Willie Smith and Louie Bellson joining my band?"

Conversations: Quite an honor, wasn't it?

Bellson: To show you what a great man Duke was—you know, for us to leave Harry James. . . that's not very nice to leave Harry. But Harry was beautiful. He said, "Look, I love Duke, and it isn't every day you get a chance to join Duke's band, so you've got my blessings. Go ahead and have a ball." Which I thought was really great of Harry to do, you know. So the three of us joined Duke— Willie Smith and Tizol and I.

Conversations: Did you succeed Greer?

Bellson: Well, no, Sonny Greer had left the band about a year and a half before that, and Duke had Charlie Smith, a left-handed drummer, with him when I joined.

Conversations: How did it feel to get into a band with such giants? First of all there was Ellington; Billy Strayhorn was still alive; there was Harry Carney, Cat Anderson, from South Carolina, Ray Nance.

Bellson: Ray Nance, Clark Terry, Jimmy Hamilton, Paul Gonsalves. Well, I'll tell you, that was one of the highlights in my career. No question about it, working with that band was just unbelievable. Right from Duke, you know, he, first of all, and Strayhorn, were such magic humanitarians. Then on top of that, their musical abilities were just—

Conversations: Which personality dominated there, Strayhorn's or Ellington's?

Bellson: Well, they were both on an even keel, because there was a respect there for one another. You never felt like Strayhorn was above Duke, or Duke was above Strayhorn, because they were like one. I've never seen a team like that.

Conversations: How does it feel to go into a band like that for the first time and sit down at the drums and Ellington calls out whatever he's going to play and you've got to start playing? Are all the eyes on you?

Bellson: Yeah.

Conversations: A new man in town?

Bellson: Right. Well, first of all, I had to pinch myself after I played with that band the first three days, because we hit it off so great. I couldn't believe that I was sitting on the bandstand with Ellington and this great band, which I had admired for so many years. Then really what made it doubly just a phenomenal thing for me was when Duke walked up to me—now here's Ellington, and Strayhorn was with him—he said, "I understand you wrote a couple of pieces, arrangements. Why don't you bring them in for the next rehearsal?" I thought to myself this can't be true, because there's no way in the world I would bring in an arrangement in front of this man and Strayhorn. They're the ultimate.

Conversations: Did you?

Bellson: I did. I brought in an arrangement of "Skin Deep" that I did and "The Hawk Talks," and he recorded both of them.

Conversations: Were you on the record?

Bellson: Right, and I just couldn't get over it. There again was one of the most beautiful things that could ever happen to me, you know.

Conversations: I noticed that you, having played with bands over a period of time, watch the instrumentalists very closely, and you almost come up with the punctuation marks for what the men are doing. That calls for tremendous discipline, but also a superb knowledge of each musician. Do you study the musicians that you play with?

Bellson: It's like a baseball team. I know exactly what the capabilities of the guys in my band are, because, being a writer, a composer, and an arranger of some sorts, you—that's what made Ellington so great: he knew every man in that band and he wrote according to their ranges, according to their abilities. That's what made it such a highly specialized band.

Conversations: That was his instrument.

Bellson: That was his instrument; that's exactly right. So when he wrote a composition, he made sure that he didn't go above a certain range for Ray Nance. With Cat Anderson he had no problem, because Cat was—

Conversations: He was a screamer.

Bellson: Yes. Super chops. With other players he found the ultimate in what they could do. He knew how to write certain

11

tunes that were well adapted to them, and he knew how to present music.

Conversations: How about you? Did he also discern what your strengths were and what your weaknesses were?

Bellson: Oh absolutely, absolutely. He knew exactly. I was in on the first sacred concert that he wrote, which was done at Grace Cathedral in San Francisco. He wrote a piece especially for that called "In the Beginning God," which is a religious piece. He said to me, "I want you to play a drum solo in church." Well, I looked at him, and I said, "A drum solo in church? Does that make sense to you, Duke?" He said, "Yeah. Let me show you what I mean." So he went on to explain "In the Beginning God," the thing that he wrote. "Now," he said, "you know, in the beginning we had thunder and lightning, right? That's you." Well, just that little explanation made me play my drum solo in church a different way—I had to imitate thunder and lightning. That's the way he was. He knew how to explain things; he knew how to put everything in its certain context so that you were always aware of what was going on. And he knew I could do that. That's what happened, and it came off great.

Conversations: Does a drummer of your ability run the risk of sometimes upstaging lesser musicians? The natural attention of any audience is on the man with the sticks. Is this a difficult thing to play down, to keep in perspective?

Bellson: Well, it is. I'll tell you why: because drums seem to be—being the second instrument (the first is the voice), drums are very exciting, and Dizzy and a lot of instrumentalists talked about this. That's why if they've got a good drum soloist—like Buddy Rich, or Joe Morello, or Joe Jones—they put those guys on last, because what's going to follow it? If he's a great player, nothing can really follow because of the excitement. On this last tour I just did, Oscar Peterson is playing piano—now you can't get any better than that—Joe Pass is playing guitar—

Conversations: Can't get any better than that.

Bellson: And Niels Orsted Pedersen is the bass player, from Copenhagen, a gigantic player. Yet Oscar said, "You're going to play your number last." So there's something about drums that

12

just creates an excitement. I will say this, though, that I agree with a lot of critics that say, "Don't tell me, another drum solo!" because they've heard a lot of drum solos performed by drummers who really can't play. That's why I respect the young drummer playing with the North Texas State Band. He doesn't really have to play a long, stretched-out drum solo, because he is taking care of what he has to do in the band, which is the primary thing of really making that band sound—playing the time or whatever he has to do, making the sound effects. If he's got the solo ability next, great. But that's why a lot of critics complain, you know, they hear—maybe there are certain bandleaders that make it compelling for the drummer: "Hey, you've got to play a fifteen-minute drum solo." Well, maybe he's not designed to do that, you know. That's why a lot of critics say, "Oh, don't tell me, another drum solo." And they're right, in many respects, because a lot of guys play them that shouldn't play them. But when you hear a guy like Buddy, or Joe Morello, or Jo Jones, or Billy Cobham, or Steve Gadd, this kind of player, then you say, "Wow! There it is!"

Conversations: Now you were away from Ellington for quite some time, and after about twelve years you went back with him.

Bellson: That's right.

Conversations: Did you find that the band was different, that it had a different sound?

Bellson: Yes.

Conversations: Was Ellington different?

Bellson: Duke wasn't different. The only difference, I would say, in Duke was—you see, with the particular band that I was in in 1951, and way before that, Ellington's band had a reputation of when you saw them on a stage—like in a theatre or at a ballroom when you first heard the band—all you saw was Duke Ellington playing piano, and maybe Sonny Greer was up there, and Carney was always there. You saw about four or five guys.

Conversations: And Hodges.

Bellson: Well, Hodges was one of the last guys to come up. You saw about four or five guys playing. Then as twenty minutes went

13

by you saw five more guys come up on the stand, and after about forty minutes the whole band was there.

Conversations: Gonsalves was last.

Bellson: Right. Even before Paul, when Ben Webster was there, the same thing. But in that particular band, Duke looked up on the bandstand at nine o'clock, and everybody was there—Clark Terry was there, mainly because Tizol was pretty much of a disciplinarian, and Willie Smith was playing lead alto. So when he started the band at nine o'clock, the whole band was there. It really made him feel good that "Wow! Man, these guys are so interested in taking care of business that they're there." And we were there every night for two years. At nine o'clock—bam!—we were there!

Conversations: Why did Hodges leave the band and Smith come in? Was there something between Ellington and Hodges?

Bellson: No. They always had a great relationship. I think Hodges decided to form a small group, which he did, and he had a couple of hit records going—"Castle Rock" was one of them, if you remember. He was doing well with a small group, and then finally Johnny just decided to go back with Duke after awhile.

Conversations: You're doing a lot of writing. Tell me about this ballet music that you are getting into. This is serious stuff for you, isn't it?

Bellson: Well, the ballet music was originally commissioned and written for Dizzy Gillespie. It was written for a trumpet soloist and for about twenty-five dancers.

Conversations: You did it in Vegas first.

Bellson: Yeah. We did it in Vegas first, right. And then I did it once, and Stan Kenton was doing a series of concerts in L.A.— they were called Neophonic concerts. I did it again with Conte Candoli playing trumpet, who was a great player. And then this last time we did it, Doc Severinsen played it.

Conversations: I think I read somewhere it's also been up in Vancouver.

Bellson: Yeah, that's right. Harriott did it up in Vancouver.

Conversations: Are you moving into the writing of classical music now?

Bellson: Well, I've been doing some writing—I've got six things to my credit for a full orchestra. In the last couple of years I have done a concert with the Milwaukee Symphony, and with the Glendale Symphony this last year. It looks like I'll be doing something with some of the major symphonies now. Pearl and I did Boston Pops with Arthur Fiedler, also.

Conversations: What's the emphasis? You've mentioned solo trumpet, but is your emphasis percussion?

Bellson: Oh, yeah. The ballet, which is initially a solo for trumpet, still employs the full orchestra; but on the ballet you have to take the entire swing band and put it right in the middle of the symphony.

Conversations: Does it fit? A lot of people say symphonic orchestras and jazz don't mix.

Bellson: Well, what I did was to make sure that all the swing figures were played by the guys in the band.

Conversations: What are you doing with fiddles all this time?

Bellson: Well, you can give them certain notes, certain notes they are familiar with playing. But it's hard to give a violin player, a violin section, a passage that you would give a reed section. It's not going to sound the same way, because when they play a dotted eighth and sixteenth, it sounds precisely measured. You can't tell them to play a rolling eighth-note style like a Basie thing, because they don't play that way. Unless you're going to get twenty-five Joe Venutis, and they're not around, you won't get that kind of interpretation. You've got to just be careful about the way you write for a string section. That's why on the things I did with the swing band, I made sure that they played the figures when I wanted to hear swing things. Then the other things that I wrote—the woodwind things and everything—are more or less in a context with the orchestra. That way you get a balance, you know.

Conversations: So you think there decidedly can be more and more interplay between symphonic music and jazz.

Louis Bellson

Bellson: Oh, absolutely. And I really feel that with the symphonies coming up in the future—we've got all young players. They're so great, because they're able to give you the interpretation that Beethoven wanted and can turn right around and give you an interpretation that Dizzy wants.

Conversations: On a recent recording with Basie you did one thing I liked very much with Lockjaw Davis and with Zoot Sims. Basie really is a rhythm section by himself. How do you adjust to him? Your drumming is very different than it was with Ellington.

Bellson: Well, all I do is what Basie always tells his guys in the band—just listen. So when a guy like Ray Brown and I play—do a trio with him—all we do is "Basie picks a tune." Of course, you must understand Basie—simplicity with him is the greatest thing. He doesn't get involved with anything like 5/4 or 15/8; he just plays straight-ahead, pure swing.

Conversations: It's not a complicated response, is it?

Bellson: That's not him—what he does up there in the top range of the piano, that's him. And so when you record with him, it's really the easiest. If you can play time, and you've got a good bass player, it's tailor-made for you. There it is.

Conversations: Do you have to adjust for him when he plays organ in some of the things you've done?

Bellson: Yeah. You just think Basie, and you think swing, and you watch him, and listen to him, and there it is.

Conversations: How about two-beat, have you been messing with that?

Bellson: Oh, yeah. We do that with Basie. We did that on that album too, where Basie will just look over at the rhythm section and go like this—play the first couple of choruses in two, and then we'll go into four, you know.

Conversations: It's really improvisation.

Bellson: But Lunceford made the two things sound, you know. Nothing can swing any harder than two, really.

Conversations: What are you going to do now for encores?

You're a pretty busy man, I gather. You're in here with the North Texas State Band, and I've just heard you talking on the sidelines about going here, going there. You're doing everything. Are you in effect jobbing as an individual talent, or are you going with groups?

Bellson: Well, I have my own big band out in California and we've been very successful the last ten years working in clubs— like Donte's; we worked Disneyland; we do a lot of colleges. Thank God for the colleges—for every band, as far as that goes. And we're able to do an album every six months or so now for Norman. And so that keeps us g〈 〉〈 〉.

Conversations: Norman Granz?

Bellson: Yeah. We don't make a〈 〉 〈 〉emendous amount of money with the band, but I'm not interested in that. I'm interested in doing something that has musical value and is constructive, because I feel that that's always going to win out.

Conversations: Big bands are going to stay alive, then?

Bellson: Oh, absolutely. I agree with Harry James—they never left. They lost their potency for a while because when the rock things came in, especially with the quartets, that was predominant. But you never lost sight of the fact that there was a Basie, an Ellington, a Woody Herman, and now there's a Thad Jones-Mel Lewis, which is a great band.

Conversations: Kenton?

Bellson: Kenton. Buddy Rich. They were always on the scene.

Conversations: But that's just a handful of names compared to the forties.

Bellson: That's true.

Conversations: Is it going to come back with as much force?

Bellson: Yeah. I believe that, because the young people are making that happen in colleges and high schools.

Conversations: Where do students that you are playing with here—from North Texas State and other schools—go? Do they go into rock, into classical, into big bands, or what?

Louis Bellson

Bellson: That's an important question. First of all, we were talking about what is happening in the schools. That's great. What's happening now is—like three years ago from North Texas State, Lyle Mays and Steve Houghton and Herbie Steward, all three, joined Woody Herman's band. Now that was a beautiful break. But five years ago I thought in my own mind: now that the music is so built-up in the schools and you've got maybe 300 college guys graduating every year—

Conversations: Who are good musicians.

Bellson: Where are they going to go?

Conversations: Where are they going to go?

Bellson: Well, that's a big problem today, because if Basie has got his guys and—okay, it's true, Stan Kenton and, I think, some guys in Buddy's band were playing in this group. But there should be maybe ten or twelve more bands on the road for guys of this caliber to be able to go out and say, "Hey, I've got a position here and here."

Conversations: I suppose the same thing would apply to people who are writing for this size group. What are they going to do?

Bellson: Right. See, an important factor in music today is when you talk about the young people—like ten, eleven, and twelve, that's where you've got to educate them.

Conversations: How do you do this?

Bellson: You see, if you've got children—like my children, when they went through nine, ten, eleven years old, I tried to educate them, to tell them, "Look, I'll listen to the Beatles and I appreciate them. But you've also got to come over here and listen to Stravinsky and listen to the Budapest String Quartet, because that's music, too." Because today, if the disc jockey is going to pump certain kids with just one kind of music, they're going to be very narrow with music. As a result, they're not going to know what's happening over here and over there. That's where we have to educate the kids, so that by the time they are eighteen and nineteen years old, or even before that, they're well versed enough that they can come hear a band like this and appreciate it.

Conversations: Would cheek-to-cheek dancing help if it came back?

Bellson: Well, not only the dancing, but the important thing is like what Leon Breeden's doing in the schools now. If you educate somebody in grade school and high school and college, so they know who the great players were and are, and they develop their musicianship, then that's the answer.

Conversations: How does what's happening in America compare to your experiences in Europe? You said the Japanese liked percussion and they dig jazz. What's happening in Europe? Are many people picking it up?

Bellson: Yeah. In Europe it's always been jazz. Europeans think jazz is a dedicated American creative form, and it is treated as such.

Conversations: Is it a good place for you to work personally?

Bellson: Oh, it's a great place. Like when a Dizzy Gillespie is announced over there, he gets a standing ovation, but the standing ovation—I don't mean to say standing ovation; it's done in sincerity. It's respect for a great man who has made a contribution. He is an artist, see. And it's getting better over here because of the young people, but jazz still doesn't quite have the respect that it has in Europe.

Conversations: Should jazz be taken into the grade schools and high schools?

Bellson: Sure, why not? Because they're finding out now that the word "jazz," like Duke used to say, was originally a dance. And now they're realizing that jazz is associated with artists. So that's why today we have the stage bands.

Conversations: You have the type of thing you're doing with Diz—a ballet.

Bellson: Sure.

Conversations: Do you run the risk of flattening the music out so that it becomes unidentifiable? For example, country music is, they say, getting flattened out; it has rock in it now, or it has folk,

Louis Bellson

or something, and it really isn't country music. Will jazz get watered down like that?

Bellson: Today the new jazz musicians are combining a lot of the contemporary things and they're calling it "Latin jazz" or "Latin rock" or whatever.

Conversations: Without being facetious, how on earth can a man of your age do what you've done? You do the equivalent, I think, of nine miles' jogging, for heaven's sake, in about half an hour. How do you do this?

Bellson: Well, you really have to build up to that, actually. You know when we were talking about drum solos before?

Conversations: Right.

Bellson: I've always been sort of a health nut. I'm careful about the amount of food and what food I eat, you know; I'm really a nondrinker and nonsmoker. Like you say, in order to perform like I do, you really have to be in physical shape. So I jog from four to five miles in the morning at home. When I'm on the road I try to do two or three miles in the morning before breakfast. I exercise a lot and swim a lot, because you really have to be an athletic person to play drums. Not only do you have to have a clear mind, but your body has got to be in shape, because everything is moving, you know—your hands and feet so. . .

Conversations: Certainly your mind.

Bellson: In the demanding pieces that you have to play these days, especially a lot of the rock things, boy, you've got to really—

Conversations: Do you play rock?

Bellson: Oh, yeah, I love to do it. I think the contemporary rock things are just like jazz when it started. There are some good players and there are some bad players. And the youngsters who are coming up today who are the good players, they are just playing some fantastic things.

Conversations: How about the technical end of the drum playing? I've talked with classical musicians who say that even though they've been on a concert stage for fifty years, they still

20

have to practice and practice and practice. Is this applicable to drums, too?

Bellson: Absolutely.

Conversations: Do you still have to play every day?

Bellson: Oh, yeah. Whenever I get a chance I practice as much as I can; I still practice sight-readings. I listen to records to see what's happening that's new on the scene. And there's always something that you can work on with your instrument. A person himself knows where he's faltering a little, and he works on those little flaws, too.

Conversations: You can sense this?

Bellson: That's right, absolutely. There's an interesting interview that Artur Rubinstein did. You know, he just retired about a year ago, after about sixty or sixty-five years of playing.

Conversations: He was over ninety.

Bellson: And the interviewer said, "Well, it's nice to retire knowing that you mastered the keyboard." He said, "Wait a minute. I didn't master any keyboard." He said, "You know how I feel about the keyboard? I've been playing for sixty years; but if I were to go back and start all over again, that piano would be just like me courting a girl. I would have to start all over again, get married to the piano, and find out what makes it tick." Now that's after sixty years of playing. So I feel that when a person reaches a certain scope—like Dizzy Gillespie, he keeps practicing; guys like Maynard Ferguson, Doc Severinsen, they keep practicing and practicing, keep the chops up, keep the ideas going. That's why I do a lot of clinics in colleges. They're the ones that keep me in shape. If I do anything for them they, in turn, keep me at a level where I'm listening. Like in this wonderful band. Look at the great things that Lyle Mays, that young piano player, wrote. When I hear something like that it encourages me to get back in and sharpen up my pencil and say, "Wow, man, here we go!"

Conversations: When you play it looks like a cerebral exercise, that you are literally composing. Is that correct, or not?

Louis Bellson

Bellson: Yeah. You see, that's what I meant when we were talking about drum solos before. One violin player came pretty close to it: he said, "You've got your own orchestra when you play."

Conversations: So are you composing, then?

Bellson: That's right, every solo that I play. It's true that there are certain things that you play, like maybe a finale or something, little things that every drummer does, but in the interim most of the stuff is ad-lib. Now tonight when we play, I may start out a phrase in 3/4 tempo and stay with 3/4 for a long time before I get into the 4/4 thing. But that's all pure improvisation.

Conversations: But it's like a story line—it has a beginning and an end.

Bellson: Yeah, that's right; that's right. Well, that's what I'm trying to convey, so if I've done that I'm glad. You see, as I said before, if you allow me to say I'm a composer or an arranger, that's the way I think. I not only think rhythmically when I play drums, but I think melodically—that is, I keep the melody line, bass line, or whatever of the tune I'm playing at that time in my mind, and I invent and play according to that tune as well as the rhythmical structure.

Conversations: So you have both things going at the same time, like playing an organ with a number of manuals.

Bellson: Yeah, that's right, because an organ player does have the top and the bottom—he's got the bass notes; he's got the melody; and he's got the in-between. And that's what I try to do.

Conversations: You mean your little injections there of your drumsticks with the bells—little bells on them?

Bellson: Yeah, with the jingles on them.

Conversations: I couldn't help but think of your statement earlier about your tap-dancing career. It comes off exactly like tap dancing. Is this intended?

Bellson: Yeah. Many years ago that was my idea, along with the two bass drums. The tambourine was always an interesting instrument to me, so I thought one day, looking at the tambourine which has a series of double jingles all the way around, I said, "I'm going to take a set of those jingles and put them on a drumstick and see what happens. And of course, when I play with Basie's band now, he always tells me, "Give me the bells." He calls them the "bells." Those sticks, when you play regular jazz, are great. They're good for rock things, too, and good for bossa nova things.

Conversations: Maybe this is an unfair question, but who did you try to emulate when you got started as a drummer? Was there somebody in the woodwork that you looked to, that you tried to copy?

Bellson: There was never one guy. I listened to all of them, because I felt that if I had one guy that I idolized, that's not really good, because then if you try to put yourself in his shoes, or try to play like him, I think that's wrong. You can listen to him and maybe pick up some ideas. But there's only one Jo Jones; there's only one Billy Cobham; there's only one Buddy Rich; there's only one Chick Webb, you know. And that's what made those guys so great—like Buddy, for instance, Buddy Rich. Now Buddy's drum set is set up exactly like Gene Krupa's was. Now Buddy will tell you he really dug Gene. A lot of things that Gene did, Buddy listened to, and I did too. But that doesn't mean that we copied everything that Gene did. There are some youngsters today who copy Buddy Rich—try to copy him right to the tee. I think that's wrong, and I tell them when I'm in their company.

Conversations: Do your own thing, then?

Bellson: I say, "You know, it's all right to respect a great man like that, but listen to some of the things that he does. You may pick out a few of them, but play the way you play, because everybody is an individual. And if you try to emulate him you're going to be criticized for it, because pure copyists just don't make it."

Conversations: What did you pull out of Webb? His quickness?

Bellson: Well, Chick Webb, to me, was—first of all, he had the affliction; he had the back problem.

Conversations: Yeah, he was dwarf-sized.

Louis Bellson

Bellson: He had to play the drums to stay alive, really. But he had what we call—you know, when we call the shout chorus in jazz, that means the guys say, "Okay, we're going home." That means the drummer, the rhythm section, has got to set it up so that when that band comes in for that shout chorus, that is the end and you're stomping. Well, usually in those days they had a four-bar break or a two-bar break, sometimes an eight-bar drum break, that led that band into that shout chorus. Well, Chick Webb was a master with that. By the time he played those two bars, four bars, or eight bars, boy, that band—well, he kept the band swinging all the time. He was a natural drummer. He couldn't read—no technique as far as knowing how to read and doing this and that. He just did it. He sat down and played. He was gifted. God gave him a gift and he just played.

Conversations: How about Zutty Singleton, Cozy Cole, and Dave Tough? Did they have something to give, too?

Bellson: Well, you know, Cozy Cole was a little different than Dave Tough and Zutty in that Cozy could read. He was a schooled musician.

Conversations: Tough couldn't?

Bellson: Dave could not read too well. In fact, Dave Tough could not really make an even snare drum roll. Now that's amazing, but he's known for the other things he did.

Conversations: How did he survive under Tommy Dorsey?

Bellson: Well, when Dave Tough had to play an act—in those days you had vaudeville to play, and invariably you played for a juggler or some kind of acrobatic act where the drummer was very important. Well, Dave used to walk up to the act and just apologize to them and say, "I can't. I'll do the best I can, but I'm not that kind of drummer."

Conversations: And they'd buy it?

Bellson: That's right. They respected Dave Tough, but when it came to playing brushes and time on the cymbals and doing his thing, he was just magic.

Conversations: Singleton, Cole, these people worked with very small groups. Were they as effective with big bands, or did they ever have an opportunity to play with big bands?

Bellson: Oh, yeah. Of course, Cozy worked with Cab Calloway's big band. And Zutty worked at one time, I think, with Louis Armstrong's big band. And then we have to mention another guy by the name of Big Sid Catlett. He was another drummer who played great in a small group and played great in a big band, too.

Conversations: There was a place in New York when bop was flowering called Minton's, where people used to jam all the time.

Bellson: Minton's. I was going there all the time.

Conversations: You too?

Bellson: Oh, man.

Conversations: Did you get up on the stand?

Bellson: I played in there once, but I was really a spectator for a long time, because you'd walk into that place and the tenor saxophone players would be, maybe, Pres—Lester Young—and Ben Webster and Don Byas and Dizzy would be there with Roy and, maybe, Charlie Shavers.

Conversations: Are you talking about Roy Eldridge?

Bellson: Yeah.

Conversations: Parker showed up there, too, didn't he?

Bellson: Charlie Parker would be in, Johnny Hodges. And when the piano players went in, it would be Bud Powell, and you'd see Teddy Wilson, and Art Tatum.

Conversations: Well, did drummers have a place to cut each other up, too?

Bellson: Oh, yeah, sure—Jo Jones—I saw Jo in there many times. Jo Jones, Big Sid Catlett, I saw them in there.

Conversations: Did you ever get into any kind of sessions like that?

Louis Bellson

Bellson: Oh, yeah, I went up there and played a couple of times.

Conversations: It's said that they used to try to cut each other pretty good, you know, the tenor men, the trumpets, and so forth. Did drummers do the same?

Bellson: Oh, sure. But, you know, the scene in those days like in Minton's and Harlem—sure, it was a competitiveness, but there was a certain tone of love in the competitiveness. Like with the three tenor men. Now if those three guys were sitting here right now, Don Byas, Pres, and Ben Webster—all three of them are gone; they are not with us anymore. They loved one another, but when they got up on the bandstand, they played for keeps. It wasn't a thing like, "Hey, I'm going to cut you." They just played. If Ben played something, then Don would play something just like, "Well, listen to this," you know. It was a competitiveness but it was. . .

Conversations: It was genuine affection and appreciation for each other's talent.

Bellson: It's like the feeling that Duke and Basie had for one another.

Conversations: Did they?

Bellson: Oh, you mentioned Basie in front of Duke, and Duke would say, "Well, Basie, he's beautiful." And then you mention Duke in front of Basie—on the tour that I made with them in Europe, he said, "Well, that was my man. He was a genius. He had it all covered." So, you know, it's beautiful vibrations.

Conversations: How about when a drummer is accompanying singers, whether it's your wife or whoever it is? This is another facet of drumming that really has to be very precise, does it not?

Bellson: Absolutely. It's really an art to back up a singer.

Conversations: What's the chemistry? Is it what's written, or do you have to get to know the singer and learn the style?

Bellson: Well, everything that you just said. Take, for instance, Sinatra and Tony Bennett—now there are two singers right there. I've had a chance to work with both of them, and mainly with Tony Bennett the last few years. He digs Basie's band and every once in awhile he'll call. We feel very honored to work with such a fine artist. He's a great guy and a great singer. But when you play for singers, what you say is right. That's an art. First of all, you have to know the personality; you have to know the singer; you have to be aware of him on stage; you have to watch his foot; you watch his hand.

Conversations: Watch his foot?

Bellson: Right. Because, you see, with Sinatra—of course, he's had the same rhythm section of Irv Cottler, Gene Sciricco, and Bill Miller, and they know him. But for any outsider, if something is not right with Frank as far as the tempo, he'll start patting his foot and give it to you. So that's one of his little ideas about watching for tempo, because there may be a lot of things that you have to cope with, like playing outdoors, or in a big hall where he's miles away from the rhythm section. And so he's got these little things that the rhythm section, especially the drummer, has got to watch for. Or Frank will give a special hand signal which means: "Come on! Let me have a little more of you, I can't hear." Sounds like a coach, you know, giving signals.

Conversations: You really have to watch him.

Bellson: Oh, yeah. Like even playing for my wife. I mean I've been playing for her for like twenty-five years, and she'll always say to me—she'll look around and she'll make a sign, which means the band is playing too loud, see.

Conversations: She has an ear for it.

Bellson: Right. Or when she starts walking fast across the stage, that means that the tempo is too slow and she wants to bring it up a little bit. So there are all kinds of key things. Like Ella Fitzgerald, there are other things that she does.

Conversations: What does she do?

Bellson: Ella pops her fingers, and if she starts doing it—

Conversations: If she wants the tempo to come up?

Bellson: Yeah. If she starts doing it for a long time and she feels a little uncomfortable with the tempo, you have to watch here, see. But if she does it where she's happy and she's got a little

Louis Bellson

smile on her face, that means keep it there. But you have to study her face—a drummer has to watch all these little things.

Conversations: Are you saying that the drummer is the key here?

Bellson: Well, the whole rhythm section is the key, really.

Conversations: But there has to be some one of them that sort of—

Bellson: Yeah, the drummer, really. The drummer has to have four sets of eyes, really, because he has to keep one eye on the conductor.

Conversations: Does the drummer also have to judge whether he's going to play sticks or brushes, for example?

Bellson: Usually, if you're playing a new chart, it takes maybe two or three times through before you realize that "Well, when I get to letter T, then I should go to sticks." Unless the part—some guys write a very thorough drum part: it's all laid out and it says, "Go to sticks at letter T." Others guys don't; they leave it up to the discretion of the drummer. So after you've played the chart three or four times—that's where a guy like Buddy excels. See, he doesn't read, but when he gets a chart like, for instance, *West Side Story,* which he did and did very well with his band, he listens to another drummer rehearse it. Then maybe after he plays it for a week or so he gets all the tempo changes. A guy like that keeps his ears and eyes open more than a guy that can read, because he knows that he's got that disadvantage. So, therefore, he's more attentive, and he picks up things faster. He picks them up real fast, you see. So as he plays it, he gets all the little accentuations that are important. After he's played it for a week or two, then he's got it.

Conversations: I saw something that was curious to me; maybe it's just a natural thing for you. When you were playing with the North Texas State Band you would count off, in fact, kick off the tempo that you wanted with the band. But you're the star attraction, and you didn't take your eyes off the conductor of that band.

Bellson: That's right.

Conversations: You were watching him all the way through. Usually the star is doing his thing. Is this the discipline that results from your band years?

Bellson: Oh, yeah. When my dad first gave me lessons, he said, "When you play and there's a conductor out front, you have to follow him." And, of course, there's another interplay on something like that. There are some conductors—there are a few of them out in California that I don't want to mention—who are really not conductors. They stand up there and they will tell the rhythm section, "Don't look and follow me."

Conversations: In other words, you're leading them.

Bellson: That's right. They rely on the rhythm section. But in a case like with Leon Breeden—Leon Breeden happens to be a very fine musician and a good conductor. So when you have somebody like that at the helm, you say okay, especially when you're playing outdoors. Now normally if we were playing indoors, Leon would say, "You got it, Lou," and he would do what he did on January 30th when I did a concert with them in Dallas, where he stands up in front of the band. A couple of numbers he didn't even show up at all, because he knew we had it covered. But being the fine musician that he is, he told me before, "Because of the fact that we're outdoors and everything, I'll just stand over there, if you don't mind." I said, "Great." Now that gives the bass trombone player, who is miles away, a little chance to know where the tempo is, too.

Conversations: He doesn't have to twist his head off to see where you are.

Bellson: Right, and this way they listen to me, and they know that Leon is listening to me, and I'm watching Leon. So it's all in teamwork. It's like a baseball team: once you've worked that way together, it comes off great.

Conversations: Your enthusiasm is almost infectious to somebody who's just met you. You look like a happy man; you really do.

Bellson: I'm doing something that I love to do.

Louis Bellson

Conversations: Is that the answer?

Bellson: Yeah. I love to play, and I love music, and I feel very blessed that I've had that opportunity.

Conversations: Is this kind of attitude a family trait?

Bellson: Yes. I would say I inherited that from my father. My father was that way. He played music all his life; he loved it; and I think that's where I got that from.

Conversations: You admired him a great deal.

Bellson: Oh, yeah. He was the one that started me.

Conversations: Did he say drums, or did you say drums?

Bellson: I said drums. At the age of three and a half he took me to a parade and I pointed at the drum section. I said, "That's what I want to play." And he said I was so definite at three and a half. That's pretty small. You're still tiny yet. And he said, "Well, okay, we'll give it a try." And I got into drums and I stayed with it for two or three years. Then he said, "How about learning a little bit of piano?" And I said, "No." He said, "Well, I don't mean play the instrument; I mean learn the keyboard. It looks like you're on your way to playing drums, and I think you should learn a little bit about music as well as percussion." So I rebelled a little bit, but he taught me theory. He started me off. But he was wise. He knew that once I got started it would be like a claw, you know. It got hold of me, and I couldn't get loose. I just started soaking everything up. Then I really got interested.

Conversations: How about the rest of the kids? You mentioned everybody was musical. Did anybody else go into professional music?

Bellson: The girls all played instruments: one girl is still teaching piano and composing and arranging in Las Vegas. The other three girls sort of dropped out and became housewives. The other two—there are two other drummers in the family. One brother works for the Slingerland Drum Company in Chicago, and the younger brother is out in California with me, and he's teaching—he's got some great students out there.

Conversations: Three drummers, then?

Bellson: And the other brother was a reed player. He gave it up. He decided that it wasn't for him, and he sort of got into something else.

Conversations: You're in your fifties.

Bellson: I'll be fifty-three July 6th.

Conversations: You're in a pretty strenuous business for a man of fifty-three. What are your immediate plans? Are you going to keep playing drums? Do you plan to teach?

Bellson: I think I'll just stay with playing, because if I get to the point where I know I can't make it, then I'll just either go to teaching or whatever. But I feel that I'll be playing drums when I'm eighty, eighty-five years old; I really do.

Conversations: Are you like a football player—you'll know when to quit?

Bellson: Yeah, I think so; I think so. I saw something very interesting in New Orleans. I saw a guy ninety-two years old playing drums. So I thought to myself: if he can do it, I can too. Of course, he wasn't doing what I do—like the lengthy solos and everything—but he was right there playing away, playing some good medium tempo. Ninety-two years old! Can you imagine that?

Conversations: Well, I can imagine looking for you at ninety-two in a place like Seabrook.

Bellson: I think that I can still be playing. Maybe not as ferociously as I am now, you know, as far as really getting the endurance and everything. But I feel that I could pick up the drumsticks and make something happen at that age.

Leon Breeden is a Texan through and through. He was born in Texas. He was educated in Texas. He teaches in Texas. Breeden is Director of Lab Bands and Professor of Music at North Texas State University in Denton, where his jazz program is considered to be the finest in the country. He is also a respected clarinetist, having studied with Reginald Kell in New York, played with the Dallas and Fort Worth Symphony Orchestras, and traveled with jazz bands in Texas and Oklahoma. He has a B.A. and the M.M.E. from Texas Christian University.

Leon Breeden

Leon Breeden's 1 O'Clock Lab Band from North Texas State University participated in the Spoleto Festival in May-June 1977 held in Charleston, South Carolina. The band served as the jazz accompaniment for such featured performers as Phil Woods, Urbie Green, and Louis Bellson. This conversation between Breeden and interviewer Zane Knauss took place in Breeden's hotel room a few hours before the band was scheduled to rehearse, then perform with Phil Woods.

Conversations: How many bands do you have at North Texas State University? I keep hearing about the 1 O'Clock Band, and you made references at your first concert here in Charleston, South Carolina, about a number of bands.

Breeden: We have nine at present. We have nine big jazz bands rehearsing daily. I should say Monday through Thursday, because Friday usually is broken down into section work, with a great number of the students often out playing weekends with some of the major orchestras that come through. Doc Severinsen, for one example, will come through and pick up maybe an entire band or the brass section or individual players for some of his engagements, and many others come through. But we have four days a week with nine bands—thirty-six hours a week of big-band rehearsals. There are times when we are under pressure with a big concert coming up, when on Friday also we'll have extra rehearsals with the full band. But the standard curriculum is a four-day week with nine bands.

Conversations: Do you handle all nine?

Breeden: I have eight graduate assistants who work closely with me. I coordinate the entire program and challenge them to meet certain demands—not demands; we're not autocratic about it—

certain criteria that I set up that we must do. One important facet of playing that I require is that we must sight-read. Hopefully, every rehearsal I'd like for each band to sight-read one number, or, at the very least, a couple of numbers a week. We stress reading, maybe sometimes to a fault, but we're trying to get them ready for any eventuality when they leave school and go out into professional playing, so that they can play anything that is put in front of them and not struggle with it. And it has worked out beautifully so far, because we've had no complaints, only excellent comments from—well, from leaders like Stan Kenton, who has called often to tell me about our students joining his band. I remember one particular call when he said, "Leon, last night three of your guys came in new to the band and I couldn't tell the difference; they were sight-reading everything in my book!" Well, to me it is important that they be able to do that.

Conversations: What's amazing to me in watching your band operate is that you have to keep in mind, after you've listened to them, that they are, after all, students.

Breeden: It's a class.

Conversations: They read and perform not at all like students.

Breeden: On concerts I usually don't introduce them as such, but I could easily say, "We now present our *class* for your enjoyment!" Think of the challenge I face walking into that class! You know, the English teacher can go into class with material that is predictable, totally. I walk in with twenty of the most capable and creative musicians. They're dynamic; they're really wanting to learn, and every rehearsal is a totally new and unpredictable experience! It's a challenge that sometimes overwhelms me. There's hardly a day that I don't go into rehearsal, really, to find the best way to pace the rehearsal, to challenge these fine performers, and to keep the motivation and drive going for the band. I am searching, mainly because I've had very little time to spend with the music. I was hired as Director of Lab Bands, with my main thrust being to serve as music director and work on the music; in other words, I was to coordinate the many details related to this large and rapidly growing area of our school of music. That growth has been so dramatic that I find my time now is so much administration that it's becoming ridiculous. Sometimes I'll be on long distance, maybe—I've had this happen recently: I'm on a thirty-minute long distance call; the call ends at ten minutes to one and the rehearsals start at one; I walk out and there are approximately 200 people sitting there who are guests. One of our rehearsals is unlike anything you can imagine. We finally had to close two rehearsals each week so we could get together and I could get to know my musicians. It was like every day was a . . . .

Conversations: People walk in?

Breeden: We have guests, many from out of town, but mostly members of the other bands. You see, we invite all the students to come in and learn from each other; so it's conceivable that on any given day—we now close rehearsals on Monday and Tuesday with Wednesday and Thursday open—anyone can come in. I have often walked in with 300 people sitting there on Wednesday; it's a packed house. On Thursday, same thing. It's not like a rehearsal; it's like a performance, almost. It's hard to really get into the nitty-gritty, never knowing who's looking over your shoulder. I mean, being a musician, I like to get with the guys and really get in there up to our elbows in the music and not worry about who might be offended if we, you know, make it a little rustic in describing something.

In education my thrust has been to try seriously to earn the respect for this music that it deserves. When I came to North Texas, I realized the first day I was there that it was not accepted by many of the faculty members. I'd already been warned by Dr. Hall, who was there. In two full days of discussions with Gene Hall, he was warning me constantly: "Now watch out for this, and you'll find that. . . ."

Conversations: The politics of academe?

Breeden: Well, there were, and still are, a lot of people. . . there were delegations going to the president's office in the early days of the jazz program at North Texas, faculty members in the school of music, trying to get this thing, "jazz," kicked out "before it takes over our school of music and destroys our good music."

Leon Breeden

Conversations: Well, let's back up then; you've been there how long, twenty years?

Breeden: I went there in 1959. I've been there seventeen years.

Conversations: Seventeen years, and was this the beginning of the lab program?

Breeden: The lab program as such started more or less informally in 1946. There was a graduate student who was directing a lab band, the first lab band, as it was, in 1946, although 1947 marks the beginning of the total program.

In 1947, Gene Hall, Dr. M. E. Hall, was hired as the first full-time faculty member whose main function was to set up a jazz program. In that year he set up a degree plan for a Bachelor of Music with a major in dance band, as it was called then. For years it was called "dance band." It was dance band in 1959 when I came, and I tried to change it. The president at that time was leery that the state legislature was not ready for the word "jazz" in there; so even as late as '59 I was told—in fact, only two years ago were we able to change it to Bachelor of Music with a major in jazz education, where I wanted it all along. But I had been there for fifteen years before we finally got it into the official program, the official bulletin, the yearbook, the catalogue.

Conversations: You went into the fifties then and had the name changed, but the whole emphasis on jazz in America had also changed. The big band era was about shot, and yet you perpetuated the so-called big band as a training force. Or do you get into small-group instrumental training?

Breeden: We have eighteen small groups now in our improvisation classes. There is no set number of groups—the number is determined by enrollment. We have two guitar ensembles, one with fifteen guitars and one with eight, I believe. And we encourage the small-group playing, but primarily in the improvisational setting where the soloist can really stretch out.

Conversations: How many people do you have?

Breeden: Well, let me give you a rundown on last fall. I have each student fill out a paper stating where he came from, what brought him to North Texas, and his instrument, and all that. So

36

when I gathered this together by instrument, I found that we had 125 saxophonists; we had 105 trumpet players; we had forty-six trombone players; thirty-five pianists; we had about sixty drummers; we had guitarists—let's see, we had about thirty guitarists, I think. Our challenge at this point was to place this very large and complex group of musicians into nine bands.

We've got 125 saxophonists—we're going to have five in each band—so we've got places for forty-five. What we do, since we're an educational institution, we try in the lower bands when we get down to the thirty-fifth student, on into thirty-sixth, thirty-seventh, thirty-eighth, as far down as we find good players, to double up some of the sections. We will have Monday-Wednesday sax sections and Tuesday-Thursday sax sections in some bands rather than deny those students a chance to play in a big band at all.

Conversations: Well, you travel with doubles, too, don't you? I noticed that you had some doubles in your trumpet section with this 1 O'Clock Band.

Breeden: Not doubles, if you mean extra players. All our saxophonists double on several instruments, of course.

Conversations: You had alternate trumpet players.

Breeden: Well, that's because some of the parts are for only four. It may look like we're using doubles, but, no, they were moving around within the section. All nine of our bands have sections of five. We've got five saxes, five trumpets, five trombones, and five rhythm: piano, bass, drums, guitar, and percussion. We've added the percussion, because we believe it's vital to have the congas, to have all the little ethnic cymbals and the Indian bells and so forth.

Conversations: Which a drummer won't have.

Breeden: That's right, and won't have time to play in addition to his set. And it's amazing how the young students today are gathering up their own collections of these. We've got a number of students at North Texas who have, I guess, $2000 or $3000 worth of all kinds of Ethiopian bells and cow bells and things; it's just astounding to me. The young man in our 1 O'Clock

37

Band, who is here at Charleston, he's—I don't know how much equipment he has. He brought just a little, small smattering of it, but he's got a whole room of it at home.

Conversations: But you have, then, an enormous number of instrumentalists?

Breeden: You asked about the big band. The reason we have the big bands is we're trying to give as many as possible a chance to play, and the big band seems to do that in the time we are allotted and in the space we are allotted. What most people do not realize is that to this very day the lab bands have operated in temporary locations. We are now in our fifth temporary home, and that's been documented; it is a statement of fact that can be proven easily.

When I came to North Texas in 1959, we were rehearsing in an old choir room: it was called Orchestra Hall, but it was built with risers for a choir. Okay, then we moved to an old lab school gymnasium—that's where our next home was. We moved down to the Music Hall Auditorium, which was a low, sunken area down underground, where the orchestra and the band rehearsed before they moved to new quarters. Gene Hall was out in an Army barracks for quite awhile. We are now in an old cafeteria.

In my office, my desk sits right where the steam table was located where the athletes came through to get their meals. And where the athletes were served their lunch privately, separate from the rest of the students, that's our lounge. We've turned that into a lounge where the kids can get together and compare notes about their scores and talk music. It's a nice, separate place from our rehearsal hall. But we are literally rehearsing in a cafeteria, and we have one room, in other words, in which all of this activity has to take place—except for improvisation, much of which we now have moved over into small classrooms in an old dormitory. Most people find it difficult to believe that we have been able to achieve first-rate results with the inadequate facilities we have had.

So many of the young educators, as I travel around the country, will. . . . I was having dinner in New Mexico recently with four young directors. One of them said, "Boy, Mr. Breeden, I'll sure be glad when I get a job like you've got!" And I just pulled closer to the table and said, "Tell me about it. What do you think I've got at North Texas?" He said, "Well, judging from the albums I've heard, you must have everything. The school must give you everything that you want. Don't you have the finest equipment that money can buy?" I had to truthfully say— and this is not sour grapes—that we have fought for almost everything we've had. I mean until the past year or so, when things have greatly improved, we have had to literally fight for everything.

I am putting no one down, but there's never been one penny of scholarship money given to the jazz area—not one cent. We have now started generating our own scholarship funds from our own friends, private sources where we can handle it ourselves and give it to worthy students. As you well know, talent does not come with affluence. Some of the best players are from the poor families where they need the help.

So in 1972, we had a big celebration at North Texas, and we called it "The Twenty-Fifth Anniversary of Jazz Education," documenting the fact that from 1947 to 1972 we had twenty-five years during which time jazz had not done what those early committees going to the president's office said it was going to do. Instead of killing or ruining or destroying or minimizing good music, it had brought hundreds of students to North Texas, so that at that time it was, and to this day is, the second largest school of music in America.

Conversations: Next to Indiana.

Breeden: Next to Indiana. And the jazz department is the largest segment in the school of music, as far as I can tell.

Conversations: Where do you get these kids? Where do they come from?

Breeden: They come from every state in the Union. We have had, since I have been there, and I've kept accurate records on this, students from every state in the Union, from Canada—quite a number from Canada. This semester we have two from England, and one from South Australia—I'm talking about players in the bands. And we have something like forty-seven states represented this semester. But we've had students from every state in the Union since I've been at North Texas.

39

Leon Breeden

Why do they come to Denton, Texas? Why do they bypass all those universities to come down there? Because I think they see we have been able, by getting that start early when Gene Hall was able to get that program—and Dr. Walter Hodgson, I would give him great credit for being the man at the point when Charles Meeks and Dr. Bain left. Dr. Wilfred C. Bain left to go to Indiana, and Meeks had started that dance band in 1946—he had been working as a graduate assistant. And Bain obviously had seen some merit to that jazz thing; in other words, "That dance band intrigues me. So, hey, Charlie Meeks, why don't you come up here to Indiana with me?" Which he did; he left.

At that point the president of the university and/or the dean could easily have said, "No more. Let's kill this. We think it's going to get out of hand." Instead, Dr. Walter Hodgson could see that this had merit. He called in Gene Hall, who was a former student and he admired Gene's work. He said, "How about coming back to North Texas and teaching arranging, setting up a program. Let's work out a degree plan, and let's get this as a valid part of our educational scene. Your main thrust will be to work in the area of jazz, or in the dance band area," as they called it then.

So in 1972, when we had this big celebration, a lot of interest was focused upon our school. Now I purposely made a big thing out of it. We had beautiful booklets printed, for this reason: I knew there were young directors all over the United States who were fighting for their lives, many of them former lab band members from whom we had heard often about their problems. They were not getting funds; they had to meet at night; they had to meet weekends. The jazz program was just barely tolerated—I mean, they were not getting the support they needed.

If they could look to one school and say, "Look, dean," or "Look, administrator, at North Texas for twenty-five years it hasn't destroyed their school of music. Look what they've been able to do there." If they could look at us, they could find support; it would give them valid documentation to get some needed support. And we had letters come in—it was beautiful to hear the comments of these young educators. They said, "This is a breath of fresh air. This is marvelous that we can say, 'Look, here is a school for twenty-five years that's had jazz and it hasn't hurt anything.'" And that's the main reason I did it.

It wasn't because it was North Texas. It could have happened at any school. Had any other school in the country had this big celebration saying, "for twenty-five years we've been in the schools and it hasn't hurt anything," I would have been elated. I'd have been thrilled to death. We needed that; we needed some solidarity; we needed some tradition; we needed some documentation that jazz will not destroy "good music."

Conversations: Well, has it now been conceded that jazz, in itself, is good music?

Breeden: By those who understand. I think there are still those who think that jazz is Dixieland; it's New Orleans. I mean some think that it began and stopped, I guess, with Bix Beiderbecke or Louis Armstrong.

Conversations: Well, if anybody looks at the complex scores that you people are playing, I think they'd understand that this is not an exercise in happy kicks, that this is serious business.

Breeden: The ones who put it down are almost always those who have no information, or wrong information about what we are doing. They have never been to a concert, have never attended a rehearsal, and have no idea what we're doing. They just know the word "jazz" represents to them something seamy, a fourth-class citizen. They've read the headlines of some charge against Miles Davis, or Gene Krupa—to this day I still hear those stories.

Conversations: That was the Dodo Marmarosa-Gene Krupa thing.

Breeden: That's right, and they remember that; they hang on to that; they want to remember that. We represent something totally apart from that in jazz education. And back to what I said: our search and our goal has been to get respect for this music— not to earn it under the covers or do anything except play music. You know, our reputation has been gained not by the spreading of sounds. We've earned our reputation through the playing of those horns, and you're right: the complexity of our music is such that I'd like for those that put us down to come up there and bring their horns and just sit down and try to play some of that music.

Leon Breeden

Conversations: You've talked about the number of instru-mentalists that come flocking to Denton, Texas, from all over the place—as far away as Australia. How about writers? Do you bring in arrangers and composers, or do you have a student cadre that develops material for these musicians?

Breeden: This has been one of the bright lights in my work there. We have had some very creative minds, some excellent writers, and we encourage it there. I have never turned down a student when he comes up to me and says, "Would you play my number?" That's why the lab band came into existence, really, to give the writer and performer a chance to get together and hear these new things coming out.

These student-written arrangements have added a tremen-dous dimension to our music, and we encourage it in every way possible. I never play a concert—and I have not in seventeen years—that I do not include as many of the student works as I possibly can, reaching into the professional ranks only when I need to change the pace or feature a certain soloist that maybe the writer hasn't done, hasn't featured. So you've hit a very salient point in that the creativity of the writing is one of the main thrusts. We definitely encourage it.

Lew Gillis is teaching arranging, as you know well. Don Gillis certainly needs no introduction; but his brother is also a very fine musician, and he's teaching arranging there. Lew had over ninety arranging students in his classes this past year!

Conversations: This raises a question: With the state of music in America today, commercial music, what's the future for all these people—these ninety arrangers, these hundreds of instrumen-talists? Where do they go after they leave you?

Breeden: You know, I'm going to recount something here that I have mentioned a few times, that really floored me. I was having a discussion at a MENC Conference with a man who had been with a major instrument manufacturing company for thirty some-odd years. He came up to me and said, "Leon, I've just been meaning to ask you how you can encourage these kids to go on and work in the field of jazz and all when you know that there are no jobs out there for them." I turned to him and said, "Do you realize that it's not something I'm talking them into?"

42

Nobody is talking these students into this. It's something they are going to do in spite of all of us. We try to take that drive and that interest and that energy they've got in this area. . . . We never know who—which one would I pick out and say, "Son, don't go into music, I mean, after all, you're not ever going to make it"; or "There's no future out there. There's nothing to do but ride a smelly bus, you know, and travel around with a few remaining bands until they all die." I can't. There's no way you can say that Breeden or anyone else is encouraging these students to do this.

By the way, let me point out something which might help to prove this point: I have never, not one time in seventeen years, invited a student to come to North Texas or to play in a band. One hundred percent are there because they want to be! I've been in music all my life, and I think that a musician is going to be a musician in spite of, and not with the help of. He's been discouraged all along the way.

I have to admire every person who has ever made it in music, because inside him there is a spark that is burning that he or she is going to become a musician. The world didn't vote a Doc Severinsen in; there wasn't an election to see if there would be a Stan Kenton. Those men made it happen. I'll put it this way: The music will be important regardless of their future, whatever they end up doing; and I think many are going to be in music, whether they are repairmen in a repair shop, whether they are conducting a church choir, or whether they are doing something else. I went into music, if they are like I was. . . .

Conversations: How did you get into it?

Breeden: When I was in junior high school I made a decision— well, let me go back to the first thing. My father was an amateur musician and played all the instruments. Didn't know one note from another. On Sunday afternoons there was a musicale in our home that was second to none, and he'd sit and play the old honky-tonk style piano. I grew up on "Alexander's Ragtime Band" and all those old tunes.

And when I was seven years old he did some repair work for a man who had come into town to organize a community band. He traded the repair work on this man's car for my first clarinet.

Leon Breeden

For one year I got pretty much interested in it and I played often. Then I laid off for about a year. At that time my books at school were becoming interesting. Well, anyway, then I skipped a year. Then at about nine I got really interested in it, and so I went on and stayed with it from then on.

Conversations: Clarinet was your instrument?

Breeden: Clarinet was my first instrument. In junior high school I can almost remember the day that I said to myself, and told one of my teachers: "I'm going to be a musician; at least, I'm positive I'm going to be in the field of music. I don't know what area; I may be selling music on the road; I may be selling instruments. I'm going into music, not because I can make a living at it, but because I can't live without it."

Conversations: And this is an important difference.

Breeden: And that is a very important difference. Today I could be a wealthy man, because my father-in-law offered me an excellent opportunity to go into the lumber and contracting business with him. I never accepted his kind offer because I could not live without music; it's my life. And it's sustained me through some tragedies in my life—without music I could never have—the involvement, the love of music. Of course, my family comes first. But I'm referring to that total involvement in the students with whom I've had the great opportunity to work.

Now so many have gone out into the—they're in all the top groups; they're just everywhere. To go back to what you were saying, all I can say is that these students, even if they never go on with their music after their experiences with us, are going to be better human beings. That music experience is going to be something that will be a vital part of their lives. You know, it just hit me. I flew to Denver last week and on the plane Ron McKeel, one of our former students—a drummer who played in one of our bands and combos and never made the 1 O'Clock Band— walked up to me and smiled and handed me his card. He is the planning engineer for Frito-Lay, has an excellent job.

Conversations: In Dallas?

Breeden: In Dallas. And he said, "Mr. Breeden, I want to thank you for all the help you gave me and for all the musical experiences I had at North Texas." I said, "But you're not in music?" He said, "That makes no difference. I wouldn't take a million dollars for my experiences in that." Here's an engineer; and there are other cases: one former student is a leading lawyer in Denver; some are deans of schools of music; they're in everything.

Conversations: Do they proselytize for jazz when they get into the other careers? Are they jazz fans always, after this experience?

Breeden: It's my experience that they are all evangelists, more or less. They are going to carry the word if they were in it because of their total involvement. I don't know of any student who is there just kind of hanging on. They're there because they want to play music, and you're right, it'll be part of their lives from now on.

Conversations: You mentioned that your father was an amateur musician and that you started out on clarinet, and clarinet, really, is your instrument. I've been told by Don Gillis that you were associated with him at Texas Christian at one point.

Breeden: That's correct. Playing with the TCU band there—back to what one wouldn't take a million dollars for, I wouldn't take anything for that.

Conversations: This was a marching band, or a concert band?

Breeden: A marching band; it was really a big swing band. Don had that band playing some swinging things out on the field, and the crowds would just go crazy over it.

Conversations: Even then?

Breeden: Yeah, and ironically, little did I know when I came there that someday I would end up being director of the TCU band also.

Conversations: At one point you went to New York and, again according to Gillis, you were a pretty fair country jazz player yourself on clarinet.

45

Leon Breeden

Breeden: I played some at NBC. Not as much as I would have liked to, because I was going to Columbia and I was commuting out to Long Island—two hours to school and two hours home every day. It was an unbelievable time. But I was able to play some; I played some up there with Peanuts Hucko's big band. He was trying to get a big band started. And I had great experiences going down to rehearsal after rehearsal with Billy Butterfield and many other great guys—Ernie Caceres and some ex-members of the old Glenn Miller Band; Al Klink was there. Some of these top guys were there. Just to meet Toots Mondello—I met him one day and I had admired him for years.

Conversations: Did you play professionally?

Breeden: In New York I didn't really, no, I didn't play any jobs except at NBC. I played some shows there. I did some of the series, *A Man Called X*, starring Herbert Marshall. We never saw the actors; they were on another floor of the TV building, but it was great playing under Milton Katims, who was a Toscanini protege.

Conversations: Now in Houston.

Breeden: My playing, really was: military band, opera orchestra, symphony orchestra, and I had my own band for two or three years in Fort Worth. To say I've had a lot of jazz experience... not as much as I would have preferred.

One thrill for me, with some good jazz opportunities, was when Ray McKinley came back to Fort Worth, and I played with his band, played lead alto and clarinet with his band for over a year. He was trying to decide whether to leave the road and come back to his hometown. He bought a home in Fort Worth. We played all over the Southwest with him; I was still teaching. See, I had the teaching and the playing in combination. I was offered a job early in my career, when I was finishing my master's, to go with Tommy Dorsey's band—it would have been Buddy De Franco's chair. I did not pursue this opportunity because something just told me that education was really what I wanted to do. And I was more of a family man, really.

Conversations: Didn't want the road stuff?

Breeden: I didn't have the hankering to get out and go on the road. I don't know, it was just something deep within me. I grew up in a large family, and, I guess, I was oriented more in that direction than to be—to have the wanderlust of moving around. Not that I didn't; I traveled with Tony DiPardo's band, a band out of St. Louis. It was a hotel band, primarily.

While still in high school I got my first professional job; I got my start in a fiddle band, for Pete's sake. I played in clubs I wouldn't go into today for fear of my life. We played with a screen, or contingency curtain: there was a chicken wire rolled up in front of the bandstand which we would knock down in emergencies. It happened only once. They had a wire around the ends of it and, when all these hillbillies and cowboys started throwing bottles and fighting, to protect our horns we'd knock those ends off and this wire would come down. It would keep flying bottles from destroying our instruments. I played in gambling casinos, joints, skating rinks, etc.

I played in a group called "Billy's Melody Five"—the number would change from time to time. Guys came in and out; sometimes they were in jail, I guess, I don't know. I was just a punk in high school, but I was earning my way through my last two years of high school. I paid for all my clothes; I bought my new horns and everything, just playing with this hillbilly band.

But get this: "Here's Billy's Melody Five—all ten of them" or "Billy's Melody Five—all seven of them" or whatever it was. They'd introduce us that way. We had a morning radio show on KGKO, which was the old station there in Wichita Falls, Texas. We played all through the honky-tonks, as we called them then, through the northern area of Texas, and up through Oklahoma. And we traveled in an old Pierce-Arrow car, with all the band inside of it and with drums strapped all over it and a bass strapped on the side. You couldn't get out one side because it was strapped; they had big ropes hanging the instruments on there. It was an absolute "grapes of wrath" band.

There were only two guys in the band who could read and write—I'm not speaking of music; I'm speaking of the English language—and that was the leader and me. The leader played bass in the band. I'll never forget the night, and I shortly thereafter quit the band, he pulled his coat back and showed me his shoulder holster and his loaded .38 that he carried at all times.

Leon Breeden

I said, "Billy, what have you got that for?" He said, "That's to protect our payroll." He said, "After all, you know, Bonnie and Clyde"—it was toward the end of that Bonnie and Clyde era when they were having these robberies out on the highway. They would have two or three cars parked across the road and they'd be standing there with submachine guns. If you tried to turn your car around they would just riddle you. While I was in the band we never experienced that.

There was another interesting thing about the time I was starting to get into professional playing. I left Wichita Falls and came to Fort Worth—that's where I met Don Gillis. But, you know, just a short time before I came to Fort Worth they were unionizing the musicians. I heard stories about the number of bands that had been waylaid after they had walked off the bandstand. Say, a union band would walk off and a nonunion band would be waiting out in the back of the place with sledgehammers, and they would take all of their instruments out and lay them on the ground and beat them into little pieces; or vice versa, a nonunion band playing and the union boys destroying their instruments.

If there were ever any discouragements about going into music, I had them. I was playing with a band that couldn't read or write—English or music; I was in an atmosphere where the gangster element was there. There was nothing in my life that said, "Hey, are you going to be a musician? Great, man! That's wonderful!"

Conversations: So education, then, sounded like a better deal.

Breeden: Well, that's right. All of my family were very strict in the Church. My father was very strict, and I was almost taught that jazz was dirty. I mean it was something seamy: "Son, are you sure you want to mess around with those underworld characters?" Even though he played those tunes, he thought of it as kind of a happy thing, a hobby instead of a legitimate job. But when he would get up to teach Sunday school, he was fire and brimstone. We were forbidden to even drive by the picture shows on Sunday—that strict, you know. When I was in high school my band director turned to me one day—we were trying to get a band together to find out how Benny Goodman and Glenn

48

Miller got those sounds, just a bunch of kids trying to learn something. The band director—I'll never forget, this was junior high—he turned to me and said, "Leon Breeden, if you bring that junk into my school you'll never play, none of you will ever play a note in my concert band."

Conversations: This is the prejudice that you've run into, I presume, all through your career.

Breeden: I have run into it all the time.

Conversations: Isn't it crazy that here is a type of music which is really an American heritage and Americans have turned against it? Why is this?

Breeden: I do not know, but I can truly state from personal experience that this is true, because I have lived it. I've been in Mexico; we played nineteen cities in 1967 for the State Department. We saw more of Mexico than most Mexican citizens will ever see in their lifetimes. We played in Russia last summer, over a month in the Soviet Union. We played in Portugal, over a week there. I've been in Paris; I've been in London. I conducted an international all-star band with *Jazz International* in 1973 in London and in Paris. . . and in Switzerland. We made a tour across Germany—we played Hamburg and Berlin; we played Munich; we played Baden-Baden. I can truthfully state that we were treated with greater respect and our music was admired, apparently, more so in those places than in America. It's not that people don't respect us. Our opening crowds here in Charleston have been marvelous, and the people who come obviously are devotees. They love jazz or they wouldn't be here.

Conversations: But it's not a knock-down-the-door type of enthusiasm.

Breeden: Let me give you an example. When I was in Los Angeles in 1975 for the founding of the World Jazz Association, it was marvelous to see—these top record executives, the top TV producers, the top people—they asked me to speak. Here was this former hillbilly getting up there to talk with these millionaires and these men who were, you know, highly successful businessmen.

49

Leon Breeden

I told them a true story which had been related to me the previous day, when I visited a former student in Los Angeles who told me of his difficulty in getting insurance for his valuable sound equipment. When he gave his occupation as musician the agent was reluctant; when he added, "I also handle the equipment"—the agent happily entered "equipment manager" under occupation. It was more acceptable than musician to his company. Ridiculous! My final statement to them was that I think in jazz education we have something that is so beautiful, and I wish that Mr. and Mrs. Middle America, the average citizen, could learn of the wonderful things which are happening in jazz education. I would hope that this would help to remove the clouds of misunderstandings. Jazz is not just toe-tapping, knee-slapping music, but is a valid art form.

Conversations: Very cerebral, isn't it?

Breeden: It is cerebral. It is very interesting, and the complexity of it is not something that one should be afraid of; it's not something so complex that you can't hum some of the melodies and find a lot of interesting things in it. I'm intrigued with it. Well, I get so excited—what was I talking about? Back to the respect and all of that. In the Soviet Union they wanted to carry us out on their shoulders. I mean we got twenty-five standing ovations for twenty-five concerts!

Conversations: You did some solo work there, too, didn't you?

Breeden: I played with a Dixieland band, yeah. They loved that, and I did it for a purpose. I wanted to show those Soviet citizens that "Herr Professor" up on that stage did not get up autocratically and tell the students, "You *will* do this," but that he got his horn out and played along with the kids. And they loved it. I wanted to show this without any announcements, just by picking up the horn and playing Dixieland with them.

Conversations: What about the name figures in jazz; are they into what you're doing at North Texas State? Do they lend a hand? Are they your best boosters?

Breeden: Yes, I would truthfully say so. We have had some marvelous commendations from people like Marian McPartland, who was a guest at our 1972 Twenty-Fifth Anniversary.

Clark Terry has been a dear friend and has touted our praises so many years; I mean he has just been one of our big backers. On and on. Ed Shaughnessy, Mundell Lowe, Pat Williams, Leonard Feather, and so many others.

Conversations: Now Kenton has been very much involved.

Breeden: Stan Kenton, as far as I personally am concerned, is one of the most beloved men I've ever known. He has set the pace for many of us.

Conversations: He told me that he gave you his music library.

Breeden: In 1960 we met Stan at the Notre Dame Jazz Festival. The night we played he came running down the full length of the gymnasium in which we were playing and threw his arms around me. I had never met the man, and I couldn't believe it. He had tears in his eyes and he said to me that night: "You have renewed my faith in music"—just like that—he made it very dramatic. And he told the guys, "I cannot get over what I've heard tonight!" He said, "I'm more excited about music tonight than I have been in years." And he was kind of halfway thinking of getting out of the business about then, according to published reports. He invited me up to his suite—he had a beautiful suite there at one of the places on the campus. So I went up and we talked. He said, "I want to help you guys. I'm so turned on by what you're doing. How could I help?" He said, "What is your biggest need?" I said, "Well, Stan"—then we had three bands, I think—I said, "with three bands we need music. It's always the battle. Every director is trying to find new music." He said, "Okay, that's solved. Now what's the next thing you need?" That's all he said.

Conversations: What did he mean?

Breeden: All he said was "That's solved," and I didn't know what he meant. The man that instant had made his mind up that he was going to give us his library.

Conversations: You mean all the original charts?

Breeden: Can you imagine my shock when a big Central Freight truck drove up?—this was late 1961 or early 1962. Here comes this big truck. I looked out the window and thought, "What is that?"

51

Leon Breeden

So they started carrying these big heavy cases in, and as the men walked toward the door, I saw "Stan Kenton Orchestra" on the carrying cases! In they walked with Stan's entire library as it was at that time—right off the road. He had told the men to pack up their books at the end of one of the nights. He had said, "We will start a new library. We're giving this to North Texas State." I spent two or three weeks carrying arrangements home. I sorted books on the floor of my living room with parts that said "Maynard Ferguson"—laying out parts that said "Bill Russo."

Conversations: Shelly Manne.

Breeden: Shelly Manne. Here were the men's names all over them. I told my wife: "I'm handling something here that is sacred to me."

Conversations: Are you talking about the Pete Rugolo arrangements, Kenton's original compositions?

Breeden: Rugolo, that's right. The whole book. Now, he had lost a lot of the music through the years.

Conversations: I'm thinking about "Opus in Pastels."

Breeden: That's correct; it was all in there.

Conversations: "Artistry in Rhythm"?

Breeden: "Artistry in Rhythm" was on some little spiral, torn-out things.

Conversations: "Peanut Vendor."

Breeden: "Peanut Vendor" was just torn-out, little spirals, where they just sketched it out.

Conversations: "Concerto To End All Concertos"?

Breeden: It was there; it was there.

Conversations: And you now have it?

Breeden: It's there at North Texas, the original parts. Now some sad things have happened. I gave Stan my word that I would guard that with my life, which I have done, personally. But we've gotten so big. We found out recently there were a few things stolen; I think just out of adulation of the man and all. Get this, here is rip-off city. I mean this is beyond belief. Whoever it was, was working internally there with me or may have sneaked in at night. They had pulled out a few of the originals there and, like say it was number 302, they substituted number 0302 back in, the zero indicating a printed *stock* orchestration so we wouldn't notice that the shelf was a little less, you know. I watched that thing like a hawk anyway. We've got a vast library of over 3000 numbers. But why go to the trouble to try to put the same number, only a stock orchestration of a printed chart, back in there? I told the guys, "I can't believe this. Let's find out how badly we've been ripped off. Go through every one of them." And we found about five or six, but even one would have made me ill, or, at least, greatly disappointed. If I had not had the foresight to realize that this might happen—I'd had them make masters on these.

Conversations: Oh, so you do have duplications?

Breeden: By masters I mean we make a master copy and we file it in another part of the building that they don't have access to.

Conversations: Do musicians such as Kenton, Louis Bellson, who has just now been playing with your band, or others of this stature come to Denton to work with your guys?

Breeden: We bring them as often as funds will allow. You might be interested to know that in our history at North Texas State we have brought many, many guests in: Oliver Nelson, we brought in Clark Terry; we brought in Leonard Feather; we brought in, from London, Henry Pleasants, the great critic—he has been a guest on our campus. We've brought in—well, Cannonball Adderley came up and just visited. He came up—this happens all the time—just because he wanted to come up and hear a rehearsal. The great one walked in with Nat, his brother; they just walked in and sat down. We all were dumbfounded. Well, he ended up talking about an hour extra, at our invitation, to the sax players. Joe Williams was appearing in Dallas—walks in with some of his new arrangements from the Thad Jones-Mel Lewis band and we sight-read them for him. When we did "It Don't Mean A Thing If It Ain't Got That Swing," he walked up to me and said, "Leon, now this is pretty—man, this thing is mean!" He said, "Thad's band was scuffling on this. You want to slow it down?" I said, "Just a minute." I walked over to the lead alto player; I said, "Joe said we ought to slow this down. Guys, what do you think?" They kind of looked at it and said, "Kick it off up to tempo."

Conversations: So away you went.

Breeden: Joe said, "Are you guys serious?" And they said, "You go ahead; we'll play it." He kicked it off up to tempo and when he got through he walked over to me and his eyes—he was just glowing. He said, "They played it better than Thad's band did after three days." Now, of course, it's a kindness of a man like that. I realize that he's probably just patting us on the back, but I didn't hear any—I heard very few minor mistakes.

Conversations: Here you are now in a situation at the Spoleto Festival where on an almost night-to-night basis you're performing with Louis Bellson; you're performing with Phil Woods; you're performing with Urbie Green. They are no lightweights. And obviously they are coming here quick-in-and-get-out. They're coming in with charts that your guys haven't had a chance really to assimilate, and they're forced to almost sight-read. This is pretty tough.

Breeden: We are playing a concert tonight with Phil Woods that we have never rehearsed. We have been over about two of the numbers, one time each. He is bringing one with him that we have never laid eyes on.

Conversations: Bellson did the same thing to you.

Breeden: Bellson did the same thing. Urbie will do the same thing. We got one of Phil Woods's things the day we left and have never played a note of it. I looked at it, and it's mean; it's got a lot of notes in there. But I have full confidence that our band is going to play that, and do it well. Now here's something you might be interested in: we've tried a little innovation at North Texas from time to time, and the one of which I am most proud is the concert where we sight-read an entire concert. I had printed programs; the band had never seen a note. We had an audience of about 400 people—we had musicians come in from Dallas. They were digging; they wanted to find out what was going to happen. We had announced that we were going to sight-read a full concert—never been done in history. Okay, I had all the parts. I had gone through personally and put the books together. I knew where the solos were—I personally typed the program up for the printer. I'll never forget: here were envelopes on the stands with ten numbers in there that the band had never seen, all in order. I said, "Your program is in order. You're going to pull it out on cue, put it in front of the envelope, and we will start with number one which will be right in front of you." And I'll never forget, I had a program lying on top of each man's big manilla folder, and the lead alto player looked down and said, "The third number is a sax feature for me, and I've never seen it?" It had his name down there as soloist. That band went through ten numbers and there were not more than five slight mistakes—and the only reason those were there was because of copy work in the parts.

We played one number that was printed in London, and when it came down to the sign indicating where the players were to return to in order to repeat part of the section, the sign was very weak and very small and any musician—I mean, it just wasn't obvious enough. So two or three guys didn't quite see it in time to jump back up; so there was a little scuffling right at the end of the concert. We all broke up and laughed. I said, "Wait a minute. Let's take the coda out; we're not going to leave it like that." But just think of that exciting achievement. I had student after student after student tell me, "That's the most exciting thing I've ever seen in my life to realize that those men had never seen that!"

Conversations: You're pretty low-key in front of this band. You don't intrude too much when they are performing, do you?

Breeden: Isn't that great? Because it's not my show; it's their show. My whole thrust has been since I came—well, I told you of the search for the dignity and the respect for this music that I love and my belief that Americans should love it as much as people over the world love it. I rarely play with the band; I just put my horn aside. "I've had twenty-five years of playing," I said, "and these men are getting themselves together." My job is to push the students, help them every way possible. My dedication is deeper than usually would be the case, with the loss of our beloved nineteen-year-old son in 1968, to a hit-and-run driver in Dallas. In every conference with my young students, I see my son and try to help them as much as I would have wanted to help Danny.

And, also, it would be ludicrous for me to stand up there and beat time for these guys. I want it to come internally, not from me, not autocratically. I'm not up there saying "You do this," or, you know, "Follow me, men," except where it demands it. There are certain times when it's very critical that I be there, and I do not shirk my duties. It's not that I'm cutting out or anything; it's just that I want it to come from inside them. The happiest music we play happens when it's something from inside the performers.

Conversations: I wanted to ask you about that. My impression of the band, in looking at the faces of the individuals as they played, for example, was so serious—deadly serious. Is this band without warmth, without emotion? Are they so cerebral, so technical, that some of the spontaneity of jazz is gone?

Breeden: We are criticized sometimes for being too accurate, too clean, too precise. All I can say is that we operate in the context of a school of music. I know exactly what you are talking about. And I know that the best the band has played was when we were in the "Jazz Gallerie" in Berlin, playing in a jazz club where Eric Dolphy had played. I told the band before we played that night: "Eric Dolphy played his last date right here in this club." A spark of electricity ran through that band; I have never heard the band play any better. Given a real relaxed atmosphere, I think this band can swing as hard as any band I've ever seen. But we're on the spot. All the time people are coming in saying, "We've heard you're great; let's see how great you are." And the pressure never seems to quite get off of us. I mean Bellson last night on that "Ellington Blues," when he started cooking that thing out there, all the inhibitions blew out the window and the band started—

Conversations: They relaxed.

Breeden: They felt marvelous and the mood just rolled through the audience and that's the way I love to see those kids play. I know exactly what you're talking about. It's not that we're trying to inhibit the. . . it's not that they are maybe too serious about it; they can play as loose as anyone. They run into our rehearsals right out of English class, out of science class, out of history class. We play for fifty minutes, and they run back out to something else. We're in an unusual setting to really get the jazz feel, I mean to really. . . .

Conversations: It's a combination of academics and jazz in a sense.

Breeden: Let me put it this way. The first day that we arrived here, after twenty-seven or twenty-eight hours on that bus, we were a little uptight. The band got together and we played with Louis at Seabrook. Last night I felt it loosening up; tonight it's going to loosen up a little more. We're getting further and further away from those books, farther away from those classrooms.

Conversations: You're a band on the road.

Breeden: We're starting to get together, and that's what we need badly. We played the first jazz performance ever at the MENC in Seattle in 1968. We flew to Denver; we played a concert; the band was good. We flew to Salt Lake City; the band was tremendously better. We flew to Seattle, Washington, the Opera House, and the band just blew the place down. Just three nights away from classes and they came together. The kids have got it; there's no question about it. But really, when we come into rehearsals and there are 300 people sitting there, you know, digging and watching, it's hard to really relax and just play. And like you say, those charts are cerebral. I don't know if we're too precise, too clean—I hope that's not a valid criticism.

Conversations: Are the charts getting away from the jazz field per se and becoming exercises of very professional composers?

Breeden: I think it's an added dimension. I don't think it's taking away from that spontaneity. I think that the great soloists are still going to be with us—hopefully, forever. And I sincerely hope that all we are doing is giving jazz an expanded voice with some of the complexity and all. It will never replace—that's been my argument about jazz in the school—we're not trying to replace the symphony orchestra; we're not trying to replace the concert band or the madrigal singers or the acapella choir or anything else. It's an added voice, an added way of making music. It takes away not at all from those other groups. I think the complexity of our charts—I just don't feel that it takes away. I sincerely hope not. To me, it gives more variety to it.

You know that jazz is an infant? Look at the history of music; we're dealing with an infant. Any growing infant has to have his diaper changed once in awhile. I mean, let's face it, when Louis Armstrong was thirteen years old, in Paris they were premiering *The Rite of Spring!* One of our founding fathers in jazz was a little child in New Orleans in an orphans home. One of the great, truly great jazz artists was just a kid when one of the major complex works of all time was being presented in the symphonic field in Paris with that big furor. So compare the two. We're talking about a baby. I mean jazz is just growing up! I hear new albums that were made just maybe a month ago in L.A. or New York that just amaze me. I mean it's moving; it's new things happening all the time.

Conversations: Is there any room for women in your scheme of things in jazz?

Breeden: Oh, yes, we've had—to give you a number, we've had probably about eight or ten young ladies come in for auditions and play well enough to make it. In fact, the first lady made our 1 O'Clock Band last year and played in it this year, until the end of the year when she graduated. But get this: she was offered a job; she flew to L.A. immediately, even before she got her graduation papers—she had finished all her work—to join the Toshiko Akiyoshi-Lew Tabackin Big Band and is in Japan right now on tour with them.

Conversations: What does she play?

Breeden: Baritone sax, the most unlikely instrument in there— the biggest, the heaviest. We've had ladies play jazz tenor; we've had one play lead alto; we've had two play piano. So, the door is open to them, you know. We have one thing that we base our membership and our bands on, one thing only—how well they play. Makes no difference. We're often put down: "Why don't you have blacks in your band?" No, there is no truth—

Conversations: I was just going to ask about that. The 1 O'Clock Band is all white.

Breeden: Yes, at present it is all white. But we have had absolutely no criteria except *how one performs* for membership. Last year our jazz trumpet player was Japanese—he is now on the faculty at Illinois, a tremendous player, Ray Sasaki. I would have to be a sociologist to discuss the facets of cruelty practiced on the blacks during the infamous slave days; I would have to be one totally involved in the commercial field to discuss the rip-offs of the blacks in the signing of recording contracts, booking of bands, managerial mistreatments, etc.

I can speak only as a musician and can state emphatically that the respect that I have personally witnessed, in hundreds of discussions with my students and with other musicians concerning the great contribution made with the gift to America and the world of jazz by our black brothers, is such that I personally want to do all that I can to erase those early days, at least in our own situation. And that is the only facet about which I can speak with personal involvement. The blacks are positively not held back, not kept out of the bands because of their color. I will meet my Maker knowing in my heart that this is a true statement.

By the way, we did have one black student to make the 1 O'Clock Band, Billy Harper—he's been with Gil Evans. He's had his own group going. He was the first and only black since I've been there—and I don't think that Gene Hall had one—who got himself together musically and academically well enough to make the 1 O'Clock Band. And he made it because he really got himself together. Not one of us would ever object to having blacks in there. But we're not going to just call them in to make us look better. I will not insult a young black player by saying, "I know we're under pressure and people wonder why we don't have blacks; would you come play with us?" Of course, I wouldn't tell him that. I won't even say, "We're going to be put down if we don't have one or two blacks in there; let's get you in here."

It would be an insult, because, first of all, the ones that we have had so far, their reading is not quite together well enough.

Leon Breeden

He would be scuffling all the time. The section would never get together. I'm not saying it's not possible; Harper proved otherwise. Nothing would thrill me more. I do everything possible to help our young black students there. Financially I do everything I can. I've cosigned notes with two or three.

Conversations: Do you have them in the program then?

Breeden: Oh, yeah, they're in our bands. I guess we have blacks in about five or six bands right now. And some get on up to the better bands. I just keep hoping: Is he going to keep going and keep his grades up? Many flunk out, or they don't do well in their academics.

Conversations: And this is a prerequisite for the 1 O'Clock Band?

Breeden: We're a school group. They've got to keep their grades up in the rest of their classes. They can't just come in and play jazz.

Conversations: Okay, you're seventeen years at North Texas State and you've turned out just hundreds and hundreds of musicians. What's the future of your program there? Is it going to grow bigger? Is the quality going to get higher? Is the marketplace going to get bigger for your product?

Breeden: One year from now we move to our first home, our first home in the history of our lab bands. We will have an area of the new building—a 7.5 million-dollar building going up—wherein we will have: two rehearsal halls, small group rooms, three recital halls, places to play. And we will be able to have two big bands rehearsing simultaneously, so that by about six in the evening we can open it up for small groups the rest of the night, with the bass and drums and all the equipment you've got to have.

The future is bright. The founding of the National Association of Jazz Educators gives us a national voice. I think we're getting better players all the time; our writers are coming in with some of the greatest new ideas I've ever heard; and I think our travels that we have done. . . when I was talking to you about our guests a minute ago—we have paid every penny of it ourselves. The school has not paid one penny. Our ticket sales

60

have paid for every guest we've had and every mile we've traveled.

Conversations: And I presume your recordings, too.

Breeden: And our recordings, strictly a nonprofit activity, which have continued since our first one in 1967 because our friends have bought them and helped us to pay for all costs, even postage stamps to pay for mailing them.

Conversations: Well, is the future of jazz in America really good?

Breeden: I think it's good. As long as we have people like Bill Moore—who literally moved mountains to personally make it possible for us to come to Charleston and be part of this famous Spoleto Festival, which had never had jazz included in its long history—jazz will continue to grow in importance and recognition. It is my feeling that we have quite a few Bill Moores around the world who truly believe in this American art form of jazz. I am positive time will prove that one of America's truly significant contributions to education is the inclusion of officially recognized instruction in this art. It is a wonderful feeling to know that I have helped my colleagues to bring this about.

Dizzy Gillespie was born on 21 October 1917 in Cheraw, South Carolina. His father, an amateur musician, died when Gillespie was ten years old. His family moved to Philadelphia, but Gillespie moved to Laurinburg, North Carolina, to accept a scholarship at the Laurinburg Institute. Gillespie started his professional career with the Frank Fairfax band. Later, he worked in the Cab Calloway orchestra, among others, and, with Charlie Parker, was a sideman in the Earl Hines band. Gillespie and Parker are given most of the credit for developing bebop. After more than forty years in the music business, Gillespie continues to be one of the most creative forces in jazz and is one of the most popular performers in the world.

Dizzy Gillespie

Zane Knauss wrote, narrated, and produced a television documentary about Dizzy Gillespie for the South Carolina Educational Television Network and the Southern Educational Communications Association. Gillespie came to Cheraw, South Carolina, for the filming, and it was there that this interview was conducted. In a small room of the Valerie Motel, owned by Gillespie's cousin, on a bleak evening in January 1975, Gillespie talked about his early years in Cheraw, Laurinburg, Philadelphia, and New York City.

Conversations: You were one of nine children.

Gillespie: I was the ninth.

Conversations: Your father was a musician. What did he play?

Gillespie: I know as a fact that he had all the instruments. He had the only bass violin—they weren't playing bass violins then in the jazz bands; they were playing tubas—but he had this old bass violin home. He had a mandolin; he had a clarinet; and my mother says he played them all.

Conversations: So of the nine children you were the only one musical, and this is where your interest came from?

Gillespie: Yeah, that is where it is. And it's a drag that my father didn't live to see me as a musician, because I imagine he would have enjoyed that, with the name that I got now—going all over the world making a living, getting into books.

Conversations: How old were you when he died?

Gillespie: I was ten. I hadn't even begun to show any interest in music, though. I remember when I was about two and a half, something like that, I used to fool around with the piano. I used to play "Coonshine Lady." I always did have a fascination for piano—throughout my whole life I've fooled around with the piano—and that's where most of my inspiration comes.

Conversations: When you were a young boy in Cheraw, South Carolina, what was life like for you and your family?

Gillespie: Scared most of the time. I was scared of my father. My father was super austere. He never did show any emotion toward us. The only emotion he showed was when he used to give me a whipping every Sunday. My brother and I used to get a whipping every Sunday morning.

Conversations: Why?

Gillespie: For what we did in the week—the previous week.

Conversations: He kept tabs?

Gillespie: No, but he just knew we had done something, so there it is. We got a beating every Sunday. Now there were some weeks that I didn't do anything, but I still got that whipping. So I decided very early to warrant the whipping. I spent the whole week putting together something to get a whipping for, and I managed to do it, too, brother. These people thought I was going to grow up to be a gangster or something, because I was pretty bad. You see, I didn't get into any serious trouble. I did things like throw rocks at girls, put chewing gum in their hair in class, if they had long hair put it in the inkwell, fight every day. I'd get a whipping in school every day.

I got to show you—this is the story of my life—the first day I went to school I got a whipping. There were two lots between our house and Mr. Harrington's home. As a matter of fact, his son, Brother Harrington, is the one who's the cause of my playing the trumpet. I'll get into that, but this is way before I started playing. Now, Mr. Harrington is a shoemaker. He owned a shoe shop uptown, and he had an ice cream parlor in the front—small, you know, with tables. My brother used to work there shaving ice and churning ice cream; then I would go up there and churn ice cream, and I would get a dish, you know.

My brother, Wesley, used to have nightmares. He'd jump up in the middle of the night and he'd see the woodman. There was an old ugly white man that used to sell wood to all the people, because all of us had fireplaces. But he was the ugliest soul—I don't think I've ever seen anybody as ugly as this guy since, after all of these years. Wesley used to have nightmares about him and say the woodman was going to get him, and I'd have to put a lock on him and hold him in the bed and wake him up and shake him up.

But one morning when he awakened I didn't get up fast enough, and he jumped up and cut his hand on one of those pitchers that you have in the house. We didn't have a toilet, so we had a basin and a pitcher. Well, he knocked it down and cut his hand very badly, and I had to go to work for him up there at Mr. Harrington's shoe shop. I got sick I ate so much ice cream that day.

But anyway, Mrs. Amanda Harrington—you see, my being the youngest child, I was home while all the rest of the kids were in school—well, Mrs. Amanda was an ex-schoolteacher and she used to teach me before I went to school. So when I went to school in the primer I was in about a second-grade level then, because I could read. I could count. I knew my alphabet. I could say my alphabet backwards, and all of this. And so the first day that I went to school I was very disinterested in what those kids were talking about because I was way up there in second grade. So I just whistled in the classroom.

When I whistled in this classroom a lady named Mrs. Strada Miller took me and shook me a couple of times, then made me get a switch and beat me. My father was furious, because I didn't know the rules or anything; it was my first day in school. But she never whipped me no more after that because my father talked to Professor Butts, who lived right across the street from us. He went over and said, "If the lady puts her hand on my kid again, there's going to be trouble." I went, "Oh, thank you." But that's the only time I heard him speak up for me; the rest of the time he was whipping me.

But anyway I stayed in that class maybe three months. There and then Professor Butts found out that I was advanced for that class, so they put me in the first grade. Then at the end of that year they put me in the second grade. That's where I caught up with my brother. I went all through school in my brother's class. I imagine he was pretty embarrassed. I could have passed him, but I didn't want to embarrass him more.

Conversations: Did you get any introduction to music in church here?

Gillespie: I used to go down to a Sanctified Church on Huger Street every Sunday, but I was a Methodist. I used to go down there to hear the music because I liked it.

There was the son of the pastor, Elder Birch—he had two sons, one named Johnny. They used to get my name mixed-up with Johnny Birch's name. My name is John Birks, but everybody called me John Birch. Right now people in Cheraw call me John Birch. But my name is B-i-r-k-s. That guy sure could play some drums—John Birch. He played snare drums.

Conversations: You ever play with him?

Gillespie: No. I never played in church.

Conversations: You mentioned the people who were instrumental in introducing you to the trumpet—the son of the shoemaker.

Gillespie: Brother Harrington was in a higher class than I. He was along with one of my sisters, Eugenia. When the state bought instruments for Robert Small School—they had all these instruments there and everybody wanted one. The bigger you were, the more chance you had to get what you wanted. I was little and they gave me a trombone; I couldn't even reach to the fifth position, but I took it. I was so mad about getting into music I didn't care. If they had given me a harmonica, I would have taken it.

So I fooled around with the trombone for a while. I learned the scale and watched other guys and used my ear and played along with them. Then on Christmas Brother Harrington's father bought him one of those shiny trumpets—long, shiny. What do you call that metal that wasn't silver, wasn't brass?—Silverplate. It was shiny.

Man, when I saw this horn under that Christmas tree I went crazy. I said, "Brother, let me try and play that." He said, "Go ahead and try it." I made a sound on it, and he said, "Oh, yeah, you make a pretty good sound." I said, "Will you let me practice on it sometime?" He said, "Yeah."

So I used to run from here to there, next door from my house to his house; when we were making too much noise we would go over to the other house. So finally I became pretty fair at just blowing into the trumpet. I learned how to read music. And that's when Miss Alice Wilson stepped in.

Conversations: That was in your third grade.

Gillespie: Yeah.

Conversations: She gave you lessons on the trumpet?

Gillespie: No, Miss Alice Wilson couldn't read music herself, but, as a matter of fact, she's a very gifted composer and has a very good ear. And she could hear songs on the radio and pick them out, but only in B-flat. Once a year we had a minstrel show at Robert Small School and it had Robert Hammonds, Ruth Bennett—there were so many names.

Robert Hammonds and somebody else were endmen. They stood on the end and told jokes, and they'd come out and do a little buckdance and jump back down, and then somebody else would come up and sing, or somebody'd come do a dance. But those were beautiful, beautiful productions.

Conversations: What did you do?

Gillespie: I played in the band. You see, Miss Alice Wilson had Tom Marshal, Wes Buchannon, Bill McNeal, and me in the band. Trombone, trumpet, bass drum, snare drum, and she played the piano. And we used to play for them to march into school every day. So that's how I started playing around.

Conversations: By ear?

Gillespie: Yeah, just playing in B-flat. She played B-flat.

Conversations: Just how did she encourage you, then, in terms of your music?

Gillespie: She taught us all of the tunes and made the arrangements. She told us what to play and we played it.

Conversations: But you did it all by ear?

Dizzy Gillespie

Gillespie: Yes. She said, "Here's the note you play," and I played it.

Conversations: Was she involved in your early training all through grade school or did she quit at the end of the third grade? Were you close to her?

Gillespie: All the while I was at Robert Small I played with Alice Wilson. Up until ninth grade.

Conversations: And when you left there, where did you go?

Gillespie: Laurinburg.

Conversations: Let's talk a little bit about the name. Obviously "Dizzy" is your professional name. Which do you prefer John Birks or Dizzy?

Gillespie: It doesn't matter to me, really. If you call me anything, I'll answer. Just call me. Of course, when I was in Cheraw my name was John Birks. All the people here call me by that name. But some of them want to be smart now and call me "Dizzy." Sounds awfully funny to hear someone that's been calling you one name all of your life all of a sudden start changing, calling you another name.

Conversations: How did you get your professional name?

Gillespie: Well, when I moved to Philadelphia in 1935, I didn't have a trumpet, and my brother-in-law went to the pawnshop and bought me one of those long trumpets. He didn't buy me a case. I used to carry it around in a paper bag, and that was unusual. They heard me—a guy down on Seventh and Pine that played the trumpet—and they didn't know my name, so they would say, "that dizzy trumpet player from down south." That developed into Trumpet Diz, and that developed into Dizzy.

But something happened in Philadelphia after working for $8 a week at Fifteenth and Bainbridge, $17, or something like that, at Tenth and Passingham. And then I got an audition to play with Frankie Fairfax's band, when he had Bill Doggett. He had a terrific band—Basie-style band. But I had trouble seeing the music because the guys notated so badly. I was reading rests—I thought that was a note. They thought I couldn't read, and they didn't give me the job. They gave the job to another guy.

Well, right after that the whole band quit. But the band was the cause of my not being with Frankie Fairfax's band. I remembered when Bill Doggett went down to the Harlem Club in Atlantic City to play, he found out that I could really read. I had only read printed music before and pr 'ed music was there. But these guys were writing so bad—Bill Doggett himself wrote good music, but very bad notation. You couldn't hardly know what it was; an eighth note looked like just a line or just a scribble. So they tried to get me to come down to Atlantic City, to play with that group. I fooled around with them and made like I was going, but I remembered. I wouldn't go.

Conversations: Let's go back. You played some gigs in Cheraw with a band which was started by Wes Buchannon. You had a small group; you played with the white high schools here; you played around; and then you went to Laurinburg, North Carolina. How did you happen to get to Laurinburg?

Gillespie: Well, it was a girl named Katherine McKay, who was studying nursing at Laurinburg. She discovered that the principal's son, Frank McDuffie, who's president of the Laurinburg Institute now, was finishing high school that year and also his first cousin, Isaac Johnson, son of the dean, was finishing high school and they went off to college. The band needed a trumpet and a trombone player to fill their places. So Katherine told them she knew two musicians in Cheraw who might be interested in getting a scholarship, and she contacted my mother. I said, "Yeah." I was glad to get out of Cheraw to go to school some place.

I stayed two years in Laurinburg. Well, I didn't get my diploma right then, but I got it later. I didn't finish high school in Laurinburg; needing several credits, I just ran away in 1935. My family had moved to Philadelphia. When I got to Philadelphia I went on to go to Europe and to New York; then I got my own small band; and then I had a big band and was on the road with Ella Fitzgerald, who, by the way, got one of her husbands from my band, and also Dinah Washington, who got one of her husbands from my band.

So anyway, we came on a tour down south, and we stopped off in Laurinburg to play a free concert at Laurinburg Institute in the daytime. In the middle of the concert Mrs. McDuffie walked out on the stage and said, "Here is something you left," and brought my high school diploma dated 1934, and my football letter and gave them to me. So now I'm not a high school dropout anymore.

Conversations: Now you've been back to both Laurinburg and Cheraw quite a few times, and in both towns they have had special celebrations for you, haven't they?

Gillespie: Yes, they're pretty nice to me down there. I'm the favorite son of Cheraw and Laurinburg. It's good to be the favorite son in two different states. It's nice to feel that they like me like that.

Conversations: But do you find your relationship to the two towns a contradiction to what a lot of other blacks who have been in the South and gone north have found in their relationships to hometowns? They have a reservoir of bitterness, and you don't seem to have that.

Gillespie: Well, no, I don't have bitterness anyway. I didn't have too much bitterness before, but my religion now teaches me—I belong to a religious faith called the Baha'i Faith—that the reason people act ungodly is because they are not spiritually developed enough to anticipate and see the joy and the goodness in acting right. They miss something. They miss life.

Conversations: After Philadelphia and your entree into the big band business, you got your major break about 1937.

Gillespie: I was playing with Frankie Fairfax in 1935, 1936, part of 1937—about 1936, really, and 1937. Charlie Shavers and Carl Warwick—Bama Warwick, came over to play in a new Frankie Fairfax band, and he got some new guys. They stayed several months, and then Tiny Bradshaw came through. Bama and Charlie left to go to the Astoria Club in Baltimore with Tiny Bradshaw, and they tried to get me to leave Philly. I wouldn't leave; I was afraid to leave home. And then they went away, and the next time they came through with Lucky Millinder's band. Well, this time they cruised me to New York to go with Lucky Millinder. That was in 1937.

Conversations: You were about eighteen, then, when you went to New York.

Gillespie: In 1937, I was nineteen going on twenty. I was born in 1917.

Conversations: Can you draw a word picture of Minton's and the chemistry that was up there at the time?

Gillespie: Minton's was just a part of the whole thing. There was another club—Minton's was the regular hours club for improvisation and creating. Monroe's Up-Town House was the other half, after hours. And I don't know whether more creativity happened at Minton's or at Monroe's Up-Town House, really, because it was seething. All the guys used to come and play down at Monroe's Up-Town House. Clark Monroe used to give us chili and hot dogs in the back. We'd eat and then we'd go on and play—never get paid. And Minton's—Teddy Hill had Minton's at that time.

    Mr. Minton was one of the first black officials in Local 802 of the musicians' union, and he had a place called the Rhythm Club. The Rhythm Club had a history before Minton's of all musicians converging—playing pool, cutting one another on the instruments. A new guy would come into town, and they would go get the best guy for him, or the guy up to that guy until they got to the top. That was the Rhythm Club. Well, Teddy was always a good businessman—not a very good musician, but a very good businessman. He knew talent, because when he hired me a couple of the guys in the band told him, "If that little guy goes to Paris, we're not going." Teddy said, "Well, I'll have to find a replacement for you, because he is going." So that's how I got the job.

Conversations: You were a young South Carolinian transferred to Philadelphia, now in New York and playing at Minton's. Anybody cut you on the horn? Did you get in on any of the free-for-alls?

Gillespie: Oh, man. You see, before Minton's when I came to New York in 1937, there were several trumpet players that were very "bad." There was one trumpet player that was better than all of us; his name is Bobby Moore, and he played with Count

Dizzy Gillespie

Basie. He played a solo in "Out the Window" with Count Basie. You can look that up and you will hear his trumpet solo and see how good he was. He knew all of Roy's solos. If Roy Eldridge wasn't ready one night, little Bobby was. Bobby was the best of our crowd. Bobby's been in the state hospital on the Island in New York since 1938, I think he went in.

Conversations: How was the setup at Minton's? How did it work?

Gillespie: I wasn't working at Minton's. I never worked there. They had the band that was comprised of Kenny Clarke, who was the leader; Thelonious Monk was the piano player; a boy named Nick Fenton on bass; Kermit Scott was the saxophone player; and Joe Guy was the trumpet player. Joe Guy you might remember as being the husband of Billie Holiday.

Monk has always been weird musically, and very difficult to follow. Monk had all these little things, and I was experimenting at this same time with my piano. Kenny and Monk used to come up to my house and we'd get together in the daytime and figure out little things; then we'd go down there and try them out at Minton's at night. I'd go down there and hang out all night with them.

Conversations: Is it true that you guys got together and tried these things out in the daytime so you could cut out the people you didn't want to play with you at nighttime?

Gillespie: Sometimes we did; sometimes we got tired. If there are eight horns on the bandstand and each guy wants to play eight or nine choruses, by the time you get to the end, man, the rhythm section is washed. So we would play some of them weird numbers of Monk's. One of those would clear off the bandstand—everybody except Johnny Carisi, a little white boy, little trumpet player. He learned all of Monk's numbers, so he never would get off the stand. He'd be right there playing all of the time—Johnny Carisi and, maybe, Don Byas. When Charlie Parker came into town he used to come by every now and then. When Charlie Parker came he rejuvenated the whole scene.

Conversations: How did you begin your association with Parker?

Gillespie: When he was playing at Monroe's Up-Town House I used to go down there and jam with them. At that time I was with

Cab Calloway. I'd go down and jam at Minton's and after hours at Monroe's. We became closely associated down there. I was playing with Lucky Millinder, with Edgar Hayes, Claude Hopkins, Fletcher Henderson after Cab Calloway, Les Hite, Boyd Raeburn—all the bands around New York—Georgie Auld.

Conversations: You were with Barnet, too, weren't you?

Gillespie: Barnet a little while, yes, and then Lucky Millinder fired me. He said I had lost my lip. Then he tried to hire me back, because Lucky would fire anybody. He would fire himself. My two weeks notice with Lucky Millinder ended in Philadelphia. By that time I had booked myself into a little club called The Downbeat Club in Philly to play with a house group there. Earl Hines came through town, and Billy Eckstine cruised me out on the road with Earl Hines.

Conversations: Eckstine was singing with Hines at that time.

Gillespie: Yes. Hines needed a tenor player. Charlie Parker was an alto player, but they bought him a tenor and he played tenor with the band.

Conversations: Wasn't Sarah Vaughan with that band, also?

Gillespie: Yes. Later all of us left Earl Hines together—Sarah, Charlie Parker, Billy. I joined Billy Eckstine's band as musical director. Then I left them and I went back to New York and got a job with Oscar Pettiford as co-leader of a band on 52nd Street. We sent Charlie Parker a telegram to Kansas City, asking him to come and join us. We didn't hear anything. He never got the telegram until about eight or nine months later. By the time he came the band had broken up; Joe Guy was playing with Oscar Pettiford; I had another band across the street with Budd Johnson.

But we got together with Max Roach in '44. And then in '45, I went into the Three Deuces—I had Charlie Parker and Ray Brown, Bud Powell and Al Haig. In '45, I took a job in California; it was a fiasco.

Conversations: This is when you went out there with Parker?

Gillespie: Yes.

Dizzy Gillespie

Conversations: That was a painful experience, wasn't it?

Gillespie: Yes, because, you see, they weren't ready for us.

Conversations: Well, I think you had some trouble with Parker, too, didn't you?

Gillespie: He was always strung out, but not in front of me. . . I couldn't say that he really was because I never saw him do anything. He always told me, "Aw, Diz, you know I don't do nothing like that," and he was so high then he couldn't even see. But I couldn't swear he was a user of narcotics because I never saw him. All the evidence was there, but I never saw him.

Conversations: Who coined the phrase "bop"?

Gillespie: That was during our stay on 52nd Street. We had numbers without names. I wouldn't call off a name: I would say, "be bop adada do bop baa bo de bop." Our music sounds like that: "ba daba do ba baba do bab baa do de bop oo bop de bam!" They would hear us doing that and the press picked it up.

Conversations: Did you object to that?

Gillespie: It didn't bother me. Duke Ellington told me, "John Birks," he said, "the mistake you made was to let them name your music bebop. You should have had them name it 'Gillespieana' and that would have been it." Like "Ellingtonia" and, you know, there is no time limit to that. But I didn't have any control over that.

Conversations: At that time you had the goatee and the beret.

Gillespie: That was part of the deal. I used to wear a beret and I used to wear horn-rimmed glasses. And everybody started doing it.

Conversations: But you still had the freedom to do your thing, didn't you?

Gillespie: Yes, because I was always funny on the stage, and I could get by with a lot of things with the music; but I played my music all the time.

Conversations: What was the reaction of your friends back in Cheraw and Laurinburg? Did you hear from them?

Gillespie: Oh, they glorified in it—"the big royal statesman from Cheraw, South Carolina." It was nice I got a good reaction from the people in Cheraw.

Conversations: Did you hear from people you hadn't heard from for a long time?

Gillespie: I kept in touch with the mayor of Cheraw, mayor Miller Ingram, and recently I've been in touch with the present mayor, Charles Jackson. I have relatives here anyway, so I am sort of close to them.

Conversations: Ralph Gleason said in a recent article that you have calmed down. You know who you are; you know where you've been and where you're going.

Gillespie: Yes, but I haven't finished creating. I know what I have to do now, and I go about doing it in a professional way.

Conversations: You take your music seriously.

Gillespie: The most seriously.

Conversations: Do you think that the audiences generally are doing the same thing?

Gillespie: Not necessarily. They look at the fringes. They take it a little lightly—even some of the critics do. But if they would sit down and listen, they'd know I am dead serious about the music. There's nothing more serious.

Conversations: Do you object to this kind of treatment?

Gillespie: No, it doesn't bother me at all. You see, history will either vindicate you or prove you're a phony. So I rely on history to do that for me.

Conversations: Most people don't know it, but you've recorded a lot as a pianist. Which instrument do you prefer, trumpet or piano?

Gillespie: Trumpet is my instrument. That's my name.

Conversations: But you do well as a head piano player.

Gillespie: I'm a pretty good accompanist, but not a soloist.

Dizzy Gillespie

Conversations: Your piano playing goes all the way back to the famous recording of "Koko"with Charlie Parker, doesn't it?

Gillespie: And "Billy's Bounce." I just happened to be there. The piano player didn't show up.

Conversations: What do you think is the most important composition you've done?

Gillespie: The one I want to write tomorrow.

Conversations: How many have you written yesterday?

Gillespie: All my yesterdays—about 200, I guess.

Conversations: What's your status from a musical standpoint in Europe? Do they appreciate you more than the hometown people?

Gillespie: Yes, I'm very big in Europe.

Conversations: Is it more cerebral there than it is here?

Gillespie: Yes, they know what's true by the test of time. As I said before, time will tell.

Conversations: Do they also know where Cheraw, South Carolina, is?

Gillespie: I tell them all the time.

Eric Kloss was born in Greenville, Pennsylvania, in 1949, and began playing the saxophone at the age of ten. He made his professional debut in Pittsburgh when he was twelve. In 1972, Eric received the Scholastic Achievement Award from Recording for the Blind, as one of the four outstanding blind college students in the United States. He has recorded more than forty of his compositions, and in 1976, a documentary film musical score he wrote won third place in the 12th Annual Chicago Film Festival. Kloss performs with his own group in Pittsburgh and elsewhere, records with internationally known jazz figures, and frequently appears in concert in the United States and abroad.

Eric Kloss

Eric Kloss was twelve years old when he and Zane Knauss first met. Kloss was just beginning to blossom as a jazz musician. In March 1977, sixteen years, seventeen record albums, and dozens of compositions later, Kloss and Knauss got together in Kloss' home in Pittsburgh for this conversation. Kloss and Knauss talked sitting on a couch in the young musician's workroom, a converted sunroom in the spacious brick home located two blocks from the campus of the University of Pittsburgh.

Conversations: You seem to derive a great deal of pleasure from your music.

Kloss: Whenever I'm writing something that I feel is worthwhile, it is exciting and wonderful to me. It's one matter to just take things and sort of put them together, and I can do that. Another way is to create music wholistically. Let's say, for example, you have an idea. You just get the initial phrase and that is the germ for a whole that you know is there; then fill in the pieces. And when you do that, then it's fascinating to just watch it come out. But sometimes it's a struggle to get it out.

Conversations: When do you know it's out?

Kloss: When the piece is finished. What happens with me is that I'll run into an idea that is slightly new to me or different. A lot of times I'll be playing the piano. . . like today I just wrote a twenty-four-bar thing. It's sort of like a germ. It's an idea that's slightly different, and then when you're exposed to that idea somehow it sets off a whole chain of creative events within yourself. But it's not perceived as one. It's many things and it's going to take a step-by-step process to get it out there; but it's all there in its essence, like a seed. And that's just what I like to think of it as—a seed or a little germ.

Eric Kloss

Conversations: How do you maintain your enthusiasm for this kind of creative process? It's hard work, isn't it?

Kloss: Well, yes, but it's what I do; that's why I'm here, basically, to create music. LeRoi Jones quite a few years ago talked about art, and he made the distinction—I don't necessarily agree with it—that the white, European-oriented listener and composer are involved with art as a product, and as something to be on display. But his contention was that art is a process; it's like our conversation here. You're capturing the process that's going on rather than the product. My feeling is that it's both; the process of art creates products as corollaries to its existence.

As part of my artistic process I did a duo album with Barry Miles. The next step in the process was to write something for a small ensemble. Then I realized: "Now wait a minute. I've got this band in Pittsburgh and I haven't really written anything for them in awhile. Why don't I come back to my roots, look at them in a different perspective, and write some things for that band." So during the last week, that's what I've been doing. Now that's another part of the process.

All these products are expressions of the process, so each product requires a certain amount and type of work. Each product demands certain things of the artist. There's a part of the artist that is always in front of himself on the path. There's a superartist inside of the artist that knows where it's going to go, at least two or three steps ahead, so it can feed information or problems or challenges to the artist. So there's no question of not being enthusiastic because, in the first place, you know that whatever you're involved with is going to enable you to create better art and to expand your art. For me, that's why I'm here: to expand my own potential and my art.

Conversations: Are you over into the black area of jazz creation; are you, as a white person, invading that area? Are you allowed into that area?

Kloss: There was an interesting statement by George Duke, the pianist. He was asked basically the same question but from the other side: Do you think that white players have a right to play jazz? He said that jazz, in its beginning, was a synthesis of European harmony and African rhythm. The instrument that I play is the saxophone. Now that's a bastardization, if you will. But someone who would look at it from another perspective would say that the saxophone is a synthesis of a brass instrument and a woodwind instrument. So my answer is that opposites, if creatively aligned, bring forth the universe. From this premise it follows that black and white musicians, though they may come from different subcultures and may, therefore, differ in some respects, can contribute together to a music that has the strength of both. Black music is black music, and I've been involved with a lot of black music. I've had many blacks say, "You really reach me."

Conversations: They don't explain it?

Kloss: They don't have to, because I understand what they're saying. I love to play for black audiences. They're really wonderful.

Conversations: They respond to you?

Kloss: They really do. Who knows what the explanation is. No explanation I've heard quite makes sense. Some people think that because a guy is black or blind, he can play. That never held water for me. It's just that for some reason or other there's a part of me that fits with the part of black music that's outside there, just like there's a part of me that fits with rock, and there's a part of me that fits with whatever. The object of the game is to take the inner pieces that I have and fit them with what's going on outside, so that it makes a whole or a unity.

Conversations: In your alto playing, have you consciously or unconsciously emulated any of the alto players you've ever heard or known? Have you picked up what they've been willing to give you through the years or what they've been able to teach you and then gone on in your own direction?

Kloss: That's about it. I try to be involved with the essences: What is "Charlie Parker-ness"; What is "John Coltrane-ness."?

Conversations: I notice you don't mention "Johnny Hodges-ness."

81

Eric Kloss

Kloss: Yes. Not so much "Johnny Hodges-ness," although I know how to play in that style; but that style has never really grabbed me. I have heard things of Johnny Hodges that I really loved.

Conversations: Which were they?

Kloss: "Warm Valley" and that thing called "Three and Six," and they were beautiful. But my roots aren't there. My roots from that direction are from Bessie Smith. Or, I feel, from my father who taught me a lot of the 1920 standards. I feel from that place, and I feel from Jimmy Rushing.

Conversations: The shouting blues.

Kloss: Yes, I feel from the blues singers of that time. Now that's something that I never thought about before. I can listen to somebody like King Oliver and groove on him intellectually; his group was doing all kinds of form things back then, but that music doesn't hit my pulse.

Conversations: You mentioned that Parker hit your pulse. Do you like his quickness, his tone, his phrasing, what?

Kloss: It's his essence. I was thinking the other day about Charlie Parker. I went back to listen to him. What Bird did, from what I can hear, was to observe his own playing. He had certain licks and things; a lot of his playing was just sort of putting these together in different creative ways, like Bach. But every once in awhile he would come out and really speak, and it blew my mind. For a long time I was thinking to myself, "That's just pure invention." But it wasn't. I can hear his pieces because I've been involved with Bird enough to know what his pieces are. Every once in awhile he'll cut through that, which is encouraging to me because sometimes I find myself playing by rearranging the parts of what I know already. Then every once in awhile that essence comes through. Somebody like Trane is so deep and so advanced harmonically. The way he constructs his solos is not as obvious to me. But I find myself relating very strongly to them emotionally.

Conversations: Did you ever work with Coltrane?

Kloss: No. I just met him and I talked to him for a few minutes. The only thing he said to me was: "If you play music, don't waste any time." That was all he said to me and that was enough. I spent a little time with Eric Dolphy, too. He didn't talk too much. The only thing I remember him saying concerned the post of his bass clarinet. He was fixing it. Now Pat Martino I've associated with a lot and we've stayed up all night talking about this type of thing—the principles behind creativity. Pat is a great inspiration to me. I look up to him.

Conversations: Well, you have little or no vibrato in your playing. This is, I guess, the modern way of using an alto sax. Do you think this is cleaner, straighter to the point in how you're developing your music?

Kloss: Oh, it's just the way I feel. Sometimes I use some vibrato. It's a slow vibrato, and it's not real wide. In that way it does differ from Johnny Hodges or some of the older players. But you know, in that respect, I like Ben Webster. Ben had a fast vibrato but he used it very tastefully; he'd use it at the end of a phrase or something.

Conversations: Sort of as punctuation?

Kloss: Yes. I liked Charlie Parker's vibrato and John Coltrane's vibrato and I think I've been influenced by them. So, in that sense, the vibrato I use has something to do with them.

Conversations: Do you consciously copy phrases or patterns from other musicians?

Kloss: It's not getting totally into the parts of their styles, but listening and trying to intuit their essences and incorporating them into my own playing. Maybe I might play a lick or so of Eric Dolphy or Charlie Parker or Coltrane or Lockjaw Davis. I like Lockjaw. I really like the way he digs in. I think Lockjaw taught me a lot about just how to dig in: how to dig in and burn, and how to make a rhythm section dig in and burn, too. Lockjaw is a master at that. In fact, I heard him in Washington, D.C., last summer, and he just blew me away. Now, to me, he is one of the older players who is a real master.

83

Eric Kloss

Conversations: Are there really new ideas in music, particularly in playing the alto in a jazz format, or has it all been stated and is it now up to people like you to rework things?

Kloss: I don't know. A lot of it is rearrangements of older forms, but then again there are other new developments, like the phase shifter.

Conversations: What's that?

Kloss: It's an electronic device that shifts the tonal quality.

Conversations: It fits into your horn, is that it?

Kloss: I hook the microphone into the phase shifter and then into the amplifier. It's not a real harsh or dominating electronic device. Unlike a lot of electronic things that I've found which are much too electronic, the phase shifter, to me, extends what I want to do on the instrument. So that's different. That's something that Trane or Bird didn't have.

Conversations: So technology has taken over?

Kloss: It hasn't taken over; it's just added new dimensions to the music. Trane did something with the lipping of harmonics: if you finger a middle F-sharp and you lip it up, since the saxophone is partly brass, you get a bugle effect, and you can get a C-sharp.

Conversations: But the notes aren't really on the horn, are they?

Kloss: Well, not per se, no, but that's something new that Trane discovered about the instrument. I have noticed an effect that Jan Hammer and people like him produce on a synthesizer. This effect can be produced on saxophone using the same principle that Trane used in lipping up. The flexibility of the tone produced on the harmonics is similar in color to the sound produced by the synthesizer. I found this effect partly because I was influenced by the synthesizer.

Conversations: Do you think the music of today is in a much more sophisticated dimension as opposed, let's say, to the music of the twenties, or thirties, or even forties when it was two-beat jazz, or stride piano, or swing?

84

Kloss: Though the forms and colors of today are more varied and complex, the emotional content and basic drive of the music, to me, remains the same. In fact, look at the rock beat. It's as basic as anything that's gone before.

Conversations: In what way?

Kloss: Just that pulse, that heartbeat. Mel Lewis and I talked about this a couple of months ago. He said that the dance music of today has basically the same pulse as the music played by Count Basie that people danced to in the thirties.

Conversations: Well, then, what makes the music of today different from the music of the thirties?

Kloss: The music of the thirties didn't have as much complexity happening on top of the beat as the music of today has. What has happened is that the rock beat has opened up a lot of things because if you have that as a base, then you can put a lot of complex melodic and harmonic statements on top of it. There's always going to be simplicity and complexity, and simplicity is going to enable complexity to happen.

It is interesting that stride pianists had to play the piano with a lot of left-hand facility to keep that steady beat going as well as playing complementary figures with the right hand. But then in the forties when everything lightened up and the drummer didn't play all four beats on the bass drum anymore, the pianist didn't have to use his left hand constantly for keeping the time and he could get involved with different kinds of chords and voicings. Then Herbie Hancock and Ron Carter and Tony Williams came along, and sometimes Herbie would just play single-note lines. He wouldn't even play chords, so it would just be lines going on.

It's always changing. It's always going to be something simple that will be the basis of other things that are complicated. Things will just be rearranged in different ways, different kinds of simplicity and complexity moving together. So music that is music at all is going to have emotion to it: soul, feeling, and body movement. But also there is the intellectual-cerebral, and there's the whimsical, the strange, and the beautiful. It's all there in the music.

Eric Kloss

You can't say that in 1940 there was no humor in music. Then in 1950 a new development—humor was created. Maybe in 1877 some guy told a joke about a carriage and then in 1977 somebody tells a joke about a jet plane, but it's still a joke. It's still something that makes somebody feel good and makes them laugh. The products of humor are going to differ, but the humorous aspects of the process are going to continue. Whether it be in music or in humor or in life in general, there will always be things that are new, spontaneous, and changing; and there will also be elements underlying these which will remain stable.

Jazz today is tremendously influenced by rock. In this sense it has taken on a new form. However, the elements of improvisation, rhythmic excitement, and the close communication among musicians remain the same as they have always been from New Orleans to the present.

Conversations: That brings up a question. Are all these musical definitions flattening out and becoming unrecognizable? For example, you talk about jazz-rock, and then there's hard rock, and then there's not-so-hard rock; there's modern jazz, and then there's not-so-modern jazz. Are all of these idioms fusing together so that you're simply playing music rather than having specific definitions for each thing you play?

Kloss: I think it's coming closer to that. One critic used the term "fusion music." I think that makes a lot of sense.

Conversations: Is it good or bad?

Kloss: Well, I think in a sense it's good, because now musicians who formerly couldn't communicate with each other can now communicate. I wrote a piece for a classical ensemble recently and I'm basically a jazz player. But because of the direction in which music is going I can do that now, where it was much harder for musicians to do this twenty years ago. People didn't know what to do. They had little sense of unity with the third stream in their attempts to fuse jazz and classical forms. But now it is getting to the point where music is music.

Conversations: You can mix it up.

Kloss: Oh, yes, but I think that at the same time there are always going to be musics happening. It's just that people who are becoming musically aware are able to draw from a lot of different sources and still make music that makes sense.

Conversations: Now is this going to produce a new type of musician? As a musician develops, is more going to be demanded of him than mechanical expertise on his instrument?

Kloss: I think the musician of the future will be called upon to keep his ears open. Even in the forties it was happening with Bird. Sometimes he was influenced by Latin American music, sometimes he played ballads, like "Laura," and sometimes he'd play his own tunes. So now it's basically the same thing. It's just an extension—knowledge itself is starting to become very global. I think it is a very natural process that when a musician comes up in a given environment, he's got certain things with which to make music. Depending on how open his ears are, there will be a lot of things for him to hear; and whatever he hears and likes and is able to put into practice, that's what he is going to play.

Conversations: A lot of the jazz you play and a lot of the musicians with whom you are associated play very complicated figures. How do you, as someone without sight, adjust to this? Do you have to memorize things or is it all improvisation?

Kloss: There's a certain amount of memorization that has to be done, but in the long run that is as much an advantage as it is a disadvantage, because anybody who wants to play something and really gets loose with it has got to memorize it anyway. If guys constantly rely on written music, they can never quite get relaxed with it because they have to be involved with something outside themselves. They have to look at the pages. My method is good for me because I just go through a piece and memorize it at first, then I never have to worry about it again. I just keep on playing it and keep on refining it.

Conversations: How do you commit a piece of music to memory? Do you have braille scores, or do you just listen to it, or what?

Eric Kloss

Kloss: I use cassettes a lot. I just make a cassette tape of the music and memorize it. Braille music, to me, has never been a necessity. You have to memorize the music anyway, and I can memorize it faster by hearing it. However, if I keep on getting into classical music, I might learn braille music to be able to check out the scores.

Conversations: Are you moving more and more into classical music?

Kloss: Well, that's another direction in which I'm moving. I find that the forms are fascinating. For example, Elliott Carter wrote a composition, "Eight Etudes and a Fantasy for Woodwind Quartet." As soon as I get done writing some material for the band, I'm going to devote myself to trying to write in a similar form. Yet there are jazz forms that are still fascinating to me. I'm coming back to the traditional AABA song form and writing some things, but this type of writing seems a lot easier to me now than it ever has. I guess I'm going to keep on checking into classical forms and try to find ways to apply them to my own music. But this certainly isn't going to exclude any other things that I'm involved in, because I love to play funky, and I love to play simply, too. There are times when, to me, I really play simply, but perhaps some other people feel that it's complicated. There are some things I play that are complicated in the sense that they take a long time to learn and you have to be on your toes playing the music, things like "Fusion Suite," a composition of Barry Miles, in which some parts are very complicated. However, I will always want to keep an aspect of my music that is very simple, like singing a song. I have always admired Lester Young's ability to do this. His music flowed so much—it was very melodic.

Conversations: You said you're probably going over to the Berlin Jazz Festival.

Kloss: Yes. In November, 1977.

Conversations: What's it like to an artist to come out on the stage and be expected to entertain, or educate, perhaps? What kind of a feeling do you get when you do this and you know there is a big audience out there? Does it have an impact on you?

Kloss: I can approach it from a couple of different points of view. One thing is that if the audience is receptive, it's really going to add to the music.

Conversations: Can you sense their receptivity, aside from the applauding and stomping?

Kloss: Oh, sure, sure. It's just a feeling. It's a collective energy that they radiate. It comes to us and we, as performers, radiate this, along with our own energy, back to them again. It's like a loop. This kind of rapport can help to create a meaningful experience for both artist and audience. If there's a dead audience, then I just say, "Well, okay, I don't really care what you think; I'm going to play anyway."

Conversations: You're going to do what you came out there to do.

Kloss: Right, because I'm basically a performer more than an entertainer in the sense that I think an entertainer is much more concerned with the impression that he makes on his audience.

Conversations: And a performer?

Kloss: A performer performs. He has grown up with what he's performed and he's lived with it, and now it's his life and that's what he does. When people respond, it gives a sense of satisfaction to the performer; he has been affirmed; someone from the outside is saying, "Yes. You're on the right path; you're doing the right thing." It is also a joy to me to have other people enjoy my music because I enjoy it. I'm happy when my joy is shared and when it can be shared in such a natural way. A lot of people come up to me and say, "Boy, you just give so much." But to me it's so easy; it's the easiest thing in the world to play. It's hard in some respects because you have to put in the time, but the actual act is so easy and feels so good.

Conversations: It's like presenting a gift, I suppose.

Kloss: Yes. There's nothing else I really want to do.

Conversations: This has been your consuming ambition since when? At what age did you start playing?

Eric Kloss

Kloss: I started when I was ten.

Conversations: Was it the alto that started it?

Kloss: Right. It doesn't matter—the saxophone. I picked up the saxophone and said, "This is what I've got to do." It took me a couple of years to get really serious about it, but I knew from that moment that music was going to be my life. This kind of feeling has come to me about many aspects of my life. When I was about twelve, before I started to shave, I thought to myself, there are two things that I want when I'm a teenager: I want to smoke a pipe, and I want to grow a mustache. So I smoked a pipe for about four or five years and experienced that, and I still have the mustache. The minute I have heard about new things, I've known whether I was going to be involved in them or not. It's just been a process of growth after that. But it's like something or someone is informing me of what is going to happen, and it feels right to me because it's right there. Another example of this type of experience is my involvement with the Transcendental Meditation technique.

Conversations: Jazz musicians always give the impression of casualness to an audience; it's almost a studied casualness. In the case of Gillespie, it was even a gimmick: the beret, the glasses, the language, and so forth. Yet when you dig deeper, you find an enormous discipline behind jazz. The facade gives way to a true professionalism, and even more than that, a very serious intent. Is this true about jazz musicians as opposed to classical artists, whom you automatically assume are serious? You guys are serious, aren't you?

Kloss: Sure. Jazz, like I said, is sort of a crossbred music, coming from a number of different sources. It's also a hybrid in that it makes full use of freedom and structure. The jazz musician is a paradox of tight and loose thinking. Traditionally the composer of classical music has had freedom within structure at his disposal; he's had structures within which to work complemented by the freedom of his imagination. However, since the beginning of the century these structures have become less important. The classical player only has room in the sense of interpretation; that's his freedom, but he can't play with the music itself.

Conversations: Can't go far away from the notes, can he?

Kloss: No, unless it's written in the score. Someone has to tell him to be free. A lot of contemporary composers are writing instructions on their scores like, "All right, now, take your bow and slap it across the strings from three to eight times." Freedom is dictated. Even to freak out is dictated and that's what's really neat, I think, about the new classical music.

Conversations: Do you dig this?

Kloss: Well, I think it's a really interesting development, but the only way I can explain it is like this. I do a little thing with my jaw, slapping out rhythms and changing the tone by moving my mouth. I was doing this at Pat Martino's house, and Pat was just getting into composing. He said, "Boy, I'd like to be conducting about twenty of you guys playing on your jaws and then just shout, 'Fortissimo!' "

Conversations: Everybody goes wild.

Kloss: Smacking themselves, you know.

Conversations: You find these gimmicks have great humor in them?

Kloss: Yes, they're great, but I'm not even sure they're gimmicks. They are the composer's attempt to free up the classical player, to try to tell the classical player to be free. But it's not going to work, totally, because the only way that you can really be free is by doing something that you want to do.

Conversations: So then you're right back to the jazz player.

Kloss: Right, because the jazz player is a spontaneous composer. He's got the elements of freedom and structure at his disposal, although even he must predetermine most of his structures. The composer of contemporary music sets the conditions for new structures when he gives the players new freedoms.

Conversations: Explain that to me. You're standing on stage with your horn in your hands and you reach a point in any given

Eric Kloss

performance where you reach what you describe as spontaneous composition, or improvisation; is that what you're saying?

Kloss: Right, but again it depends on the form. There are some forms that are much freer than others. I can use different approaches to even, say, a song form. I can stick closely to it while improvising or, if I feel it's in good taste, I can play anything I want to. But then I have to come back. I always have to know where the structure is. If I'm playing in a free form, then the only thing I need to do is to listen to the other players. A lot of the free music that I really dig is just music that grows out of the communication of the different musicians.

Conversations: I've heard that real jazz comes from the street. What do you think?

Kloss: The man who knows the world of the street as well as the academic world is further ahead than the man who has knowledge of either the street or the college exclusively. The academician, if he's been into it all his life, knows only one side of music, and he's further into that side than the guy who's been on the street half of his life. But the guy who's been on the street half of his life knows what the academician doesn't know. And if the guy has been on the street all of his life, then he doesn't know any of what the academician knows.

Conversations: You're talking about blends, then.

Kloss: Right. Jazz has always been a blend; and the jazz musician is a blend of the ridiculous and the very serious, of the formal and the informal.

Conversations: But you're not a man of the street.

Kloss: No, but I've been involved with people who are from the streets. Although I haven't experienced a lot of that, I know a lot of the philosophy, at least in a theoretical way, and I can use that kind of thinking in what I do.

Conversations: Has your blindness at all affected your attitude toward what you compose? Does any of that spill out into your instrument?

Kloss: No. I think that's irrelevant.

Conversations: You mentioned the rapport with your fellow musicians. I've seen you perform in situations where you were surrounded by musicians, but you also were wearing earphones. Do these things tend to intimidate a performance or do they help you in hearing the other musicians around you?

Kloss: Are you talking about in the studio?

Conversations: Yes.

Kloss: Well, in the studio it's a different kind of situation because of the physical setup. There are baffles between you and the other musicians, so there isn't any leak. But because of that it's very difficult to hear, so earphones in certain instances are an advantage. You put your phones on and you can hear the whole group. You might be referring to the TV session with Barry Miles.

Conversations: Right.

Kloss: The earphones were very useful to me in that situation, because if I hadn't used them I would have overblown even more than I found myself doing to compensate, because there was all that brass and just me.

Conversations: As a soloist.

Kloss: Right. Therefore I really needed the phones to hear the balance. But on a stage, especially if you're close together, there is no need for phones. There are some instances on certain stages where phones would help. It's only a question of hearing. That's the only thing the phones are for. Anytime I don't think they are going to help me hear the music, I'm not going to use the earphones.

Conversations: Are you working with other electronic devices? You mentioned the phase shifter that you use with your horn. But how about a synthesizer and other things? Are you used to working with these devices?

Kloss: I think there's some place for a synthesizer, but so far I've directed the synthesizer player to use it like a horn. I've always tried to be very musical with it, musical in a conventional sense. I

Eric Kloss

still don't hear pure electronics enough to use them in a general way in my own music. But I have, however, written a film score in which I used qualities other than the hornlike ones of the synthesizer.

Conversations: Well, is this something that you're going to get into more and more, this fusion of the alto—or any horn for that matter—with electronic music?

Kloss: Well, probably.

Conversations: Do you feel compelled to experiment with electronic devices?

Kloss: No, not really. The only thing that I feel compelled to do is to keep my ears open and listen to what different people are doing with the synthesizer so that if there's anything there I can relate to, I can pick up on it. Now I do feel compelled to do that, to keep aware of the trends.

Conversations: Do you visit or do you have associations with people in academic life, who are in the music schools messing around with these things?

Kloss: Some. I've met a couple of people, but I guess I'm thinking more in terms of the jazz-rock trend where there's a lot of synthesizer used. The real practical application of all of this, for me, has come basically from rock because the rock musicians have explored how to use electronic music, applying it to other forms akin to jazz. Composers of movie scores have also used electronic music to good effect. Academicians, or the guys who have written purely electronic music up to this point, have just been involved with it as an end in itself, like Stockhausen; what I've heard of him is just electronic music and it's beautiful because it's electronic music. But this type of music is basically different from either rock or movie music. Wedding it to any other form necessarily creates a blend.

Conversations: We're back to the blends again.

Kloss: Right.

Conversations: It sounds like that's what this is all about.

94

Kloss: But it's sort of a blend of well-developed differences; without the differences, you couldn't have a blend, you see. So I can't see everything going into an amalgam. That's Muzak. Muzak draws from many styles. When you think about it, there are few popular styles that Muzak doesn't use. But it's all blended into that thing which doesn't make any sense to me. It's all watered-down pabulum. You might hear a little synthesizer thing, a little nice, watered-down jazz, but whatever it is, is watered down. Music isn't to be watered down, although music isn't to be totally harsh, either.

Conversations: If music isn't to be watered down, then people have to sit down and pay attention to it, don't they? Muzak is designed specifically for people to take rather casually.

Kloss: It's a very subjective thing. But Muzak makes me nervous.

Conversations: How?

Kloss: Because it's just so sweet, and I can hear the contrivedness of it. But obviously the Muzak business is successful and there are a lot of people who can take Muzak for granted. There are people who can take TV for granted, who can turn a TV on and just let it happen and then do whatever they want to do. But I can't. TV impinges on my consciousness; I'm uncomfortably aware of it most of the time when it's on. There are some good programs on TV, especially the educational stations, that are giving invaluable service to the country.

Conversations: Does it bother you at all when some critics or people who hear your work try to build messages into it? Is there a message in your music or in other jazz?

Kloss: Well, I can't think of any specific instance when a critic has said that my music had a particular message.

Conversations: Would you like them to?

Kloss: Well, it's up to them. Do I have a message? I think so, but what it is only the music can say. In certain instances I have used music to express a philosophical idea.

Conversations: For example?

Eric Kloss

Kloss: Well, the last album that I made was a duo album with Barry Miles, and we played a composition of mine entitled, "The Goddess, the Gypsy and the Light," which I drew partly from the idea of the loss and recovery of the knowledge of the Absolute, from the TM conception of things. This work is concerned with two forces, the Goddess and the Gypsy, with a third transcendent force, the Light, integrating the first two. The Goddess symbolizes order and structure and going to bed early and everything nice. The Gypsy symbolizes a vital, passionate, and, at the same time, destructive force. The Light is what brings them together; this is the transcendent Absolute. Meditation, too, helps to integrate opposite values.

Conversations: *Are you into meditation?*

Kloss: Oh, yes. I've been doing TM regularly for three years.

Conversations: *What does it do for you?*

Kloss: I think it has put balance into my life; it has helped me to think more clearly; it's made me more aware.

Conversations: *Has it done anything for your musical development at all?*

Kloss: I think it has benefited my music in subtle ways, enabling me to make clearer musical statements. Indirectly it has affected it by making me more aware of my creative cycles. There are times when I'll write something very extended, a little on the heavy side. That takes a lot of energy. But then, again, there are times when maybe I'll write some lighter or shorter pieces. It depends on where I am in the cycle.

The music I listen to seems to follow patterns, too. Like I was listening to Elliott Carter, Morton Feldman, and Michael Tippett during the time I was writing a contemporary piece of my own, "Environments for Alto Saxophone and Small Ensemble." Then I realized it was time for a change, and I went back to listening to Bird and Trane and to the writing of original tunes for the band. The artist would like everything to grow in straight lines, to move from here to there. But it grows in circles. One thing develops while another thing waits. I like to think of it as a spiral movement, sort of an upward movement. That seems to be what's happening.

Conversations: When you write music, do you get an idea for an extended piece as you described, and if you can't quite cut it, do you leave it and go to something else? Can you do two or three things simultaneously?

Kloss: Sure. In fact, I memorized two pieces from Yehudi Menuhin's and Ravi Shankar's album, "West Meets East." The first one I learned easily, but I had a hard time mastering the technical intricacies of the second.

Conversations: Were you trying to transpose it to alto?

Kloss: Right. So I let three or four months go by and came back and tried it again but I still couldn't get it quite right. Now it may be time to try it again.

Conversations: Do you worry about these things?

Kloss: No, I don't worry about things I can't do because I know they'll always be there. They'll be there for the rest of my life and I can keep coming back to them. If there are some things I can't do, at least I can say that all my life I've tried to do them. I don't have to feel frustrated because I've tried my best. In the meantime I've made a lot of music that has made myself and other people happy.

Conversations: What are you looking for from your music— fame, fortune, satisfaction?

Kloss: I want to play music. Any fame or fortune that comes for me is only to help the music grow. A long time ago I remember hearing one person praise my music and another put it down. I was about twelve or thirteen then and was considered a child prodigy. Child prodigies get a lot of praise and blame. So I made the decision that I would listen to praise or blame but not necessarily pay attention. It's the same with fame and fortune. The more fame and fortune I have, and I can still play the music that I want to play, the better. Because then I'll have more chances to develop my own music. But fame and fortune, in themselves, I don't find myself concerned about. I want enough money to live, and I want enough fame so that I can have as few blocks as possible in producing the music that I want to produce.

James Duigald McPartland was born in Chicago, Illinois, on 15
March 1907. As a teenager, he switched instruments from the violin
to the cornet, and since then has never played anything else. Early
in his life, McPartland developed a fascination with jazz. He formed
a band in high school, quit school to play with the famed
Wolverines, and for more than fifty years has been one of the great
practitioners of Chicago-style jazz. He now makes his home in
Merrick, Long Island, plays the jazz club circuit on Manhattan, and
occasionally joins ex-wife Marian McPartland for club dates around
the country.

Jimmy McPartland

Jimmy McPartland and Zane Knauss first shook hands in Rockefeller Center in Manhattan on a hot, humid Wednesday afternoon in July 1977, moments before McPartland began performing on a program in the "Music for a City Evening" series. The two agreed to meet for a conversation later that night at Jimmy Ryan's, the famed jazz room on 54th Street. Then the lights went out all over town! But they burned candles at Jimmy Ryan's and McPartland continued to play. Between sets, Knauss and McPartland retired to Jimmy's station wagon parked across the street, sipped tea, and talked in the midtown darkness.

Conversations: I listened to you play today and the kind of exuberance you threw out to the audience in Rockefeller Center belies the fact that you were born in 1907. Where do you get all of your energy?

McPartland: I guess from breathing. No, I think number one: I don't drink any alcohol; I haven't had a drink in about twelve years, I guess.

Conversations: That helps?

McPartland: I think so. And I've been on a diet. I swim as much as possible; I do quite a bit of swimming.

Conversations: How do you maintain your chops? People who play trumpet sometimes worry about their teeth when they get up in years. Charlie Spivak worries about his, but he says, with a great deal of pride, that he has his own teeth, so he can play his own horn.

McPartland: That's the same thing with me. I have my own teeth, and I'm fortunate, and I practice a lot. Oh, cripes, every morning for about an hour. And then, when I get back from swimming or something like that, I'll drink tea and I'll practice another hour—

two, three, four. Just over a space of time. Drink tea or read or watch television or do what I have to do around the house. And I skip rope at home and I exercise—do sitting up exercises. I actually just really devote myself all the time to the horn. You have to; it's like an athlete being in training.

Conversations: Somebody introduced you today as playing Dixieland; I don't think you like that term, do you? That's not your style, really, is it?

McPartland: No, not really. If you want to, call it Chicago style; it's swing, actually.

Conversations: Is that Chicago style?

McPartland: Yep, that's Chicago style. The difference between really old Dixieland, where they used to play the two beats on the bass drum and the string bass. . . . You know, it was draggy, like: "bonck-bonck bonck-bonck bubump-bump boomp-boomp!" But in Chicago style, when we'd play a Dixieland number, shall we say, like "Jazz Me Blues," like: "bedeedle-do-do bedeedle-do dedoodle-da-da da-da two-three-four bedoodle-da-da dedoodle do-da"—it's got a swing. The drummer played four-beat, not two, and we'd call it "swing." Benny Goodman sat in with us, a lot of the time.

Conversations: Bud Freeman was in that group, also—

McPartland: Oh, well, that group: the original group, before we even met Benny. At Austin High School, when we first heard the New Orleans Rhythm Kings, I think I was about fifteen years old and it was Frank Teschemacher who was there. We already had a gang of guys who liked music. We'd go over to a little after-school store, and we'd get malted milks and sandwiches—remember?—after high school. Why we'd go over there and listen to. . . they had a bunch of records laying on the table there and we'd just put one on and listen to it and have our malt and sandwich and so forth.

Conversations: And this is what started to turn you on?

McPartland: Well, we heard the New Orleans Rhythm Kings. That's the first band we heard, you know, with Paul Mares, Leon Rappolo, and George Brunies, and so on and so forth. Well, when we heard them play "Farewell Blues" and "Tin Roof Blues," we said, "Let's form a band!" You know, oddly enough, we were all fiddle players; we were all violinists.

Conversations: You were playing violin?

McPartland: Yeah, violin. Not very much, but Jim Lanigan was an accomplished violinist, and so was Frank Teschemacher. Now, my brother and I—Rich and I—we were all right, you know.

Conversations: What prompted you to switch to cornet?

McPartland: The music, the jazz music. What we heard; that was it. We said we'd form a band. My father was a professional musician, teacher, professional boxer, and a professional baseball player. I was trained to be an amateur boxer since I was six years old—and a violinist and a baseball player. My brother, the same thing. We used to work out every day. We used to box amateurs—they call them the "Golden Gloves" today. And I never lost a fight as a kid there—

Conversations: A lot of musicians from Kansas City and New Orleans finally wound up in Chicago, did—

McPartland: Well, they came up to work. The New Orleans Rhythm Kings, they came, too; and then, they called themselves the Friars Society Orchestra and played at the Friars' Inn. They were in Chicago and we could hear them from the outside; we weren't able to get in. But we could go out to the Southside and we could hear King Oliver and his Creole Jazz Band, with Louis Armstrong on second cornet. When they came out with tunes like "Snake Rag" and things like that—why, man, we heard they were in town and we'd go out there and we used to hear them.

And then, we'd copy these numbers off the records that they'd make. We'd sit down—we'd practice. We'd practice, practice, every day, man—day and night after school—until we'd get two bars off that old 78 machine. We'd get two bars at a time for the different instruments on the ensemble, and we'd play it right off. You know, play it and play it, over and over again, till we got the whole thing! I think the first tunes we ever learned were "Farewell Blues," and then, "Tin Roof Blues." They were easy blues and we got to learn them quickly, oh, in a couple of months, I'd say. Then, finally, we would work up every tune we'd hear: the tune, "Snake Rag," and stuff by King Oliver and Louis Armstrong—and then, the Wolverines came out with Bix Beiderbecke. We copied all the numbers off their records and we knew them all.

But my brother said to me, "Nobody plays another guy's solo. This is jazz; you've got to play your own solo. You know, you've got to express yourself in what you play. You can't play what he's playing—it doesn't mean a thing." So, that was our creed: You've got to play your own solo. So what happened was, I decided I was very apt, I guess. I mean, I got ahead of everybody else, and I was cocky. I got a job with a band called Al Haid and His Society Orchestra.

Conversations: In Chicago?

McPartland: Well, at Fox Lake, Illinois. Thirty-five dollars a week, room and board. I worked up there for one summer and then came back. Then I worked at a place called Eddie Tansel's; that's where I met Benny Goodman. Capone moved in and killed this guy, Eddie Tansel, and we—

Conversations: So you ran some risks making music, then?

McPartland: Well, they didn't hurt us. They came in—they had brass knuckles—and they hit guys in the head and the face with seltzer bottles, you know, those little seltzer bottles which explode and all that. Eddie Tansel wasn't there, but the next day they killed him—shot him and took over the place. So we were out of a job, but that's where I met Benny Goodman. And Benny Goodman came out and sat in, but I was the leader of the band.

Conversations: Did Goodman play in it?

McPartland: Yeah, sure. And Bud Freeman, Frank Tesche-macher, Jim Lanigan, Davey Tough, and a guy by the name of Dave North on piano. Jim Lanigan played bass; Davey Tough on drums—he was from Oak Park, the next school over, and used to run a Saturday afternoon "tea dansant" in Columbus Park out there in Chicago, at Austin High. My brother and I, being amateur boxers. . . . The reason they called us the Austin High School Gang was because when we first started playing, we'd go and play at any place where anybody would ask us.

Conversations: For nickels and dimes, I guess.

McPartland: Hey, for nothing! But we used to make money on those "tea dansants" every Saturday afternoon. We went to play a fraternity dance one night—not a dance, just a fraternity meeting—and one of these wise guys who we went to high school with said, "Hey, what kind of music is it that you guys are playing?" I said, "Well, it's jazz." And he said, "Jazz? It stinks." So I said, "Hey, Rich, this guy says we stink." And he said, "You know what to do, Cocky." And so I went bang! Bang! Oh, I laid into him; I knocked him on his cannetta. Some of his buddies started to come in and my brother got up and we mopped 'em up. We were boxers.

Conversations: So you had to defend your music?

McPartland: Well, we defended our music; you're damn tootin' we did. This happened twice, and from then on they said, "Don't fool with those guys; they're a gang. That's the Austin High School Gang"—and that's the reason they called us a gang.

Conversations: How did you happen to get involved with the Wolverines?

McPartland: Well, I went to a New Year's Eve job one night out in Lincoln Park West. The guy playing drums was Vic Moore, who had just finished playing with the Wolverines down around Cincinnati, in Hamilton, Ohio. When they went to New York they got Vic Burton on drums and let him go.

Now Vic Moore heard me when we got on this job. I've forgotten, Murph Podolsky, I think, was in this band, and Benny Goodman, and myself, and a guy by the name of Joey Quartrelle. We had a front line, you know, everybody used to hire us: the guys out at the University of Chicago, the guys out at Northwestern University, the college boys. And we played; we were like pros. We were better than the pros—I mean, we were going to high school, but we were better than the professional musicians around there! And we could play jazz. You used to get $2 extra because you could play an obbligato. That's the truth; it was the union scale. So, this guy heard me—this Vic Moore, the drummer—and he said, "Hey, kid, you sound just like Bix's band." And I said, "Oh yeah? We got the numbers off the records."

Jimmy McPartland

Conversations: How old were you then?

McPartland: I was sixteen going on seventeen. And so he took my name and address, and then I got a wire when I started back at school there in September or October. October it was. I was seventeen years old then, and I got a wire saying: "CAN YOU JOIN THE WOLVERINES REPLACING BIX BEIDERBECKE AT THE CINDERELLA BALLROOM NEW YORK CITY ANSWER YES OR NO."

Conversations: What did you do, quit school?

McPartland: Well, sure! I thought it was a gag at first, but the guys said, "Well, answer them." So I said: "YES I CAN STOP SEND TRANSPORTATION." I got a wire back saying: "MEET US AT THE SOMMERSET HOTEL DICK VOYNO"—he was the leader of the band. I just got on a train. Everybody saw me off; I got to the South Street Station, and I went. Benny Goodman was there and Joey Quartrelle, and Jim Lanigan, Teschemacher, Bud Freeman, Davey Tough, my brother, my family. I took off and went.

Conversations: And never got home?

McPartland: Oh, yeah. Yeah. I played with 'em. Matter of fact, when we got there and I auditioned for them—went up and played in the afternoon—I hadn't met Bix yet. You know, I kept saying to Dick Voyno, "Where's Bix?" And he'd say, "Oh, that's all right. Let's play another number. Which one do you want to play?" I said I knew every number that they played on the records, so all they had to do was to start beating it off and away we went. But, when it came time for my solo, I played my own solo. So, man, they were very happy. After the thing was over I said, "Where's Bix?" And he said, "He's sitting right over there." Bix was listening all the time.

Conversations: Why was he leaving?

McPartland: He was going with Jean Goldkette. Finally, we walked across the floor, and I'm going over to meet Bix. He put his arm around me and he said, "Kid—" And I said, "It's nice to meet you, Bix. Gee, you're wonderful; you know, we've listened to you on the records and everything." He said, "Well, kid, I like

104

you"—he put his arm around me like his kid brother, you know—"I like you," he says. "You sound like me but you don't copy me. You're okay." So Dick Voyno set it up and we lived together for about a week there, and Bix showed me their other arrangements that they had not recorded.

Conversations: Was Dorsey in the Wolverines at that time?

McPartland: No, but I met all those guys at that time around New York. I mean, they introduced me.

Conversations: Did you stay in New York, then?

McPartland: Well, no. We played a couple of months there at the Cinderella Ballroom, it was. Bix was kind enough to give me his girl. Bix says to me, he says, "Gee, kid, do you like my girl?" I said, "Sure." And he said, "Well, you can have her when I go." So he told her, he said, "Take care of the kid, now, you know." So that was it. He really treated me like a little brother.

Conversations: Did Beiderbecke teach you anything on the horn?

McPartland: Oh, yeah, yeah. He showed me a few little runs and things; he showed me the false fingering on the cornet. Also, he showed me. . . he said, "When you're playing along and you can't think of anything, just play these little figures here"—and he showed me: "dadoodle doddle dum doddle doodle dum." I still play those things, but I've never heard anyone else play them.

Conversations: You've always played the cornet?

McPartland: Yep.

Conversations: Never trumpet?

McPartland: Nope.

Conversations: Why?

McPartland: I don't like the trumpet; I don't like the sound of a trumpet. I like a big, round, full tone. And it sort of sits in close and feels comfortable and snug; it feels snug right in there: in my hands and down at my side, it feels close to me, you know.

Jimmy McPartland

Conversations: Is your cornet custom-built for you?

McPartland: No, Getzen. This last one they gave me, I told them I wanted a large bore. There's a pretty big tone there, if you'll notice, and it takes a lot of air to fill it. So you have to try to keep in shape.

Conversations: Is the mouthpiece bigger than usual?

McPartland: No, no. I have an excellent mouthpiece: Jet Tone, it's an alloy thing. But, Bix showed me some things.

Conversations: We're talking now about the twenties, aren't we?

McPartland: Yes, we're talking about 1924. I was seventeen years old. On March 15th, 1907, I was born.

Conversations: A pretty big jump for a seventeen-year-old: all of a sudden to be in New York, playing with a major group.

McPartland: Yes, it was.

Conversations: Did it go to your head?

McPartland: No. No, I just wanted to play. I always have... I enjoy someone playing well, listening to anyone—I don't care. As a matter of fact, doing anything well. I'm one of those guys who enjoys sports: I was a swimming and a judo instructor in the Army, trained with the Rangers down at Camp Gordon Johnson in Carrabelle, Florida.

Conversations: World War II?

McPartland: World War II. And, I wasn't a kid; I was thirty-five years old—right on the line there, thirty-four or thirty-five, I was. I've always been in sports, you know, a boxer and played handball and golf. I won the Austin High School Golf Championship with a seventy-three.

Conversations: When did you evolve into big-band work, or have you always been, more or less, wedded to a small group?

McPartland: Well, I like a small group better, but I went with Art Kassel in Chicago in August '27, around in there, and I worked with Art about a year or so. Then Ben Pollack wanted me to come with his band.

106

Conversations: Did you join the band?

McPartland: Glenn Miller and Benny Goodman were with Pollack. Sure, I went with them and came to New York with the band. And when I was with them we worked The Little Club first. We were there for a few months, and then we went to the Park Central Hotel and we were a hit in New York—worked in a show called "Hello Daddy" with Lew Fields and played at the Park Central Hotel. We'd get up every day and record in the morning; record in the afternoon; and then, go to work at night at six o'clock at the hotel. We'd work up until one o'clock and, at the same time, we'd double in the show: work at the hotel from six to eight; go over to work from eight-thirty to eleven; come back to the Park Central Hotel and work until one; and then, frankly, we'd go up to Harlem and sit in.

Conversations: Who were you playing with in Harlem?

McPartland: Oh, Willie "The Lion" Smith, and then I've forgotten the name of the band at Small's Paradise, and then Louis Armstrong at—

Conversations: Did you get to know Armstrong?

McPartland: Oh, I'd known Louis since I was a kid. Remember, I was talking before about Louis Armstrong and King Oliver coming to town there at the Lincoln Gardens? Well, that's where I met Louis. And Louis even came out to our house for dinner. My mother loved him. He came out to the house for dinner. I came up and picked him up—I had an old Rio; I picked him up out on the Southside and took him to the house. My mother had cooked roast lamb, and she just loved Louis. She said, "My boys love you so much and I love your records, too. I just had to meet you."

Conversations: Did you ever work with him?

McPartland: Yeah, jam session style—I mean, in concerts. We played in Philadelphia. That's perhaps the biggest compliment I ever had in my life, like the one from Bix, you know, saying: "You play great, kid. You sound like me, but you don't copy me." Bix autographed a copy of "In a Mist" for me and he said: "To Jimmy McPartland—the greatest white cornet player living."

Jimmy McPartland

That's what he said. To me, Bix was the greatest. Red Nichols—I never did care too much for him, personally, because he used to copy Bix, really.

Conversations: What kind of jazz did he play?

McPartland: Well, I don't know; I don't know. He didn't play with a. . . . You know, he played well—don't get me wrong—I mean, he played fine. Jesus, he played a beautiful horn—

Conversations: He didn't have the spontaneity, though.

McPartland: He didn't have the spontaneity or style. He couldn't improvise as well. And he cried once: he sat down with me in Chicago, there at the Sherman Hotel, and was crying. And I said, "Why in the hell are you crying?" He said, "Jesus, I don't know how you do it; you and Bix and these guys—you just—I can't improvise." He used to practice these things at home, he told me. Then he'd go and play them on a recording date. You know, he'd practice runs and so forth. He just was not creative, but he knew it. Now he played that horn well—don't get me wrong—he was a fine player.

Conversations: Did you check out one another? Like, for example, if Muggsy Spanier was around—

McPartland: Oh, yeah. Yeah. Muggsy played great, but his great influence was Louis Armstrong. Well, Louis was one of my influences, but so was Bix. I mean, these were the guys that you'd be influenced by; I don't think you could have better influences, but you gotta go your own way. I mean if you don't play what's inside of you and how you feel, I mean, forget it.

Conversations: Did you and Wild Bill Davison complement each other? He has a style completely different from yours, really.

McPartland: Oh, sure. I mean, he's expressing himself. That's fine; that's fine. It's sort of rough sounding and all that, but fine; it's good. It's his style.

Conversations: It's sort of a "dirty" horn.

McPartland: It's dirty, yeah. You know, "Rhurr-rhurr-rhurr"—snarling and all that, but it's fine. I like that; I like anybody who plays well, plays their own way.

Conversations: Did you ever get into the big bands of the thirties or forties with your cornet?

McPartland: Oh, sure, yeah. I used to play in the pit; I used to play in the shows on Broadway. Once I played in the New York Philharmonic Orchestra an original composition by some Jewish composer—it was a song about Israel. He heard me at the Park Central Hotel and he kept saying, "Your tone, your tone!" He said, "I have a movement in my symphony that must have that tone." I have a straight, legitimate tone, believe it or not.

Conversations: What does that mean? A tone that would match up with a symphony orchestra?

McPartland: That's right—a legitimate tone, with no vibrato. Bix told me about that.

Conversations: But you can put a vibrato in when you want to.

McPartland: Oh, I can put a vibrato in, but it's very minor; I don't use too much of a vibrato; no, no, no.

Conversations: So how did you meet Marian McPartland?

McPartland: I'll tell you what happened to me. I had been working a year and a half with Jack Teagarden's band in 1940, traveling all over the country. Jack had just finished making a picture with Bing Crosby and Mary Martin, *The Birth of the Blues,* and they had a number in the show called "The Waiter and The Porter and The Upstairs Maid." And Kitty Kallen was with Jack singing, and I sang Bing's part in "The Waiter and The Porter and The Upstairs Maid."

Conversations: You sound like Teagarden, a little bit.

McPartland: Yeah? Yeah, well, I sing my own notes. You gotta sing just the way you feel, you know, because I don't have a voice or anything like that.

Conversations: But you have a style.

McPartland: Style, that's right. Well, what the heck you going to do? But I sing in tune. Now, what happened was this: we had been on these one-night stands—Charlie Teagarden and I were helping Jack—we drove the truck with all the instruments and stands and the music and things. And we were going along there but, man, the war came on and everybody was trying to duck it. And I said, "What's the matter with you guys? What's going to happen with everybody trying to duck the Army? You got to fight for your country." Well, I was drinking a lot then, so I called myself the "drunken patriot" for this reason: because I went in and I wanted to enlist. The man at the draft board said, "You've got to go *now*." I said, "Well, I want to enlist." "So enlist; you're gone; you're in now." So I went. We came to Chicago, as a matter of fact, and I checked in at the draft board. So I told Jack, "I gotta leave; that's it." I said, "I'm glad to go in."

Conversations: You didn't go into Special Services, then?

McPartland: No. We got in there and I was with an outfit called the 462nd AAA—Automatic Weapons. We used to have these .450-caliber machine guns mounted on a half-track and the 40-millimeter Bofors guns. So we trained; we had a lot of training, oh, all over at different camps.

Conversations: And you weren't playing?

McPartland: No, no. No band. This guy by the name of Brubeck, Sergeant Brubeck—it was Dave Brubeck, I found out later—came. We were out at Camp Hahn in California; he came out to the outfit and wanted me to transfer to the band. And I said, "No, forget it, man." I said, "I want to be a soldier; I want to stay with the outfit. I've already got some friends here. I'd rather do this, you know." Which I did—stayed with the outfit.

I could have gone in bands; they wanted me to go with the 28th Division down in Florida. "Forget it," I said—I don't know.... Anyway, then we went over to Scotland and we went down to Wales and trained there: making landings, climbing cliffs, and everything like that. I came in Normandy D plus 4, in a combat team. At the time I was driving the colonel and I had a jeep with a .50-caliber mounted on the thing. It was rough, believe me. And I was scared: I saw a few guys getting hit close by, and a couple of guys got killed. I was scared, but I prayed and I got an answer—I'll tell you that. I was scared and God just said, "You're okay, Jimmy." I said, "Oh, God, what shall I do?" And I got the answer: "You're all right. I'm with you, Jimmy; you're trained for this and I'm with you." And I just relaxed and I haven't been scared since. Really, it's the truth—and I was sober.

Conversations: How did you get in the USO?

McPartland: Well, I got five battle stars. We hit Normandy, and I was in the Saint-Lo ordeal; then all the way through the Falaise gap, and to Paris; and then we went on up in the Ardennes Forest, and we were patroling the Ardennes Forest there. By that time I had had it, and I told the colonel: "I want to get the hell out of this outfit; I want to play that cornet again." He said, "Oh no, Mac," he said, "we need you out here." But I made my deal and the thing came through.

I came off patrol one morning—from a half-track patrol in the Ardennes Forest—and I got called to the colonel's office. He said, "Mac,"—I got busted in Paris, by the way, I got drunk, so I was busted from a sergeant back to a private again. So now, he says, "I got this thing from V-Corps Headquarters; they want you up there to go in the Special Services." I said, "That's it!" He said, "Mac, if you don't go, I'll make you a sergeant again." I said, "Forget it; I want to go play that horn again. Forget it. I've had enough of this."

Conversations: Did you have your horn with you?

McPartland: Yeah. They always let me carry my horn, because I blew bugle calls, in different camps—you know, big deal. So I went to V-Corps Headquarters and the first gal I met. . . . They wanted me to play, you know, get my horn out and play in this pyramidal tent. I said, "I'm not playing until I get a drink. I want a drink." Then some officer came over with a bottle of Scotch and I said, "Now, we're talking business." I had a few slugs and started to have a jam session with this band; and this girl came up and said she wanted to sit in.

She had a USO camp shows outfit on. She wanted to play "Honeysuckle Rose," and she played it, rushing like mad. She was going: "Er-umb a-dumpf a-dum." And I said, "Oh, Jesus, help!" But I could hear her playing was good, so I said, "Listen, let's play something pretty like, 'I Never Knew Just How Much I Love You.'" She played that and I heard those beautiful harmonies and I said, "Oh, man, this gal is a killer. All she needs to do is have a beat and she's got it." So that's what happened; that's where I met her. And I think I proposed about three or four weeks later.

Jimmy McPartland

Conversations: How do you pick the musicians you play with? Do you look for something besides musical ability?

McPartland: Oh, yes, definitely. You can tell when someone respects you—likes you as a person and respects you. You can feel that, if you're sensitive. Good Lord, years and years of mingling or associating with people, and so on and so forth. See, you can feel it; you know that. You can tell when someone has a chip on their shoulder, more or less. . . .

Conversations: Are you playing a type of music that's going down the drain for a lack of young people coming along to pick it up?

McPartland: No. No. I meet a lot of young people who listen to it, especially in college and in high school. And then there are marvelous young players like Warren Vache and Ed Polcer, who's at Condon's.

Conversations: Are they actually playing Chicago-style jazz?

McPartland: Well, I wouldn't call it Chicago style; it's just straightforward, classical American jazz to me. It's standard, or sort of classical, I would put it. Billy Taylor said that on the air the other day and I thought of the same thing: "What would we call American jazz of that era, or of two or three eras so to speak, from the twenties to the thirties to the forties—even to the fifties." It's, to me, standard; it's swing—I don't know—it's Chicago. And everyone seemed to adapt it from the next ten to twenty, thirty years. Just like at the end of the war when bebop came out—why then, it switched to the pyrotechnics and running around on the horn of Dizzy Gillespie and Charlie Parker. Now, this is good music.

Conversations: Did that put your type of music on the back burner for a while?

McPartland: I don't think so, no.

Conversations: You stayed busy?

McPartland: Yes. I think, really, when rock 'n' roll came out the young people said, "This is in!" and they went along with it for a while—"That other stuff, that's old-fashioned." But now, they're listening to the music we play. If anything is good, to me, basically it's sound, if it is well played. Painting is comparable: if it's good, it's gotta stay good. Jazz has its own place as an art form, and the individual expresses himself in whatever he's playing. He tries to express his inner feelings—not only harmonically but with his phrasing—and in anything, painting as well as music. So go ahead and express how you feel; let Dizzy express how he feels; let Charlie Parker express how he feels. It's fine; it's interesting.

Sometimes the harmonic clashes are pretty rough to take. I mean for someone like myself. I listen and I'll try to see what's good about it. There are some things good about it—by George, they get over those instruments beautifully. But those who have tried to follow them, who are influenced by them, most of them don't come up to that original standard.

Conversations: Yeah, there's only one Gillespie.

McPartland: Okay, there's always one guy like that. Well, there was only one Louis Armstrong, one Bix Beiderbecke, Paul Mares—whoever you want to say. I was influenced by these guys, but you have to, to me, go off on your own. I can't express your feelings. It's got to be your own: "This is me; this is the way I am."

Conversations: You've had a long day with playing at Rockefeller Center, and then playing a full gig here at Jimmy Ryan's. How do you keep your spirits up?

McPartland: Well, it's easy to keep up when you're with quality musicians, no matter who's there. Now, we were all pretty tired, you know, but I can still play, and I was doing my best and it sounded fairly good to me. I mean, I'm a critic of myself. But it's easy to keep your spirits up because you're with your peers and you want each other to play well. It's a matter of musical empathy: we're talking to each other; we're conversing on our instruments.

Conversations: It seems that you have an inborn affection for each other, too, don't you?

McPartland: Right, that's correct. An inborn affection, it's true. We know what each one of us goes through, because we're all

113

the same. We're always trying to play well and do our best for ourselves, basically. We try to let each other know: "Let's play well; let's do something well; let's have a lovely conversation or a happy conversation—whatever the tune calls for." Like that last thing we played, "Got a Right to Sing the Blues"—I always think about Jack Teagarden. He played it so beautifully.

Conversations: Sang it, too.

McPartland: Yeah, he sang it; I sing it too. I didn't get a chance to sing it, because there was no microphone tonight and I didn't want to foist that on anybody at this time of the night. I just didn't feel like it, but I love to sing it; I sing it my own way. But the important thing, when you're with a group like that, is, man, you want to hear each other play well.

Conversations: Are there certain things in each song that must be played, or can everybody take liberties?

McPartland: Well, yes. You must establish.... It's just like a team, you know, the quarterback calls the signals.

Conversations: And you're the quarterback?

McPartland: I'm the quarterback; I'm the leader; I'm the cornet player; I'm the loudest. I play the melody, and let the guys know that I'll play the melody. In other words, I was calling the signals on the first chorus: I was just sort of phrasing the melody— nicely. You know, a lot of phrasing with feeling. "I got a right to sing the blues"—but I don't have that right if my ass is dragging. That's the way I feel.

Conversations: Who calls the signals for the next player?

McPartland: Oh, I call 'em. I call 'em; I just point. I mean like the last couple of bars: "Da do da da da da do da da dedoodle doodle da da"—and I'll gently turn around to the clarinet player, or, if the trombone is on, I'll go over to him.

Conversations: How do they know how long to play?

McPartland: They're on their own, then—long as they know who's next. But I just point over, like if the clarinet player's finishing, I'll just point over to the trombone. You know, you

114

usually get it set like that because a brass instrument is pretty rough; your chops get pretty tired. A clarinet player does, too, but not in the same category as a brass man.

Conversations: You have said that your chops are comparable to a pitcher's arm; but when your chops get tired, you can't take yourself out of the ball game.

McPartland: You're darn tootin' they do and I can't get out of the ball game; I've got to stay there and do the best I can. But you learn after many years of playing: Don't try to overdo it at that time, because you've got to last the whole ball game or else the whole team will fall apart.

Conversations: Do you pace yourself?

McPartland: I have to. I have to pace myself, but the guys feel you: the drummer feels you; the piano player feels you; the bass player and all the other horns feel you when you come in on that ensemble. If you come in strong and assert yourself, saying, "Here's where it is—'da doop da dadoop da dey.' " They'll get it going. They can just swing it, but you've got to set that. If I'd come in halfheartedly with: "Tee dee dee tee dee da da dee"— it'd just drag and nothing would happen. Same thing in "Louisiana." Now I just do this naturally, because I'm the leader. I mean, they're all going to follow that cornet—I don't care who it is, you've got to follow him. That's it; you're the front man and they're going to follow you. If you're wishy-washy and you don't assert yourself with firmness or with authority, say, "Here's where it is, guys. Let's lay it right in here"—but you do that on the horn. I mean, you're saying that on the horn and everybody goes right along with you. But the important thing, all the way around, for any different kind of number is—the most important thing is empathy. Each guy in the band. . . . You see, we're not using music; we're using our ears and our sensitivities, our feelings— we listen to each other; we inspire each other. That's the whole story; that's the whole ball game.

Conversations: You're seventy years old and you've been at it a long time. How long do you plan to keep it up?

McPartland: I'm going to keep on till my teeth fall out or I die.

Jimmy McPartland

Conversations: No plans for retirement?

McPartland: No, oh God, no. Jiminy Cricket, I feel like I'm twenty years old—up in my skull. And the body is, fortunately, still responding to about a forty-year-old guy, I should add.

Conversations: And so are the chops?

McPartland: The chops are good because I practice my ass off. I have to. If I want to come out and play, and I don't have any chops, man, it's a bringdown—not only for me, but for everybody in the band, you know. You gotta be out in front there. It doesn't mean a bloody thing—what you've done in the past, forget it—I never even listen to the records that I've made. They're gone; that's gone. Now is now. I mean, now is the time to play. All you can do is give it your best and your best shot—that's all you can do. As long as you've given it your best—that's all.

Barry Miles is a native of Newark, New Jersey, and still makes his home in that state. Miles started his musical career in grade school as a drummer, but switched to piano and studied musicology at Princeton. Now thirty, he has his own group, which uses both acoustic and electronic instruments. He also performs regularly as a pianist on recording sessions with other artists.

Barry Miles

Zane Knauss met Barry Miles through Eric Kloss, Miles's good friend. The two have performed together in concert and also have recorded several albums of their compositions. This conversation took place in Miles's rambling wood and stone house near the little town of Stockton, New Jersey. Miles's complicated directions from the Newark airport to his home included the description of a covered bridge over which the interviewer had to travel, the last such bridge existing in the whole state of New Jersey.

Conversations: I'm curious about the term "fusion music." What, exactly, is it?

Miles: Well, I had started a term a little bit before the term "fusion music," which was "syncretic music." I developed that term around 1964 or '65, and, basically, syncretic means a fusion of various styles and elements of music. For instance, at that particular time I was interested in taking certain elements of classical music, jazz, rock, folk music, Indian music, and, oh, a lot of different influences that I had, and trying to meld them into a personal sound of my own that had all of those elements, but wasn't necessarily any one of those things. Then later, in the early seventies, a lot of other people began to get involved with that type of thing, too, and the simpler term, "fusion music," sort of came about. Unfortunately, fusion music has a slight connotation of being very loud, electric jazz-rock. But it can be anything, really. Like there's a group called Oregon, a totally acoustic group, which plays what I would consider fusion music. There's the new John McLaughlin group, Shakti, an acoustic group with Indian musicians plus himself, which also plays fusion music. So it can be a lot of different things, depending on the people who are playing it.

Barry Miles

Conversations: How do you maintain the individual identity for something that you have created?

Miles: Well, some of it you can actually copyright, if there's a certain composition that you've written for it. But, a lot of it has to do with your own personal sound as an improviser. And that, of course, you can't copyright. It just has to do with your particular style.

Conversations: Your composition, "Cityscape," has all kinds of things in it. Was it written out from start to finish, or are there wide areas for improvisation in the body of it?

Miles: There are lots of spaces for improvisation, but there is a full score which I had written out. That piece was written about 1973—I forget. I think the scores are like forty pages of score paper, and the brass parts are totally written out, because there isn't any improvisation for them. On the album, Eric Kloss is playing alto sax, and he has some actual written parts, which he learned off a tape that I had given him, and then, of course, he has a lot of improvisation on it. So it's sort of both. There's a lot of improvisation and a lot of written sections. But as far as the length of the piece, everything was worked out.

Conversations: I'm curious about several parts in it. Toward the end, you literally have a cacophony of sound, in which everybody seems to be going every which way.

Miles: Right.

Conversations: Did you write that, or did you just write instructions?

Miles: There are a lot of instructions on the final section of that piece, but what actually happened was I gave the brass players a motif to improvise on within whatever range they wanted to play it. So the effect was cacophony, but there were actual notes, or instructions, which they played.

Conversations: I am sure there are time frames, too—the number of bars in which they are to do this.

Miles: That's correct. That whole section is conducted. There is a certain pulse that is going on, and the musicians are watching the

120

conductor to know how long to play that particular section. Certain written sections are sort of interspersed in this improvised section. But it's not totally improvised. There is certain thematic material that they're improvising on.

Conversations: You mentioned a number of influences on your music, including Indian music. Are you professionally schooled in these influences?

Miles: To a certain extent, especially in classical music. I've had a lot of training, private training, through my teacher, Olga Von Till, and scholastic training in that area. I went to Princeton University and I majored in music, which was basically composition. I studied with Milton Babbitt, J. K. Randall, E. Cone, and some other people who are teaching at Princeton. So I became familiar with classical music there—professionally, in a way—although I had a great interest in that type of music from the time I was about eight or nine years old.

Conversations: You started out playing the drums. When did you start playing the piano?

Miles: I actually started studying piano when I was about four from my uncle, who is a jazz pianist. Even before that I had started listening to jazz—from the time I was about one or two— because my father had a record store and he used to bring home Charlie Parker's records.

Conversations: Where was this?

Miles: This was in Newark, New Jersey. I just had this little 78 record machine, and I listened to a lot of swing things—like Benny Goodman. Then, later on, the bebop thing with Dizzy and Bird.

Conversations: So by the time you got to Princeton you were into jazz?

Miles: Oh, yeah. That was the first kind of music I was into. Then later on, when I was about eight or nine years old, through my own interest in listening to classical music I got into other kinds of music—you know, other than jazz. Then I started studying drums when I was about seven. I got into the musicians' union when I was nine.

Barry Miles

Conversations: You were playing professionally?

Miles: Right. I was doing a lot of concerts and things locally.

Conversations: On drums?

Miles: Yeah, on drums. And one particular thing: I got a chance to sit in with Woody Herman. He liked me so much that we worked some other gigs together, and then he recommended me.

Conversations: And you were how old?

Miles: Around eleven. This was around '58 or so. Then later on, until I was about fourteen or so, I did a lot of playing with him and a lot of other musicians which was a great experience.

Conversations: Well, did you go to Princeton with the intention of studying composition?

Miles: I went to Princeton for two reasons: First of all, I knew that there wasn't going to be any jazz type of thing happening there—I wasn't going for that type of thing because there really wasn't any particular school then where I could learn jazz. I had studied jazz privately—some improvisation from John Mehegan, some arranging at the Eastman School of Music. But when I went to Princeton I wanted to get a liberal arts education in things other than music. And I wanted to learn a lot about music's past, plus certain techniques in composition, especially twelve-tone composition.

Conversations: Were you into Schoenberg?

Miles: Right, and a lot of the people who taught there were very much involved with that type of music, and so I wanted to learn their thing. And the jazz, I continued while I was at school on my own—like playing concerts on weekends and bringing in musicians. We did a lot of concerts down at Princeton with some very great musicians. There was one album that was a live recording of a concert at Princeton in 1966 called *Syncretic Compositions*, which was never really released, except through a mail-order type of thing, but it got a very good response— excellent reviews.

Conversations: Artistically a success, then?

Miles: Yes. Someday I may get a chance to rerelease that.

Conversations: Did you write the stuff that was on the album?

Miles: Yes.

Conversations: There seems to be a tendency among teachers to look down their noses at jazz. Did you run into that at Princeton?

Miles: Some of them did, to be honest. Some of them said, "Well, I don't really follow that type of music, and I don't quite understand it, so I don't want to make any comments about it." Other people felt that any improvisation results in relying on cliches. I totally disagree, because there are cliches in everything.

Conversations: Well, the original cadenzas were supposed to be improvisations.

Miles: Right. Depends on who is improvising. I remember one guy—the dean of the music department. I was in his office, and he said, "You know, I used to play jazz piano myself when I was in school, and I sympathize with you."

Conversations: Well, there are cases to be made for his argument; for example, Mel Powell gave up jazz—walked away from it and won't touch it at all. Andre Previn really won't pay serious attention to jazz. There are people who feel that somehow jazz is the stepchild of music.

Miles: It depends on who you are and how you feel about it, but I don't put down any type of music because of what it is. I have a great respect for every type of music. What I don't understand sometimes is people from other walks of musical life looking at jazz, or looking at certain kinds of music and saying, "Well, this isn't really a together art form."

Conversations: Improvisation is a highly intellectual process, isn't it?

Miles: Jazz is a different type of thing. I can't compare any type of music to jazz—or any type of music to any other type. I found when I was at Princeton that my background in jazz gave me an immense advantage in the development of my ear. I remember when they were trying to place us in certain classes by giving us

123

musical dictation, and they played a line of some Bach piece. I just wrote it out from what I had heard, immediately. All the other people, who were involved in atonal composition and everything, took hours to get this, because their ear wasn't developed toward hearing intervals that another musician would play. That's one of the things jazz really develops: it's a totally aural experience.

Conversations: A lot of your playing is fugue-like. Are you conscious of your classical experience when you write this sort of thing, or even when you improvise it?

Miles: To a certain extent. I like to hear a lot of lines going on counter to one another. That was always something I was trying to do in some of my pieces, especially in the middle sixties. There was a piece that I wrote that was on the syncretic music album called "Exposition and Development." I wanted to get away from having a jazz piece which would have just the head arrangement, where the horns would play the line in unison, and the piano would play the chords, and the bass and the drums would do the rhythmic things. So I would work on things where I'd have two horns—in this particular thing we had Lew Soloff on trumpet, Robin Kenyatta on alto sax. A lot of the written sections were very polyphonic, where sometimes one guy would take the lead and sometimes someone else would. So, it wasn't very parallel.

Conversations: But there's a melody line somewhere in there.

Miles: Right.

Conversations: And you have to pay attention to find it. It's like a musical mystery, isn't it?

Miles: They are sometimes almost like a crossword puzzle. But then sometimes I like to write totally linear compositions—a single-line type of writing.

Conversations: When you write, do you write, as the Princeton guys might say, for cliche effect? Are you a serious composer in the truest sense?

Miles: I'm very serious about what I do.

124

Conversations: But there are a lot of people who separate jazz composers from "serious musicians."

Miles: Well, I think one of the major differences, at least as far as I'm concerned for my own type of writing, is that I write for a particular musical personality, a soloist. I write for the improviser.

Conversations: Like Ellington did?

Miles: Right. And I'm very concerned about continuing to further the art of improvisation. I'm not as much concerned about writing a piece of music with a little bit of improvisation in it, or writing totally for the composition itself. I consider my compositions as a framework for the improviser to bring out his musical personality.

Conversations: Before you begin writing, do you have a particular soloist in mind, or are you thinking about a particular instrument?

Miles: A lot of times I'm thinking of a particular soloist; sometimes I'm thinking of an instrument, but it has to do with the actual personalities, the actual musicians whom I'm writing for.

Conversations: How does this exercise begin? Does it come in the form of a commission to write for a particular soloist, or a suggestion, or does the A & R man say: "Do this"?

Miles: A lot of it has to do with the group that I have. A lot of my pieces are written for my musicians, the people in my group. A lot of them are written for me as a soloist. I've always wanted to be in a position where I could write and perform my own music.

Conversations: When you talk about "my" musicians, this is to say, then, that you have a regular coterie of musicians who work with you all the time?

Miles: Right. Since around 1962 or '63, I'd say, I've had a band.

Conversations: Silverlight, has he been in the band a long time?

Miles: Well, my brother, Terry Silverlight, who is the drummer with my present band, has been with me on and off since, I'd say,

125

around 1969. He recorded an album with me when he was fourteen called *White Heat*, which was on Mainstream Records.

Conversations: He's on your newest album.

Miles: We began playing together when he was in high school, and then he went to Princeton for one year. I've had other drummers and other bands in between.

Conversations: Now there are other Silverlights involved in your recording.

Miles: Well, my father, who has informally managed me for a long time, is Art Silverlight. He's not managing me at the moment, mainly because he's so busy with his own work. Actually, the person who is managing me is a guy named Hermie Dressel, who also manages Woody Herman.

Conversations: Did that come through your experience with Herman?

Miles: No. That's purely a coincidence. It's very interesting how things come back around the circle. At one time I was managed by Woody Herman's manager, who was a different person—a completely different person. Somehow it just worked out that Woody Herman's present manager and I made contact. It was just a coincidence.

Conversations: So, then, the Silverlight family is very much involved in your career?

Miles: Right. Then I have another brother, Ron Silverlight, who is a trumpet player. He had a rock band in the Midwest for a while. But he isn't playing trumpet presently; he is involved in another line of work.

Conversations: But how about Juris, the guitarist?

Miles: Vic Juris has been with me now for about a year and a half. The present group, of course, is guitar, bass, keyboard, and drums. But I've had many different types of groups. A lot of the groups that I had in the middle sixties were basically trumpet, alto sax, piano, bass, and drums—totally acoustic groups. A lot of players went in and out. I couldn't work real steady during that time, because I was still in high school. But at times my groups included trumpet players, like Woody Shaw and Jimmy Owens and a great trumpet player who's now in Carolina—I think it's North Carolina—Ray Codrington, who was originally with a group called The J. F. K. Quintet from Washington, D.C. Also bass players like Eddie Gomez and Richard Davis and Ron Carter and David Izenson; Walter Booker, and a lot of different sax players—I have mentioned Robin Kenyatta and a guy named Bob Porcelli and Andy Marsala.

Conversations: Where do you find these people—or do they find you?

Miles: Well, it was sort of both ways. A lot of these people at that particular time were very young also. I remember when I started playing with Eddie Gomez, he was about nineteen or something, going to Juilliard at that time.

Conversations: Is there a grapevine among musicians that says, "Hey, that guy's playing this kind of music and you ought to look in on it"?

Miles: Yeah, in a way. Like with Woody Shaw—again, he was about eighteen; he was living in Newark, and I had been involved with a lot of musicians in the New York and Newark, New Jersey, area. I just knew who was doing what. Some of them I might have seen playing somewhere. I just knew who the younger musicians were. In a lot of cases, of course, it was before they were really well known. Later on, around the late sixties, I had a group more like the one I have today, which had the guitar, keyboard, bass, and drums. There were a lot of very good guitar players that went through that group—a lot of them before they were really known: John Abercrombie and Al DiMeola, who later played with Chick Corea's band, and Jack Wilkins who's a very fine guitarist. Pat Martino recorded with me, although he never worked with my band.

Conversations: Is this the key group that you make personal appearances with?

Miles: Well, the present group, which is named Barry Miles and Silverlight, came about around January 1973. It's gone through certain personnel changes since that time. But the present group—with guitar, keyboard, bass, and drums—is what I perform with.

Conversations: And then it's augmented for your recording dates?

Miles: Right. There were two albums, however, that were done for London Records with just the quartet, which at that time contained Bill Washer on guitar and Harvie Swartz on bass. The new album on RCA, called *Sky Train*, is not necessarily a Barry Miles and Silverlight album. That group is called Barry Miles and Company.

Conversations: It's really a full orchestra, isn't it?

Miles: Right. It's sort of like a solo album of my own, with members of my present recording band plus guest artists and friends.

Conversations: I noticed that you had Phil Woods conducting your "Cityscape."

Miles: Right. I've known Phil for a long time. We played together 150 years ago.

Conversations: You're not all that old. How old are you?

Miles: I'm thirty. And I played with Phil, it must have been in the late fifties. And then we hadn't seen each other for a long time. That was another coincidence: he was recording for RCA and he was, I think, a good choice to conduct this particular piece. He will be doing some playing on my next album.

Conversations: Now, you're doing some accompanying work. I gather you're going to be recording with Mel Torme.

Miles: Right. There are some other albums that we are going to do.

Conversations: Are you writing for Torme, or what?

Miles: No. I'm not writing on any of the albums that we are going to be doing over there, other than mine.

Conversations: This is in London?

Miles: Right. We were in London in January mixing my album and recording an album of Phil Woods's, which will be out sometime in the fall, called *The Seven Deadly Sins*. There was one piece that I wrote and arranged for that album, which was for a full orchestra.

Conversations: A musician today who is into the things that you are into can't just be a musician. He almost has to be an electrical engineer; he's got to be an acoustical engineer at the very least. Do you do all of your mix downs and supervise all your tape editing and so forth?

Miles: It depends on the album, but I'm always present for any of the mixing and editing that is done. And I work very closely with the engineer. I don't think I could sit down by myself and turn on all the equipment, with all the knobs and stuff, but I really have a certain sound that I hear in my mind that I want to get onto the record. It's the whole idea of trying to communicate that to the engineer, which I feel I never have a problem doing.

Conversations: There are a lot of classical musicians who seem to have the right, whether by contract or otherwise, to actually withhold a performance from the market if they don't think it's up to their standards. Do you have the same latitude in your contracts?

Miles: Pretty much. In my particular contract, I have the right to choose material, to choose the musicians, to accept or reject the cover of the album, and other things like that. And if I'm not happy with a particular performance, I can say I don't want it on the album. So RCA doesn't have the say over what is going to be on the album. I have the control over that.

Conversations: Including the material itself?

Miles: Right.

Conversations: How does that work? You are not only a performer but a composer—in effect, a contractor, too, because you bring along your own musicians. How do you get along with the A & R man, the guy who is usually the boss in a situation like this?

Miles: Well, in this particular case for RCA Records, it's under Gryphon Productions, which is coheaded by a guy named Norman Schwartz. He has been involved in producing for quite some time, and produces my albums. We get along very well. He understands my music and his whole thing is to make happen what I have in my mind. If I need sixty string players, if I need certain musicians, he will organize the whole thing, the whole session. Also, he might have comments to make, which I'll either accept or reject. I respect his opinions, you know, in an objective way, and his feelings about certain things. We work very well together.

Conversations: Is Gryphon contracted by RCA to produce your records?

Miles: Right. Gryphon works exclusively for RCA: they record for RCA, and I record for Gryphon and RCA.

Conversations: Does your agent also get involved to a certain extent?

Miles: My agent and my manager get involved.

Conversations: You have a manager in addition to the agent?

Miles: Yes. In other words, it's the manager's job sort of to hire agents—I'm not signed to one particular agent. I have an agent whose job is to get college things; there's another agent who is to get club things. Each person has different experience in different fields.

Conversations: You're practically a conglomerate, then, aren't you?

Miles: Well, you know, hopefully you don't move to that point, but the whole thing is that I have to have certain people around me whom I can communicate with—who understand what I'm into; who understand about the musical field that I'm into; who can help accomplish a lot of things that an artist needs to accomplish and will be able to save me the time to write and practice and perform and rehearse. There are so many business things around the career end of it; it's very hard to do it yourself. I can do it myself; it's just the amount of time that it takes to do all of those things. If it were a full-time operation to do that, then I would have no time to write. I want to be in a position where the only thing I have to do is to write and perform and rehearse. Of course, it's never going to be that simple, and I understand that, but the goal is really to get the business matters tied together so that everybody is communicating with one another.

Conversations: You talked about being able to have the time to do what you have to do creatively. How much time do you spend practicing? Are you disciplined to the extent that you spend X number of hours a day at it?

Miles: Well, it's a little hard to do that sometimes, because a lot of time is taken up on the road actually performing live, which keeps your chops in shape. Sometimes working on certain compositions specifically for my instrument accomplishes a lot, again for the technical end of keeping your chops together. But whenever I get the opportunity to practice, I practice as much as I can. A lot of musicians feel that after a certain point they just don't have to practice. But I think a lot of that has to do with the fact that they are performing constantly, which is a form of keeping your technique together, if you're an improviser.

Conversations: Is your writing schedule predictable? Are you a methodical writer, or are you an impulse writer?

Miles: Both ways. A lot of the inspiration for writing comes when I'm sitting around somewhere and an idea pops into my head. I might write it down or I might go over to the piano and work with it. Sometimes I work at the piano; sometimes I work totally away from it. Sometimes in jamming with my brother I'll play keyboards and he'll play drums, and I'll come up with some kind of idea which just has to do with the improvisation. We'll just be playing off the tops of our heads. I might have the tape recorder running, and I might say, "Hey, that's a great fragment. How can I work it from there?"

Conversations: You record practice sessions, and store them away for further use?

Miles: Right. A lot of times I'll do that. Sometimes a full composition or a full song or something will pop into my head immediately. The thing that gets very methodical is when you're actually writing it down for other people to play.

Conversations: When you write, do you start out by putting the first thought, which is the melody, down, or do you score as you write?

Miles: It depends on what it's for. Sometimes I will be scoring or sketching for the entire combination together—well, say, with a piece like "Fusion Suite," which was conceived, as you know, as a piece that featured a small group plus brass section, I was thinking of the entire thing. Sometimes the piece of music will just be melodic lines with certain harmonic implications, which later on I will write for, say, the small group. On the album that I'm working on presently with strings and brass, a lot of the pieces were conceived as music in its abstract sense—not for any particular instrumentation except for the group itself, or a couple of pieces which are featuring acoustic piano with strings, flutes, and harp. If I know I have a certain deadline to meet with that particular thing, then the writing gets very methodical. I sit down and say, "Okay. Today I have to score this thing out for an orchestra"—or for strings, or for brass, or whatever.

Conversations: Are these deadlines why you're out here in the hills of New Jersey?

Miles: That might have something to do with it. Another thing is that we rehearse a lot out here, and I have enough room here for people to stay overnight and things. The only neighbors that I have are Ronnie Glick and his family. Ronnie is an old friend of mine. He's a great jazz drummer, and he rehearses with his group next door, so we don't bother each other. And at this particular point it's financially a lot easier for me to live here than to have some place in the City to do the same thing, because it runs into a lot of problems—you know, instruments going in and out. If I were living in New York, had a loft or something, and I was working out of town, then I'd have to have a van in the city; I'd have to have a building with an elevator; I'd have to worry about all kinds of details. I'm in the City quite a bit; I'm in New York maybe half the time. And it is quite a drive into the City. I hadn't expected to be in New York quite as much, but I had been doing a good amount of studio work. I'm not doing as much now, and this place is perfect right now for what I want.

Conversations: I've noticed in your recordings you have a tendency sometimes to blend an acoustic piano, an electric piano, and a synthesizer. Do you have a rationale for using all three?

Miles: All of them are different instruments. I don't consider an electric piano a piano—it's an electric keyboard instrument. I think an acoustic piano is a much more highly developed instrument. It's had more time to develop; it's a much more sensitive instrument than, well, say, a Fender Rhodes electric piano. However, there are electric pianos coming on the market which will rival acoustic pianos. If I had my choice on a recording to play an electric piano or an acoustic piano, I would choose the acoustic piano in an ideal situation.

Conversations: Where they can mike it properly, and so forth?

Miles: Right. In a concert situation, for some reason, technologically they haven't been able to come up with a setup where the acoustic piano can be amplified properly to compete with the drums—which has a lot to do with why there are a lot of electronic instruments. Regardless of a PA system, the group has to come up to the volume level of the drums, and the drums have changed—their style has changed a lot since the bebop era. In the sixties, especially, the whole style of drumming became a lot more dynamic, and, of course, the suspended cymbal, which is the loudest instrument in the orchestra, can drown out an entire orchestra. It's not that drummers have become less sensitive. Their whole style has changed to a much more dynamic thing. The drum stands out a lot more.

Conversations: Their equipment has improved, hasn't it?

Miles: Oh, yeah, sure. When I was playing with my brother in the middle or late sixties, it was always a struggle for me with the acoustic piano, when I didn't have any electric piano at all, to reach the dynamic level of what he was doing. He had to play real soft for me; but if he really wanted to come up dynamically, it would waste the acoustic piano. And there are a lot of people

133

who have developed their style—their piano style—purely on the dynamics of the drummer. In my opinion, the reason guys like McCoy Tyner play so strong is because of the drums. A lot of times you go to a concert, or you go to a club, and you can't hear them play; hence, the electric player, who can do the volume thing. However, the electric piano doesn't have the dynamic range that an acoustic piano has. An acoustic piano can play very soft and it can play very loud. If you have an electric piano, when you turn it up it can play loud; but if you hit the note real soft, it still comes out very loud. However, there's a new Yamaha electric grand which has an action like an acoustic piano, has a sound like an acoustic piano. I can play a record of Herbie Hancock playing the thing and you'll swear it's an acoustic piano. In this way, they'll be able to solve that problem—they'll be able to get an instrument. It's just a matter of time in electronics for them to develop the techniques to be able to come out with a sophisticated instrument.

Conversations: You use a synthesizer for effect in what you compose.

Miles: That's a totally different instrument. Synthesizers can be guitar synthesizers, horn synthesizers, and keyboard synthesizers—which don't necessarily sound like a piano; they just happen to have a keyboard. They don't use strings or anything. It's totally electric, using oscillators. And they're much more sophisticated electronically than, well, say, the electric piano.

Conversations: Well, do you sit down at some point and go fishing for sounds from a synthesizer?

Miles: Oh, yeah. The synthesizer is unlimited in the types of sounds that you can get. But it's a very expressive instrument and I have found that I have been able to develop my own recognizable sound on that instrument. A lot of the criticism of electronic keyboard instruments was that you take piano players whose style you can recognize, put them on an electronic instrument, and you can't tell the differences among them.

Conversations: It flattens them out.

Miles: Basically, they're talking about the Fender Rhodes electric piano, which is not a very acoustically sophisticated instrument—there are just certain technical things that you can't do on it; you can't play it like an acoustic piano. You play a lot of runs or arpeggios and they get muddy—it's a slower action. But on the synthesizer there are certain players, now, whom I can hear play that instrument and say, "Yeah, that's Jan Hammer; that's George Duke; or that's myself." It's a lot more sophisticated; it's got a lot more things that you can do with it, and a lot of people have developed their own type of sound.

Conversations: Well, is the sound that you identify with based on technique, or is it based on the music that is written for the sound?

Miles: Both. All of that is developing right now. It has to do a lot with the technique that players are using on it—the different parts of the instrument that they tend to gravitate toward.

Conversations: How about you?

Miles: Well, I don't really use the synthesizer for sound effects.

Conversations: Do you mix it into your overall score?

Miles: Right, I like to blend it with acoustic instruments. A lot of times there are pieces on which I'll have the synthesizer and acoustic piano—which I feel can blend very well, depending on what types of settings you have on the synthesizer. I use it more as if I were, say, a horn player. The synthesizer I have is a mini-moog, which is a single-line instrument: you can get certain harmony things out of it, but they're all parallel. But I use it as if it were a horn, or a flute, or something like that. I don't try to imitate the sound of those instruments, but use it as a new type of instrument, a solo voice.

Conversations: With all these new developments in instruments and compositional style, what kind of reaction do you get from the old-line musicians? In the classical field, there are symphonic conductors who stop in the fifties, because electronic music doesn't interest them. Do you find the same thing applicable to the old-line jazz musicians?

Miles: Some of them, and some of them not. I wouldn't make any generalization about that. I'm concerned about developing what I feel is right for myself.

Conversations: Does the word "jazz" really fit what you and your contemporaries are doing in music?

Miles: To some people it does and to some people it doesn't. There are certain jazz people who will listen to what I am doing and say, "That's not jazz; that's rock." There are rock people who will listen to my music and say, "That's not rock, that's jazz." There are certain elements in my music that I consider jazz. I think there's a great jazz influence in what I do, but I think there are other things involved with it, too. I don't like to label what I do.

Conversations: Is jazz becoming a very sophisticated breed of American music?

Miles: Some of it is, but it has always been heading that way. They had Third Stream music, back in the late fifties, and a lot of it in the early sixties. And yet, there are certain kinds of jazz now that are very much disco-oriented. I see it moving in two directions simultaneously.

Conversations: Is there such a thing as commercial jazz and commercial rock versus not-so-commercial; and, if so, where do you put yourself?

Miles: It has to do a lot with exposure as to what is commercial. If you have a big exposure and marketing is emphasized, something can become commercial that wasn't commercial the year before. There are other things that are not intended for certain kinds of audiences. I don't consider my music intended for the same audience that Grand Funk Railroad is into. However, I feel there's a very large audience for the type of music that I'm into, and it's up to me to try to get that music to those people, to make them aware that it exists.

Conversations: Is it tough? Do you consider yourself a loner in this respect?

Miles: A lot of jazz people are always attempting to reach a larger audience for their music or to reach the audience that is out there for their type of thing. I feel my type of music has been getting a lot more exposure recently. It's a very gradual process, but I like to delve into both fields. I like a lot of things about rock music; I like certain kinds of disco music; I like funk—I like to play that type of music. And because I like to do that, it doesn't mean that if I'm going to write what I consider a disco piece of music that I'm selling out or something. I just play the music I get off on.

Conversations: How about the blending of what you do, with the type of instrumentation you're working with, and a symphonic group?

Miles: Well, that's basically what I'll be doing on the next album. I'm having basically the group, plus a large number of string players, woodwind players, brass players, harp, and I'll be doing some things along those lines.

Conversations: Have you been able to figure out how best to use strings? That seems to be the stumbling block for many jazz musicians who try to write for a big orchestra.

Miles: Well, the whole thing, to me, has always been a rhythmic problem more than anything else. A lot of the string players do not have the concept of the syncopated rhythm in jazz. Now I have heard recordings of real good jazz violinists who can play a piece as if they were a saxophone section and make it swing. It is possible to make a string section swing.

Conversations: You mean like Joe Venuti?

Miles: Right, or Jean-Luc Ponty. It just has to do with the type of playing. So if I'm writing for string players who I know do not have a jazz background, I'm not going to write those types of lines for them. However, a lot of the music that I'm writing that these players are going to be on does not have the old swing jazz rhythmic thing happening. It's a more of an even eighth note type of thing. Therefore, they can do a lot of syncopated things, but it's not really a jazz feel. I can move it more into that direction without making it sound corny, but it is a difficult problem—it always has been.

Barry Miles

Conversations: You say you don't want labels, but isn't it a fact that as a commercial composer you're a victim of the interest of the moment? You were talking about the cymbals dominating a band, for example, when that didn't happen so much in the bop era. Won't that trend be replaced with something else?

Miles: Well, before I used the cymbals to illustrate the dynamics of the drums. What really happened was that in the bebop era the drummers were really playing cymbals, with accents on some of the other drums. But the cymbal was the main thrust of the music. Then, when a lot of the influences of rock or Indian music or other things came about, drummers started playing the drums, and the cymbals were used for the accents. So the whole emphasis was away from the cymbals for timekeeping and onto the drums for timekeeping, especially a lot of bass drums and snare drums—back beats—and the cymbals are used more for accents. What will happen next depends on individuals. I don't see any general trend. You can't look at this type of music and feed it into a computer and say, "Well, what's going to be the next thing?" It depends upon certain individuals and their influence on other people.

Conversations: What are you, as a composer, pushing toward?

Miles: That's really hard to say—

Conversations: Well, you're certainly not a follower. You must be plowing some new ground somewhere.

Miles: Right, it has to do again with—like I said, I don't want to get too technical—keeping a certain interplay that happens within a group in improvisation, plus writing pieces to utilize that interplay. What's missing in a lot of present-day fusion music, or even in a lot of newer jazz, is that the soloist is out there and the rhythm section is backing him up. The rhythm section is playing a fairly set type of thing, and the guy is soloing in front of it; or, in a group like Weather Report, there's a lot of short soloing fragmented or soloing together. But I'm really into the idea of the soloist having a lot of interplay with the rhythm section. The soloist can be out in front, but that rhythm section, to be doing things right with the soloist, shouldn't be doing the same thing all the time.

138

Conversations: Countersoloists would you call them?

Miles: Right. And I find that a lot of my group's success in that regard has to do with the rapport I have with my brother on drums when I'm soloing, either on the synthesizer or the piano. We have a lot of rhythmic interplay, which I find very intriguing.

Conversations: This is bred through familiarity, then?

Miles: Right. It has to do with playing together a lot.

Conversations: How did you meet Eric Kloss and what's the musical relationship there?

Miles: Well, we've known each other for a real long time, because we both started very young. I heard his records when I was young, and he heard mine. We met through a mutual friend, Bob Miller, who's a saxophone player from Westfield, New Jersey. I forget the exact circumstances, but I think Eric was either playing out in New Jersey or visiting Bob Miller. Anyway, he was staying with Bob Miller, and Bob just brought Eric over to my place, which wasn't far from where Miller lived. And the first few times we got together, we just improvised freely. We just played sax and piano for hours. Of course, we had similar backgrounds as far as our influences, and as far as our goals and everything. So it was just an instant rapport and a real friendship, which has developed in the last seven years. We've always been doing duo things together, but not in front of an audience. I recorded on an album of Eric's a couple of years ago. He has worked, on occasion, with my band. We've jammed together with a lot of other musicians, but we've done a lot of jamming, just the two of us, for the last seven years. And then, finally, we got an opportunity to actually do a duo album on Muse called *Together*, for Joe Fields. That's how that album came about; it was just the time to do that. I have the feeling sometimes that some people say, "Well, you're doing a duo album because there are a lot of duo albums that are coming out now: there's Jan Garbarek and Keith Jarrett, and there's Gary Burton and this guy, and whoever." And yes, that's true, and maybe that's one of the reasons we've gotten an opportunity to do a duo album; but it's not because we looked at them and said, "Oh, wouldn't it be nice. Why don't we do that?" We've been doing that all along, and the time was right for us to record.

Conversations: It's apparent, then, that Kloss' playing is compatible with your musical thinking and with the musical thinking of the other people in your group.

Miles: Right. We have a great musical rapport. And the same thing between Eric, myself, and my brother. Again, that interplay is always happening, and we think very much alike. There are a lot of differences in our styles and our playing, but they sort of complement each other. It makes a sum larger than the separate components. I add certain things to the total experience when the two of us are playing together—or the three of us—and Eric adds his thing, and Terry adds his thing. What comes out is something which is very cohesive in itself, but goes in many directions.

Conversations: Are these ideas articulated verbally before you articulate them musically?

Miles: Maybe a little bit. If one of us has a piece and wants a certain idea out of it, we may talk about what it is; but most of the concept is expressed purely through the music. We might play something and Eric will say, "Well, I'd rather hear this voice singing in your left hand," or I will say to Eric, "Well, I'd like this line legato and certain written sections should be softer here or louder there." But in trying to get across the idea, most of it is actually doing it and then maybe sitting back and saying, "Well, what can we do to make this better?"

Conversations: How much showmanship, how much show business do you have to inject into your performances to hold an audience?

Miles: Well, I think one of the features of our performances is in the audience automatically picking up on a certain rapport that the musicians have with one another. They can sense it. There are certain visual things—like if there's a line we play we might smile and say, "Well, that felt good to play that"; or if I'm doing a certain musical duel with my brother, there might be things back and forth that visually would be exciting to the audience. It looks like we really have a rapport with one another, and the audience can hear that we have a rapport. That's one aspect, I think, people pick up on right away: that all musicians in the group are happy about playing, that they enjoy playing with one another; they enjoy being up there. You can't really lay back with the music as a musician. It's very intense, even though at certain times it may be very mellow. But it's more than just sitting around jamming or something. You have to be very conscientious in the playing or else you're going to get lost.

But another thing is that I'll announce pieces—I'll explain who's in the band and tell maybe a slight bit about a certain piece, although I don't go up and do a whole monologue and tell jokes and stuff like that. But just acknowledging the audience and saying, "We're glad that you're here, and we hope you enjoy it." And the feeling that when the audience likes what we do and somehow shows its approval, either by applause or being attentive or by just being there, makes a difference to us—it makes us feel like playing more. Although, if there's nobody there or if there's one person there in the audience, the group is still going to get off playing, because we enjoy playing with one another. We enjoy being in a position where we can do our own thing. But it's not so much to try to please everybody in the audience and say, "Well, what are these people going to like?" We play what we enjoy playing, and we try to present it in such a way that people can have some understanding of what we're trying to do, and we hope that they like it.

Conversations: I imagine the people who represent you have to pay pretty strict attention not only to what you do, but to the type of hall they put you in, so as to maximize your effectiveness.

Miles: They really have to have an understanding, first of all, of what kind of thing we're into—what the music is; what direction it's going in; and what type of audience is going to enjoy what we're into. If we got a gig that was booked opposite a group that drew an audience that was not into what we were into, it just wouldn't go over. Or it may go over, but it wouldn't be right.

Conversations: Do you have any say about the other groups you appear with?

Miles: Yeah. If we are headlining, obviously, we would have that type of say. If I'm not headlining, if I'm opening up for somebody, I would want to know who it would be. I think, especially this fall, that will be one of the things that we are going to do: to work opposite some groups who are better known than we are—who, generally, are in a similar field of music that we're into and who are going to draw people who would like what we're into. That's a move at this point for us to get a little bit more exposure. Probably the major problem that I've had in the area of exposure, and perhaps one of the reasons I'm not as well known as I feel I could be, is that except when I was very young, I always had my own group. I never got my exposure through playing with somebody else. I didn't go on the road with, let's say, Miles Davis in 1966 and make my name that way. I got a chance to play with a lot of those people as a drummer when I was very young, and it was almost as if I had a different life. I got that experience at that time and I didn't want to do it in 1966 for the experience, because I already had it. I felt it would be a dishonest move to myself just to go out on the road with someone to become famous, to use somebody else's name to get my own name. So because of that, I did my own albums; I had my own groups. But the people who came to see me had never heard of me nor my music, so I was always drawing an audience that in the very first couple of tunes was saying, "What is this going to be?" I have been very lucky to gradually build a following. But it has been a very slow process, and sometimes it's been difficult—say, doing a concert and having four people in the audience. So what we're trying to do now is not for me to join somebody else's band, but to work opposite a band that would draw the type of people who would enjoy our thing, so eventually they will know the name and then will have a familiarity with the type of music that we are playing.

Conversations: You're going to be performing in Europe. Is this your first excursion into Europe to concertize? Do you have an audience there, or do you have to go do this musical salesmanship in Europe?

Miles: Well, a lot of it is going to be doing the musical salesmanship over there, which we understand. That's sort of why we're laying the groundwork. I have worked with my own group at Ronnie Scott's in London in early '74, which was a good gig for us. And I did go over to Europe in 1961 on a State Department tour of seven countries. Of course, I was very young. I was a drummer at the time, and John Mehegan was on piano, and John Handy was the saxophone player. That was a very good experience for me, but that's been so long that the people in the audience are probably over here now. The tour was "Visit USA."

Conversations: Why do you go to London to do your recording—for economic reasons, artistic reasons?

Miles: Both. First of all, we're recording some other albums over there. There is a studio called Olympic Sound and an engineer by the name of Keith Grant, who does all the engineering for Gryphon Productions and is an excellent engineer. He happens to be a part owner of that studio, so he has a great familiarity with the equipment there, what the studio can do. It's a very well known studio over there; a lot of different things have been done there: jazz, movie scores, the Rolling Stones have recorded there. So it has all the capabilities that anything in the United States does. Because we're doing five albums in a month, to get this whole studio for a certain length of time is less expensive. It's also more convenient, because you have the studio night and day during that time.

Conversations: So you have a block booking, then?

Miles: Right. I'm bringing over the musicians from my group, and the brass players over there are all the finest players in Europe. A lot of them have been on the road with all kinds of big bands in the United States.

Conversations: Who picks these people for you?

Miles: Some of them, at this point, I pick myself, because I'm familiar with them now since I've been over there—was over in January. The others would be picked by Norman Schwartz, who has recorded over there a lot of times.

Conversations: What's in the future for you? You're only thirty years old, but you've been at it a long time. You're helping to legitimatize jazz. Do you intend to teach down the road? Do you have something to say in print about your music?

Miles: I think all of those things. I have taught, to a certain extent, before; I have written—I wrote an instruction book on improvisation back in '63; and I've done a few articles for a couple of publications in the past. I'm not into doing that right now, because I want to do one thing at a time. Eventually I'd like to write movie scores. And I'd obviously like to write pieces for other groups and other people—some big bands, an orchestra, whatever. It's only recently that I've gotten back into doing the orchestrating-arranging thing, which I was doing in the sixties before I got very much involved with the small group. Now I'm getting back to the arranging. I'm also into writing songs with lyrics. I don't write lyrics myself, but I work with a lyricist—you know, to write pop tunes or whatever.

Conversations: Are you easy to collaborate with?

Miles: Yeah.

Conversations: Is your temperament the type that allows you to collaborate?

Miles: Yeah. I don't think there's a problem with that. I don't like to collaborate very much with people writing music. A lot of times a lyricist will come to me with a set of lyrics, and we can work from there; or I'll come up with a melody and they'll write lyrics to that, with a few changes along the line. But to collaborate with someone in writing music, I'd have to be very close to them. That might present a little bit of a difficulty, because I have my own set ideas. I like to work by myself in that respect.

Conversations: Is this future you're carving out for yourself on a predictable schedule?

Miles: I don't want it on a real predictable schedule, but the first goal that I want to accomplish is to be able to maintain a working group on a full-time basis and to be in the position to record and to perform my own pieces, whether they be for the small group or for the small group plus a larger combination. Then, after that, I'd like—for instance, over this summer I will be writing a couple of compositions for Woody Herman's orchestra, and several other writers are going to be doing that, too. Chick Corea is supposedly going to be writing something for him also. And I already wrote this other thing for the Phil Woods album which will be out in the fall.

Conversations: How do you get these commissions? Did Herman call you up and say, "Hey, write me something"?

Miles: In this particular case, yes. The same thing with Phil Woods. Of course, I have known these people for a long time, but they were interested in having some of my music on their recordings. I'm really up for doing that type of thing.

Conversations: How would you like to be recognized, as a composer primarily, then as a performer?

Miles: No. I think it's really an equal thing between being a performer and a writer, because at this particular point in my life I'm really concerned about performing as the improviser, the soloist; there's a certain vitality there. I think the important thing about music is not so much that it's made sitting down writing something or it's made recording something in the studio, but that it's made actually performing things in front of people on the road. That, to me, is an important thing, and it seems that it could be a lot harder that way because you always say the way to really make it is to get an album on the charts—everybody would love to have an album on the charts. But, to me, to keep that thing happening by performing in front of people—to be a live performer—is very, very vital.

Conversations: It keeps your creativity going on?

Miles: Right. The writing all comes from that. It's like coming back and saying, "Hey, that felt really good. Maybe we can try to capture that, to put a framework around that, and to be able to utilize what was happening at that moment the other night."

Conversations: Can you go back and recapitulate a performance and get something from it?

Miles: To a certain extent. You can't recall that moment forever, but there are certain things about that: it's something new; it's something that happened. That whole idea of improvisation is very important to me.

Conversations: Is your music all-consuming, or do you have other things that you like to do?

Miles: It's pretty much all-consuming. I like to go for a walk; I like certain sports; but music is a full-time thing with me, especially in dealing with the performing and dealing with the writing and trying to keep the whole business running. I could get into the business thing a lot more than I do. I consider that I have a certain business sense, but I don't use it because I don't like to do that. I don't like to get on the phone and say, "Hey, we need thirty-five albums out to this guy." But I realize that it's very important to do that, only because I want to be in a position to do my own thing musically. But I don't do it just to become a star, although a lot of people say that your main thing has to be to become a star. I'm afraid that that isn't my main goal. My main goal is to be in a position where I can do what I want, and where I don't have to do another thing, somebody else's thing.

Conversations: There seems to be a humanity about jazz musicians that, somehow, is not found in other musical pursuits. Jazz people seem to like one another. Do you find this so, by and large?

Miles: Well, I can't really say, because I don't know too much about how people feel about each other in other fields. I found when I was a kid drummer that the better the musician, the more famous he was, the nicer he was to me, the more he tried to help me out. I admit that I had an ability in that field—they weren't ashamed to play with me, because if I wasn't any good I couldn't get up on the stage with Buck Clayton or someone and make a fool out of him, or Coleman Hawkins, or whoever. Somewhere along the line they knew that I was good enough, at least, to play with them. But they were very helpful, and they gave me the opportunity to get that experience. They were very nice to me. And I found that type of thing happening, yet there are lots of jazz musicians, especially some of the city guys, who are very competitive. There are guys that put down everything. I know a couple of guys: "Oh, this guy stinks! This guy is no good!" And then there are other guys: "Everybody's great!" And then there are other people who have their own opinions about things. Like, for me, the whole thing between electronic and acoustic music: I like both. There is certain music that I love that is electronic, and I love acoustic music. I don't think acoustic pianos grow on trees and come down from heaven. They are man-made, and so is the synthesizer: they're both dealing with acoustics. Yet, someone like Keith Jarrett, who's a master of the acoustic piano and a master of electronic instruments, too, says he doesn't like any electronic music whatsoever, and anybody who plays it, forget it—it's no good. He's entitled to his opinion. But for someone who's an expert to say that, and then someone else to come along who is also an expert—well, say, like Chick Corea—to say he likes electronic and he likes acoustic. . . . To me, here are two experts who have totally different opinions, and that's the way it is. There are all kinds of directions going on at once.

Conversations: Do these opinions get personal? Do you still manage to respect one another, or, at least, have an empathy for one another as musicians?

Miles: Well, again, I don't know how Keith Jarrett really feels about anybody playing electronic music. I think he just feels that's the work of the devil or something like that—that's his own opinion. Yet he has played electronic instruments on many records. So, for him, it isn't the right thing, which I can understand. But I feel, in general, that the musicians are much nicer to one another than, we'll say, critics, who try to make musicians fight with one another. Like I'm supposed to hate Chick Corea, because certain critics have said, "He copped this from Chick." In reality, I might have done something before Chick did it, you know. "He put his group together because Chick had this type of group," and my group got together before Chick's group was together in that form. So I'm supposed to hate Chick Corea now, because I was accused of copying off of him. But that isn't the case.

Conversations: Do you hate him?

Miles: It isn't that way at all. Some of his influences are the same as my influences, so there are going to be similarities in our styles to a certain extent. There's a lot of difference in our styles. I love the way he plays; I love his music. I like him as a person, and I think the feeling is mutual. We don't know each other well, but anytime that we have been together it's been a nice experience. I know he speaks very highly of me to other people, and vice versa. Other people are entitled to their opinions, but I'm not going to let people who have wrong factual data, you know....I know that they are not capable of doing criticism because they have the wrong facts.

Conversations: How about critics in general? Do they have too much clout?

Miles: No. They have very, very little power in the jazz field. In some other field they may have a lot, like with a Broadway show—the guy doesn't like it, that's the end of it.

Conversations: The audience is ahead of the critics in jazz?

Miles: Yeah. The audiences are much hipper; you know, it varies. There are some critics who, you know, make some very good—it's not that I'm against critics totally; sometimes they might have objective remarks about things. But I find a lot of the jazz critics today go by little gossip things that they hear from one musician, then it gets to be third hand; by the time it gets into *Down Beat* it's wrong. It's just not right. A lot of times you'll see a guy who will write his review off of the liner notes of an album. I remember on one of Eric's albums in the liner notes it said that Vic Juris holds his guitar high, like a classical player—giving it as if he had classical training. So the review came out and said, "Vic Juris, who was classically trained"—and Vic Juris never studied classical music in his life. So how does this guy know that he's classically trained? It's just not factual. The other day someone showed me an article about me in *Down Beat* in 1963. When we were down in Allentown this drummer from the other band came and said, "Hey, remember this?" I was just looking through the record reviews in that issue and there was a nice review of a John Coltrane album, which got two stars out of a possible five. You read *Down Beat* now, they make it sound like they discovered him, you know, "Coltrane is the greatest thing that ever happened, and we were hip, too." When he was around they were putting down everything that he did, right across the board.

Conversations: Do you discount what critics say and go on and do your thing and let the audience decide?

Miles: Right. Exactly. I'm much more interested in what I feel. I've been around long enough to be able to look at things objectively myself and to know if something that I'm playing stinks—whether it's good, or whether it's bad. I've seen enough criticism to know that one guy will say it's great, and another guy will say it's lousy. One guy will say it's great for the wrong reasons; another guy will say it's lousy for the wrong reasons. It makes no difference. Plus, there are a lot of things that are very relative in the music. There was a review of one of my albums in a publication, and the guy called me up and said: "I reviewed your album. I loved it. I'm going to give it five stars." I said, "Oh, that's really nice. That's very good." Then came the review, and it was four stars—which doesn't matter to me either way. But I just was curious as to why it was four stars, so I asked him. He said, "Well, they reviewed a Chick Corea album in the same issue and they only gave that four stars, and if they gave you five and him four it would look funny, so we had to give you four." I said, "Okay." If a review is purely relative for whatever issue it is in, depending on who else is being reviewed, then there is no standard of criticism. I just think the level of criticism and journalism is a little bit amateur. I don't feel that I can respect their opinions when I know that they don't have their stuff together.

149

Melvin James (Sy) Oliver was born in Battle Creek, Michigan, on 10 December 1917. He grew up in Zanesville, Ohio, and was introduced to music by his parents, both polished musicians. He had rudimentary trumpet training from his father, but no formal instruction in composition or arranging. He made his big-band debut with the Cincinnati-based Zack Whyte band, and, soon thereafter, in 1933, he joined the Jimmie Lunceford band as a trumpet player and vocalist. His arrangements became identified with the famed Lunceford band sound. In 1939, Oliver joined Tommy Dorsey and the arrangements and compositions he wrote for Dorsey have become big-band classics. In the mid-1940s, Oliver won both Metronome and Down Beat polls as the outstanding arranger of the year. Oliver currently heads his own band.

Sy Oliver

Sy Oliver and Zane Knauss met in Oliver's bright and spacious apartment at 102nd Street and West End Avenue in New York City in July, 1977. Oliver was on vacation from his three-year engagement in the Rainbow Room at the RCA Building. For this conversation, far removed from the opulence of the Rainbow Room, Oliver wore sandals, walking shorts and a short-sleeved sport shirt. The atmosphere was pleasantly informal.

Conversations: Early in your career, you were the arranging voice of the Jimmie Lunceford Band.

Oliver: Well, there were two arrangers in the band. Ed Wilcox also did a lot of the writing. The things that are mostly identified with him are the beautiful saxophone choruses—things like "Sleepy Time Gal," "Sophisticated Lady," those things. Wilcox wrote all of that stuff. But I did most of the—well, I did all of the vocal trios, and most of the novelty sort of things.

Conversations: Like "Cheating on Me"?

Oliver: "My Blue Heaven."

Conversations: The trio had a sound that I don't think can ever be copied.

Oliver: No three people sound alike.

Conversations: It had an almost whispery quality to it.

Oliver: Well, we were always compelled to sing in that manner, because none of us had voices and the idea was to sing softly to get a blend. If we had sung in our natural voices, in a robust fashion, it would have been terrible.

Conversations: I've read that you were quite hesitant about

Sy Oliver

*taking trumpet solos on your own, and that you used to write
your solos a lot of times. Is this so?*

Oliver: Well, yeah. In those years I was not what you might call
an ad-lib soloist like so many of the fellows, principally because I
had very little expertise on the trumpet. I had never spent any
time studying trumpet. From the time I got into the business I
was always interested in writing. I remember when we were
youngsters, I was in the band in Cincinnati.

Conversations: That was the Zack Whyte band?

Oliver: Yeah. Roy Eldridge and Reunald Jones were in that area,
and many times we'd all be living at the Sterling Hotel there. Roy
and Jones and the other fellows would be in their rooms blowing
all day long, and I was sitting in my room trying to write. They
used to tease me all the time—said, you know, "Get with the
horn; you'll never be able to play." That's just about what
happened.

*Conversations: You were born in Michigan. Your father was a
singer, and both your mother and father were teachers.*

Oliver: Yeah, both of them were. My father was a singer, and also
he played everything—brass instruments; he even played the
violin.

*Conversations: Was the orientation toward the classics, or was it
toward jazz?*

Oliver: Well, semi-classic. He also did pop music. As a matter of
fact, he and my mother had an orchestra when I was quite young.
They used to play for dancing.

Conversations: In Zanesville?

Oliver: Yes.

Conversations: How did you gravitate toward jazz?

Oliver: I sort of drifted into music. My parents started me on
piano when I was quite young. I didn't like to practice and they
didn't insist; they were fairly enlightened for the times. They
didn't insist that I practice piano. My father told me at the time
that if I ever wanted to play an instrument to let him know, and

he would get it and teach me. As I say, he played everything: he played the brass instruments; he played saxophone—in fact, I still have one of the first saxophones ever made by Conn, a double octave key tenor.

Conversations: Which he owned?

Oliver: Yeah. My father used to demonstrate the saxophone for Conn. He used to travel and demonstrate it around the country—Atlantic City, New York, everyplace. During those days they didn't even write music for saxophones. He used to play with martial bands and play the baritone horn parts, because it's the same register as the tenor saxophone, you know. But at the time he first started with the tenor saxophone, they actually did not include the tenor saxophone in orchestrations. However, I had never had any inclination to take up an instrument until many years later. I was in high school—I was a freshman in high school, I believe. And my best friend was a fellow named Al Sears; he played tenor saxophone with Duke Ellington. He was playing with the local orchestra. They rehearsed at night, and I wasn't allowed to stay out at night, you know, unless there was a very good reason. So my interest in the orchestra was to be able to stay out at night; that was my sole interest.

Conversations: No musical interest?

Oliver: None whatever. That, and I wanted to hang out with my buddy, you know. So they needed a trumpet player, and I told my father that I wanted a trumpet. He got me a trumpet and showed me how to run the scale. And almost immediately he became seriously ill. In fact, he never recovered. Well, by then I had gotten hooked on the horn. After he showed me how to run the scale, I began fooling with that. I lived with the darned thing. I was playing it very shortly. Of course, I was also motivated by the idea of playing with Cliff Barnet's Orchestra.

So after I was able, I began playing with the school orchestra, of course—the school orchestra and the school band. And I went to my father and told him that I had a new job. He said, "Well, what are you doing now?" I said, "I'm going to play with Cliff Barnet's Orchestra." He said, "Oh, no, you aren't." Because back in those days that wasn't—of course, their plan was for me to go to school. However, as I say, Dad got sick, and I began playing with the orchestra. It was the only way I could earn money and stay in school, and that's what got me in the music business.

Conversations: Necessity, then?

Oliver: Every year, after my brothers and sisters began growing up and I had things fairly well in hand, I planned to go to college. But something always occurred.

Conversations: You never did go to college?

Oliver: Never did, no.

Conversations: Well, are you self-taught as an arranger then, too?

Oliver: Yeah. I stupidly did it the hard way. I was playing with bands, and I bought books written about arranging. But they were so complicated in those days—if you could understand one, you could write one. They really weren't very helpful. So I wound up, through trial and error, discovering things, you know, over a period of years that I could have learned in five minutes.

Conversations: Is that really so bad, though?

Oliver: Well, it might be bad for a lot of people; it worked for me. You know, it's a funny thing about this business: as Duke Ellington said, "There's no formula for success in this business." It's different for everybody. The way I learned to arrange... now, I was fortunate in that I was always working with good bands, highly imaginative musicians.

Conversations: Was the Zack Whyte band good, too?

Oliver: One of the best bands that ever existed in the Middle West. Many of the top musicians in the country today came through that band—guys like Vic Dickenson. I played with Vic in Zack's band back in 1929.

Conversations: Now this was a black band?

Oliver: Yeah. They weren't great musicians from the standpoint of training—technical training—but most of them were talented musicians. Of course, there were just as many bad musicians then as there are now; the percentage never changes. But somehow most of the very talented guys through the Middle West, at one time or another, played with Zack's band. And I was also helped by the fact that most of them didn't have any more technical knowledge than I did. Things that I wrote that were wrong from the standpoint of writing, they didn't know were wrong any better than I did. I could tell by sound when I was not getting the effect that I wanted, but that was it.

Conversations: But your approach, then, to harmonics and chords and even sections was simply trial and error?

Oliver: Exactly. I didn't realize it then, but, basically, the criterion for producing music—composing, arranging—is: Does it sound good? Are you getting the sound that you want? If you are, then it's successful.

Conversations: Is it true, then, that each arranger has in his own mind a particular sound he wants to achieve?

Oliver: Sure. A guy that arranges with Guy Lombardo doesn't want the same effect as a man that arranges with Benny Goodman.

Conversations: Well, can you juggle instruments then to get that sound? For example, like with Ellington's band, you were always conscious of Carney's baritone sometimes leading the section, having the melody.

Oliver: Well, there's a perfect example of what I was talking about awhile ago. If you achieve the sound that you want, then it's successful. Many things that Duke did in his band—many things in the way of orchestration and so on—were completely unheard of. Nobody else has ever done it or ever will do it, in all probability. It has nothing to do with the so-called rules. You know, that's always amused me, too, about—you really can't teach anybody to compose, to arrange; you can provide them with the tools, but there's no way in the world to teach anybody to compose. And arranging is composition in a great sense.

Conversations: A lot of people don't think of it as that.

Sy Oliver

Oliver: It is. For instance, suppose I were to make an arrangement today. The first thing I would do is write the introduction. Where does the introduction come from? It's composition.

Conversations: It's not part of the tune you are arranging?

Oliver: It certainly isn't. Where is the background behind the vocalist or soloist? It's composition. The countermelodies? It's all composition. The modulation to go to the next chorus? It's composition.

Conversations: So you're not a re-creative person, you're a creative person?

Oliver: That's right. Of course, you also have to combine it with—you require a bit of the talent of an architect, you know. The thing has to have a basis; it has to go some place; it has to make a complete picture.

But to get back to what I was saying, it's almost impossible to teach that sort of thing. For instance, you go to a conservatory now and you study theory and so on. Most of the rules that have to do with the construction of music—none of those rules were devised by people who create music.

Conversations: Or, even more specifically, people who improvise.

Oliver: That's right. There's a great master of sound who wrote the symphony, and then somebody who couldn't write a symphony sat down and analyzed it and came up with a set of rules and said, "This is the way." But he couldn't take his own rules and write a symphony.

Conversations: The people who are the spokesmen for the profession are not the professional composers?

Oliver: Very rarely. A successful teacher in this business is one that knows how to free a guy; if a fellow has talent, a good teacher shows him how to get out of his own way and use it, you know. Take a writer, for instance: he writes. Well, when you're going to write a piece you can't sit down and analyze it; you just sit down and start writing. And somebody says, "How did you happen to write that?" That's the stupidest question. How do I

156

know how the hell I wrote the thing? You can't explain it; you can't explain it yourself. And that's what I meant about getting out of your own way. If you have talent, if you have creative talent, it's an integral part of you that you have absolutely nothing to do with. All you can do is to develop tools to use it, then stay the hell out of the talent's way and let it come out.

Conversations: Have you ever been in a position to do as you suggest? Have you ever worked with students?

Oliver: No, not really. A friend of mine, Dick Jacobs, and I used to—we had an office together; we taught an arranging course. Actually, Dick did the teaching; we sort of devised it together, and he did the teaching. I didn't have time to bother with it, number one. The other thing was I was never interested in that sort of thing. But to make my point, you know, 90% of the students were men who had graduated from a conservatory or had finished the Shillinger course.

Conversations: And they came to you.

Oliver: Found out they couldn't write, then came to us to find out how to write. That is the literal truth.

Conversations: You can't do it in the laboratory?

Oliver: You know how Dick used to teach? I made an arrangement some years ago for Tommy Dorsey's band on a tune called "Swanee River," which you've probably heard of— "Swanee River" that is. It's a very simple arrangement. All footballs, very simple, and that's all he ever used.

Conversations: For his teaching instrument?

Oliver: Just used that for examples, and we wrote an arranging book together and used that arrangement for the demonstration exercises throughout the book.

Conversations: In "Swanee River," for example, you had this pause with just the rhythm going in the second chorus before the sections pick it up again. Is that your signature, more or less?

Oliver: I don't think in terms of signature, but one thing that I've always believed in, as far as arranging is concerned, is white space. Take advertising: You take a whole page of a paper and put three words on it and everybody sees it. Then when you make a statement, everybody hears it. People can't hear but one thing at a time. That's the first thing I—anytime I talk to an arranger. . . . Kids come to me; a lot of the guys helped me when I was coming along and I always try to help the kids. But as I say, you can't help them but so much—just point the way and they have to do it themselves. But one of the things that I tell them is: Don't try to put it all in the first chorus. I remember this fellow— he's a very famous arranger; he's written for all the big stars. He came from—I think he went to Clemson, either Clemson or North Carolina State. But when he hit New York—incidentally, he's out of the business now; he became very rich as a stockbroker. But he got off the train and came straight to my office. Nice kid. He pulled out his briefcase—that was always the case: every time a young arranger came to New York, the first place they would come was straight to my office.

Conversations: You had a big name on the door.

Oliver: Well, that—I'll tell you about that, too, that big-name bit. But this guy opened his briefcase and began showing me his scores, and I looked at one—and the guy really was a brilliant writer—but he had put in too much stuff. I told him to take that score home and cut it up in bits and pieces—he had enough stuff there for his next 200 arrangements. And he got the message— became one of the most successful arrangers in the business.

Conversations: You obviously took a great deal of license with the vocals—I assume these were your vocals.

Oliver: Yeah.

Conversations: When you arranged "Sunnyside of the Street," was it for a particular group?

Oliver: It was for the group that was with Dorsey's band at the time. They were called "The Sentimentalists"—Clark Sisters, really.

Conversations: In Zanesville, Ohio, and then with the Whyte band down in Cincinnati, you had, in effect, almost what Ellington had: a band to work with and a chance to experiment.

Oliver: Yes. That's what I started to say awhile ago. I've been very fortunate during my whole career in having good musicians to work with.

Conversations: And they allowed you to experiment?

Oliver: As I say, they were coming along at the same time I was; they were all youngsters. Back in those days, bandleaders rarely knew anything about music; they were usually businessmen or showboats. Duke Ellington and Fletcher Henderson were the only two musical bandleaders I knew at the time. The rest of them were just front men, you know, in one way or the other— either as a businessman or as an MC and so on. They rarely had anything to do with the music of the band. And as I said, the fellows in the band, they were coming up; we all came together. So they were tolerant of my inadequacies and mistakes, they didn't know any better—I didn't either. We were all learning at the same time, you know.

Conversations: You heard the Lunceford band and then decided that you wanted to work with them. Is that how it really went?

Oliver: That's true. I was in Cincinnati and they came through there. They were on their way to Buffalo, actually, where they settled and stayed for several years. I heard them rehearsing in the Sterling Hotel and their rehearsals were meticulous. Lunceford conducted a rehearsal as though it were a classroom, and I was very impressed. While I was working with good musicians—they were all talented guys, and they were also pretty wild—one of my problems was to get them pinned down to something.

Conversations: And the Lunceford band was disciplined?

Oliver: It had discipline—the first organization of that nature that I had ever run into. As I say, I was very impressed; however, I had no intention of going with them. I left shortly after I met them; I left Zack's band. I was in Columbus, Ohio. I wasn't even playing anymore; I was arranging, and I had some students from Ohio State—that sort of thing. And I did have a group in one of the clubs there, Hill's Restaurant, and I was writing for them— just sort of organized the thing. And Lunceford called me and asked me to do some arrangements for him, which I did.

Sy Oliver

Conversations: You had already met him, then?

Oliver: Yes. I did several arrangements for him, and then he offered me a job. I joined the band because they were coming to New York. And I joined them for a free trip to New York—to come here and go to college. I had no intention of staying with them. No. I joined them that summer and they were due in New York in the fall.

Conversations: Had you gone to school, would you have studied music?

Oliver: No, I had planned to study law; but, first, I had to go to college. I was just going to college, but I always wanted to study law. However, to get back to Lunceford, we came to New York and the band was an overnight sensation, literally. It just turned this town upside down.

Conversations: Why? What were the ingredients?

Oliver: Well, the band was unique—people had never heard anything like it. That caliber of musicians, caliber of men, Lunceford himself, what we were playing—it was all new. It literally brought something new to the business, in fact. . . .

Conversations: Did it overshadow Ellington, for example?

Oliver: Well, in a different sense. You see, when you speak of bands, you don't speak of Ellington. Ellington was unique, in the literal sense of the word. I mean, that covers it. It just can't be included in any generalizations.

Conversations: So, then, everybody else starts somewhere else.

Oliver: That's right. Lunceford's band was the first band to bridge. . . . Well, let's see, I'll put it this way: at that time there were two worlds, a black world and a white world, in every respect—entertainment, music, everything. There was music above 110th Street and music below 110th Street, and they were completely different. Many years later Glenn Miller came up with hits like "In the Mood," "Tuxedo Junction," "Don't Be That Way," and "Stompin' at the Savoy." The guys that wrote those things wrote them for black bands; black bands had been playing them in Harlem fifteen years before Glenn Miller was

160

ever heard of. Before he even had a band. They were all recorded, too, and practically the same arrangements, because Miller's arrangers copied the original arrangements, except in instances where the black guys did the arrangements themselves. However, my point is that at that time there were two worlds, and Lunceford's band was the first band that bridged those two worlds. He appealed to both worlds. That was amazing, too. Many of his hit records were hits uptown and downtown at the same time, and that had never happened before. Had never happened before.

Conversations: Did the record companies take notice?

Oliver: Of course they did. Prior to that time all record companies had what they called a race record section. There was another thing that made the band so popular: it was not only a fine musical organization, but also it was a fine entertaining organization in a sort of formal, classy way.

Conversations: Well, Miller stole stuff from the band—the hat trick with the trumpet.

Oliver: Sure. In fact, I think that's the word that best describes the thing that appealed to Harlem so much about Lunceford's band—"class." Also, without anybody ever making a big thing out of it, they discovered all the guys were college guys, you know—well, that they were gentlemen. And it really made a difference.

Conversations: From what I've seen of the band, it was one of the most charismatic groups ever to get up on stage.

Oliver: It was. All the fellows were attractive; they all dressed well; and they all dressed at all times, you know.

Conversations: Was this the kind of discipline enforced on them by Lunceford?

Oliver: Well, you know, Lunceford's leadership was. . . to me, he was the perfect leader in that he didn't even state a position. He took a position and he just followed it.

Conversations: Did he give you guys enough running room so that you could exercise your artistic talents?

161

Sy Oliver

Oliver: He never said a word to me about making an arrangement; neither did Dorsey, for that matter.

Conversations: Before you got to Dorsey though, how did it work? Did you decide which pop tunes you wanted to arrange for the band, or did you arrange originals?

Oliver: I arranged things that I liked; I simply wrote what I liked. When I wrote originals it was just something that I liked, and usually something predicated on what the fellows played. For instance, the thing that I did—an instrumental that I did which became one of our big records was a thing called "For Dancers Only." Most of the riffs I incorporated in that thing were things that I had heard the fellows play. Somebody organized it—it was Lunceford; it was the Lunceford guys. Oddly enough, they talked about the Lunceford band, the Lunceford style, when he contributed absolutely nothing musically; yet, the whole thing could never have happened without him.

Conversations: He was the catalyst.

Oliver: It was Lunceford the man. He was an amazing man. As I say, he was a great leader in that he never had to impose himself or his ideas or his discipline. He didn't impose it; he just established it. It was there.

Conversations: Yet, the band probably missed its greatest fame because the big rooms around the country were not really available to it.

Oliver: That was the two worlds I was telling you about.

Conversations: The exposure on the air, all the accoutrements that the white bands got—

Oliver: No way. The thing that really launched them was the six months we were in the Cotton Club. We were on the air every night from there and that established the band nationwide. But after that, of course, as you say, it was impossible for them to get into the hotels and so on; it was unheard of. The two worlds still existed; however, people were coming to hear the band.

Conversations: Did this damage the morale of the band?

Oliver: It didn't work that way, because they were a part of a

162

world—they were living in the world as it was; you can't go around worrying about things—

Conversations: You mean you were all pragmatists as well as good musicians?

Oliver: You're bringing up something now that I could never explain if I talked for 1000 years—there's just no explaining it. People live in a world and accept the world the way it is, or else they're going to knock their brains out.

Conversations: Is it true that there was a time when Dorsey said, "Whatever you're making, I'll give you five G's more if you'll join us"?

Oliver: That's what he said. That's why I didn't get to school at that time. Everybody thinks I left Lunceford's band to go to Dorsey. I didn't. I left Lunceford's band to go to school again. I had put in my notice. It was in July and I was going to school and I left. I wanted to take the summer off because I was going to school that fall. And, oddly enough, Dorsey's manager was there that night, a guy named Bobby Burns. We were at Brighton Beach. He heard the fellows talking; he asked me to ride back with him. This all happened the same night; it's funny. No, I didn't leave Lunceford to go to Dorsey.

Conversations: Had you known Dorsey?

Oliver: Oh, sure. I left the band. I put in my notice. I was going to school that fall—there I was again. Well, I finally did get to school, though—after I came back. I was in Paris for a couple of years—'68 and '69—

Conversations: Was this with the Olympia?

Oliver: Yeah. Olympia Theatre, yeah. And when I came out I had finally gotten enough music. I just had it up to here, and I came back to New York. I closed my office—I had had an office in the Brill Building for years. I closed my office and said, "That's it." And I started taking classes down at The New School—things I'd always been interested in and never had the chance to pursue: beginner philosophy, advanced psychology, some of the humanities courses, planning a new life-style, things like that. I enjoyed it for a while, but then—

Sy Oliver

Conversations: You missed music?

Oliver: Not especially. But it just didn't occupy me enough; I'd waited too long. It's like so many things that you look forward to all your life and when it happens. . . . I'd been too busy, too long. I thought about it: "Now, what will I do?"—I was taking that course planning a new life-style; I enjoyed it, too.

Conversations: So you took it to help your own life-style?

Oliver: Yeah. I started thinking about it and I didn't decide to do anything particularly, but since the thing that I knew most about was music, I was curious to see if I could re-create the big-band sound with a small group. Big bands are out of the question; they're just no longer feasible, economically. I decided to use nine pieces—two trumpets, two trombones, two saxophones, and a vocalist—I'm going to use the trio, of course. And I sat here and wrote a book—oh, about 100 numbers—did it myself.

Conversations: Did you go back through some of the old songs that you'd done?

Oliver: Yeah. The basis of the library was all the standard things that I had done down through the years: all the hits I'd done for Lunceford, all the things I'd done for Dorsey, that sort of thing. I did; I broke them all down and made them over for the nine pieces.

Conversations: That was a job, wasn't it?

Oliver: Well, I didn't have anything else to do, and it kept me occupied.

Conversations: I know you've also had groups, recently, of eight and six pieces.

Oliver: Well, that's part of the story. I got some guys together, friends of mine, fellows that had worked with me in the recording industry for years—George Dorsey, Budd Johnson, Monty Johnson—guys like that, you know, top musicians. We started running these things down, and it worked! It really sounded like a big band. And as I say, I still had no idea of pursuing it, because I had never wanted to be a bandleader. I had wanted a band like I wanted a hole in the head. That's what's so funny about this situation now. If anybody had told me I'd be standing up in front of a band playing a trumpet six nights a week, I'd have laughed like Little Audrey.

Conversations: You're not only playing, but singing.

Oliver: Yeah, well—"singing." But it really worked. And the guys, of course, were very enthusiastic about the band—just knocked them out, because we all came up together, you know; we were all good friends.

Conversations: Does playing in the smaller groups give the individual musician a greater part to play or more prominence?

Oliver: No, we were playing the same arrangements, exactly the same. Before I broke the thing up, we were offered an engagement at the Downbeat—it was a club, sort of a jazz club—on East 42nd Street, I think it is. We went in there for six weeks to give the guys a chance to—you know, pay them back for rehearsing. As a matter of fact, I paid them considerably more than scale out of my pocket—that six weeks cost me quite a bit of dough. The thing was a big hit, a big hit, and the people who handled the talent there also handled the talent at the Riverboat and the Rainbow Grill. Oh, before I knew it, I was in the band business.

Conversations: You went in the Americana, too, the band—

Oliver: Went into the Riverboat and went back on the Riverboat; went into the Rainbow Grill and back on the Riverboat and—

Conversations: You also had an eighteen-piece band that you've used for this jazz repertory thing and at Newport.

Oliver: Well, that was something else, that jazz repertory thing. Oh, you asked me about when we were in the Americana. I went in with six pieces; we played the same arrangements. I broke them down again into six pieces and my wife—who is a pianist, by the way—said, "Now, first you took the fifteen-piece orchestrations and you broke them down to nine pieces; now you're breaking them down to six pieces; now, how about making piano duets out of them so we can play them." Most guys start with small bands and work up to big ones; I took orchestrations that I'd made for fifteen pieces and made them for nine and for six.

Conversations: It's tougher, isn't it?

Oliver: It requires much more expertise, much more expertise. Now, I couldn't have done that years ago, you know, which bears on the point that we were talking about—how you go about studying arranging. For the benefit of anybody who may read this sometime, if you are interested in learning to arrange or in any sort of creative work, there are only two ways—assuming you have talent. There are two things that you must do: you must acquire the tools one way or the other—either by studying with somebody who can teach you, or by trial and error. And you must work at it—you must write. There are no other ways. There's no other way. It's sort of like—any sort of creative work is like.... You could have the greatest style in the world and rarely will your first efforts be as good as your final efforts. It's sort of like learning to drive an automobile: you can read everything that's ever been written about driving a car, but until you get behind the wheel—forget it.

Conversations: Does an arranger have to have a keyboard instrument to arrange? Did you also have to play piano, in addition to your playing the trumpet?

Oliver: Nope, I don't play piano. There again, it's different for everybody: some people don't use anything; some people use a keyboard; some people use a guitar. When I was in Paris writing for the Olympia Theatre shows I didn't—there wasn't a piano available to me for the first six months that I was there.

Conversations: You just heard it in your head, then, and put it down?

Oliver: That's right.

Conversations: One of the beefs, I guess, you had with Lunceford was that there was so much traveling to do. You were on the road constantly, playing trumpet as well as arranging.

Oliver: That's the reason I left the band. Yeah, I was in that band for six years, and I had had enough of it.

Conversations: With Dorsey, since you were just doing the arrangements, did you also have to travel every place they went?

Oliver: No, no. I didn't travel with them except when I wanted to, or sometimes, when they'd go to the Coast. They were doing radio commercials for Raleigh cigarettes, also some movies, and I had to go out there then. But when they were on the road I didn't travel with them.

Conversations: You just had to go listen occasionally and—

Oliver: I didn't have to do that; I just sent the arrangements to them.

Conversations: Did you write "Well Get It"?

Oliver: "Well *Git* It." That's a very funny story.

Conversations: You know, some of the labels are wrong.

Oliver: I know it. I know it—very well do I know it. We were broadcasting from some place—the band was broadcasting from some place—and this announcer's stentorian voice boomed: "And now, Tommy Dorsey and 'Well Get It.' " And the thing is a slang expression, "Well Git It."

Conversations: Was this written with Ziggy Elman in mind? Was he in the band then?

Oliver: Sure, sure.

Conversations: Did you write with specific players in mind?

Oliver: You always do, of course.

Conversations: I suppose "Hawaiian War Chant" was written with Buddy Rich in mind.

Oliver: Well, I didn't do "Hawaiian War Chant," but—

Conversations: You did "Quiet, Please."

Oliver: I did "Quiet"; I wrote that for him. Here's a case in point. Tommy called me one day—I think they were in the Palmer House in Chicago. He said, "Sy, Buddy Rich is joining the band tomorrow"—this was five o'clock in the evening—"could you make an arrangement and bring it out here for him tomorrow?" I said, "Tommy, you've got to be out of your mind." He said, "Yeah. You can do it. They'd like to have something for him for rehearsal tomorrow." So I got on the plane and I wrote "Quiet, Please" on the plane. We got to Cleveland and we were in a terrible storm; the plane landed in Cleveland. We took off for Chicago—there was nobody on the plane but me and the crew. I was writing. And I got to Chicago and the guys met me and they took me to the hotel. A copyist met me and copied the arrangement—I finished it just sitting there and we had it for the rehearsal the next day.

Conversations: How about when Sinatra joined the band? Did you write for him, too?

Oliver: Oh, sure.

Conversations: Is there a different approach when you have to write for someone who has a particular style? Do you have to sit down and listen to their style before you start writing for them, or do you make them sing your style?

Oliver: Well, it's a little of both. Usually, with the sort of arranger that I am—I'm kind of a producer and director, too—you know more about what a guy can do than he does himself, you know.

Conversations: That's to his advantage then, isn't it?

Oliver: Oh, yes.

Conversations: Was Sinatra tough to write for?

Oliver: Not for me.

Conversations: Tough to get along with?

Oliver: I've never had any trouble with any of these bad-tempered people that you hear about. The only musicians that I've ever had any trouble with are poor musicians. I don't have any trouble with good musicians.

Conversations: Dorsey had a reputation for being volatile and sometimes difficult.

Oliver: A general pain in the neck, yeah. He was, but not with me. I've never had any trouble with good musicians, never.

Conversations: Were you the only arranger with Dorsey, or were there others?

Oliver: Oh, no. When I joined the band, he had two other arrangers, Paul Weston and Axel Stordahl. There were three of us.

Conversations: Stordahl also sang, didn't he?

Oliver: No. Well, he did—he sang on one of their early records; I think it was in a trio on "Once In Awhile." But at the time I joined the band, he wasn't singing with the band. Jack Leonard was the vocalist.

Conversations: When did you start singing with the band? You did "Yes, Indeed!" with them, didn't you?

Oliver: I never sang with them. As a matter of fact, that was an accident. We were recording the thing and we were running out of time. The part that I sang on the record was supposed to be the band singing in unison against Jo Stafford. They weren't picking up on it very fast, so I just did it to save time.

Conversations: Have you any desire to work within the classical idiom?

Oliver: One of the things that has always amused me about people is the length to which they'll go to make themselves miserable. I've seen so many fellows. . . . For instance, a man who is, say, a very successful sportswriter—probably one of the best sportswriters in the world—well known, very successful, and that's his thing. He does it very well, and spends his whole life miserable because he hasn't written the great American novel. Well, I'm very happy about one fact: no, I'm not one of those. I'm a jazz arranger. A pop arranger. A very good one and very happy about it—and have no interest in writing a symphony. Furthermore, I don't think writing a symphony. . . to me, that doesn't represent the epitome of achievement. These guys that write symphonies couldn't do what I do.

Conversations: And yet, you wrote some very good things with strings.

Oliver: I've written for symphonies.

Sy Oliver

Conversations: Even with the Dorsey band when he put strings in—that "Mandy, Make Up Your Mind" was recorded with strings, wasn't it?

Oliver: That amuses me; people used to ask me: "Mr. Oliver, can you write for strings?" So I'd get out something that had numbers for a fifty or sixty-piece orchestra some place and play the first eight bars and say, "Does that answer your question?" Confident arrangers can do anything.

Conversations: What about today with people experimenting with electronic instruments—does this interest you as an arranger?

Oliver: No, I'm not particularly interested in it. I'd do it if that's what the client wanted, but that's not to my taste. I don't care much for electronic music; that's a field unto itself. It has its place and it has a reason for being. You see, people make a mistake: they close their minds and something that they don't like, or can't do, they say is bad. There is no bad music; there is only badly performed music. And it's very stupid to put something down simply because you don't know about it or can't do it. I listen to everything. Some things I enjoy; some things I don't. It's just a matter of taste. But if your taste is not. . . . That's one of my criticisms of the critics. A critique based solely on your personal taste is not a valid criticism.

Conversations: Are there qualified critics around looking at jazz?

Oliver: There again, there are some who approach it with an open mind, and in judging a performance use as criteria that criteria which applies to that particular thing—but very few. As I say, most of them are people whose criticisms are based just on their personal tastes. In fact, the whole field has always amused me. Years ago, about the time the Lunceford band came along, kids began following bands around, you know, young college kids and so on, gathering around the bandstands. And then it became sort of a faddish thing. So because of the great interest some of these smart guys—you know, they were pretty bright kids, some of them—began writing about the bands, started magazines like *Metronome* and *Down Beat*. Of course, the public ate it up. So these guys, because they had access to print and because their names were before the public, became authorities. People believed everything that they wrote, which was quite all right, because the American public is geared to believe what they read, anyhow. But when the musicians began believing them, I thought it was a little much. Oh, they were good for the business; gee, they kept interest in bands alive, but Jesus—

Conversations: You won a Metronome *poll; you won a* Down Beat *poll.*

Oliver: I won a *Down Beat* poll seven or eight years in a row. I started to mention that awhile ago, when you talked about guys coming to my office and you said, "the big name on the door"— that was a direct result of publicity. Before Dorsey began publicizing "Sy Oliver," nobody knew what an arranger was; he was the forgotten man. Nobody ever mentioned the arranger; Lunceford never mentioned the arrangers. And when I went with Dorsey's band he set out. . . that is, I didn't make an issue of it; it was his idea. And every time he played one of my arrangements on the air: "A Sy Oliver Arrangement. . . . A Sy Oliver Arrangement." And of course, as a result of that, the other bandleaders began to see how important it was, and they began doing the same thing; but it was too late by then. I was in on the ground floor. As a consequence, everybody in America knew "Sy Oliver, the Arranger," and it wasn't that I was better than anybody else. My name was just publicized, and that's why I would win all those polls. Somebody said, "Arranger?" and everybody immediately thought "Sy Oliver," you know. They thought I was the only arranger in the world. For instance, at the same time—even before I went with Dorsey—Jimmy Mundy was writing for Benny Goodman; nobody knows who Jimmy Mundy is. Nobody knows who Jimmy is.

Conversations: Fletcher Henderson got a little bit of fame, but not as much as you had.

Oliver: Well, he was his own leader, and he was Mr. Music Business—he was ahead of Duke Ellington, you know. His was the top band in the country in the days of Paul Whiteman, in the black world, you know.

Sy Oliver

Conversations: Is it true that Henderson went to Goodman because he just hadn't been able to get the support he deserved on his own?

Oliver: Oh, I have no idea. It's a very romantic story, but a lot more like so many of these romantic stories about this business: it's a crock—probably.

Conversations: You wound up writing for a lot of different people; you were even writing for Charlie Spivak—who had an entirely different kind of band than Dorsey's.

Oliver: I am a professional arranger, just like some people are professional writers. If somebody wants you to sit down and write for a medical journal, you'd do some research and you'd write it; if somebody wanted you to write a book on sports, you'd do some research and you'd write it; and I'm a professional arranger—whatever you want written, I'll do it.

Conversations: Did you sit down with Spivak and discuss what the band was supposed to sound like?

Oliver: I didn't have to. I knew what his band sounded like; I'd heard his records. Of course, that's not what he wanted from me; he was trying to get other things—he wanted Sy Oliver. Of course, in so many instances. . . . This reminds me: for years—to show you the difference in people—at one time Dorsey had the whole top floor of the Brill Building as his office, the whole top floor.

Conversations: Is this when he got into the publishing business and the record business?

Oliver: Publishing business, yes. He had the whole top floor. He had one tenant who had a suite of two small offices—Guy Lombardo. And Guy Lombardo had nine-tenths of the money in the world at the time. But the point of my story is that every time Guy would see Dorsey he would say, "Hey, Sy, when are you going to make an arrangement on 'St. Louis Blues' for me?" And it got to be a joke. Though a lot of people would come to me and say, like this Charlie Spivak, for instance, that they wanted me to write Sy Oliver for them—well, a lot of people can't play Sy Oliver. I went with Dorsey's band, and I had been with the band

172

about six weeks when I heard them broadcast from the Pennsylvania Hotel one night. I was in bed, and I got up and got dressed and went down and quit. I said, "I will not be associated with this." Tommy said, "Now, Sy, when you came with the band I told you that these guys would not be able to play like Lunceford's band." He had a Dixieland-oriented band, you know—"Song of India," boogie-woogie, that sort of thing. They couldn't play the sort of thing that I wrote; they literally couldn't. He said, "Now, I told you these guys would not be able to play like Lunceford's band. You'll have to have patience. I've given them a few weeks, and if they don't pick up on it, I'll get you some guys that can play it."

Conversations: And did he?

Oliver: A year later there was one man in the band that had been in the band when I joined it. And they were swinging by then—turned out to be a great band. He just went out and got guys that could play it. Well, there's a case in point: now, when I joined his band I could have written for the band that he had, but that's not what he wanted.

Conversations: And it's not what you wanted either, is it?

Oliver: No, it didn't make any difference to me. I don't know where people get that idea. People are always. . . . There is so much romantic nonsense about this business. Just why do people think I go to work—to get my jollies?

Conversations: You go to work to get paid.

Oliver: You're goddamn right—solely. People are always coming up to me down at the room: "Don't you get so"—There's some creepy broad that always the reviews of the band. She's always—I don't understand her. She's down there every week and writes a review for some paper out of town every week. And she spends her whole review talking about what great musicians they are and how frustrated they must be, sitting there playing dinner music all night long. But she keeps coming back, you know. Well, now I say, "Here comes Georgia somebody have a breakdown from frustration." They got the best job in New York, for Chrissakes. There's not—oh, well.

173

Sy Oliver

Conversations: I guess the Rainbow Room is the prestige room in the city, isn't it? It pays well.

Oliver: That's not the point. Where else could a musician work in New York three years on one job?

Conversations: Right, unless you're a single doing the Carlyle or something.

Oliver: Name me a jazz club where they could work.

Conversations: I can't.

Oliver: "Aren't you frustrated sitting there playing?"—I get so sick of that.

Conversations: Well, you're no spring chicken; how long are you going to work?

Oliver: I don't know why I'm doing it—I'll tell the truth. Well, I do know, because as I said—I did try doing nothing and I can't. I've been too busy too long. I can't sit around doing nothing. As lovely as this home is, I've just got to get out of here sometime.

Conversations: Are you still writing things for other bands?

Oliver: No, sir. I don't write for anybody but myself.

Conversations: And this for the small band?

Oliver: That's right.

Conversations: Now what about the Newport Jazz Festival? You went back in with the big band—I assume it's a big band.

Oliver: No. We played the last night at the Newport Jazz Festival last week, the Fourth of July.

Conversations: With your small group?

Oliver: Yeah, same group we have every month. My band and Count Basie's band. You know the high point of the evening? When my band was on the stand—you're darn right.

Conversations: Well, Basie doesn't have the same band he used to have, does he?

174

Oliver: I don't know what his band is now. I didn't stay to hear it. After we finished, I left.

Conversations: So you just went in and did it and got out of there?

Oliver: That's right. Incidentally, I was just teasing about that now. That reminds me of the time we were invited to do a concert for The Duke Ellington Society. The fellow who was the head of the organization didn't know me, and he got in touch with me through a mutual friend. So he called and spoke to me about it, and I agreed to do it. He said, "Well, Sy, what should we call the concert? 'Sy Oliver Plays Duke Ellington'?" And I said, "No, call it 'Sy Oliver Improves On Duke Ellington' "—very seriously, you know. So in a few minutes the woman who had gotten us in touch and gotten us together called and said, "Sy, what on earth did you do to that man?" She said, "He called up and says you're crazy; who is this crazy man?"

Conversations: Did you know Billy Strayhorn very well?

Oliver: Sure, very well. He used to live right around the corner. He was a great musician—the only man in the world that ever understood Duke Ellington.

Conversations: Is that right?

Oliver: Sure. Nobody else could write Duke Ellington—nobody. When I did that concert I just mentioned, I had occasions to listen to some of the things very closely, because I took a good bit of it off records, you know. Amazing, truly amazing.

Conversations: Did you get to know Ellington very well in your career?

Oliver: Oh yeah.

Conversations: Was he difficult to know?

Oliver: No. One of the most charming men I ever knew—warm.

Conversations: Some say he's probably the greatest American composer of the twentieth century.

Oliver: Well now, that is a nonsensical statement.

Sy Oliver

Conversations: Is it?

Oliver: Of course it is. How can you compare Duke Ellington.... Well, I gather from that, that whoever said it took all the composers in America and said Duke Ellington is the greatest. That's ridiculous!

Conversations: Perhaps, Ellington, for this particular reason: most of the other American composers are writing from a European point of view in their instrumentation, their approach—

Oliver: I think, in his field, he was probably the greatest creator that ever existed. And his field was Duke Ellington's band— period. He has probably more standards—as many standards as any composer in this business. But when anybody plays any of them, it's just somebody playing a beautiful song—it doesn't sound like Duke Ellington.

Conversations: Do you think that a lot of his material will end up on a shelf because it was written for a particular band?

Oliver: No, that's not true. Many of his songs are quite successful just as songs: "Sophisticated Lady"—well, Jesus, if I'm going to have to start naming them, I'll be naming songs for the next 200 years. But I don't care who plays them, it don't sound like Duke playing them.

Conversations: So he was one of a kind, then?

Oliver: I said that in the beginning: Duke Ellington was unique; his orchestra was unique; he was his orchestra.

Conversations: So then, your career is just going to go as written, right now?

Oliver: Well, I'm going exactly. . . as long as I must be involved, this is exactly the way I prefer to be involved: doing something that I find pleasant with pleasant circumstances and pleasant people, playing for pleasant people. We've been at that place for three years, and I've seen no unpleasantness, no bad vibes, nobody coming in there drunk. It's a pleasant—it's a beautiful room; we play beautiful music. If we get a Saturday night crowd and people want to jump, we play "jazz." We play waltzes; we

176

play polkas; we play cha-chas. We play whatever the people want to hear. And the people who come in there are not music aficionados; they're just people, just ordinary people like you and me. When I'm listening to music, I'm just an ordinary guy. I don't listen to music as a professional musician. My tastes are just like any other person's. I don't know anything, and, oh, I'm constantly amazed at the so-called authorities. I've been in this music business all my life. I'm sixty-six years old and been a professional musician since I was thirteen, and I don't know anything about music. These authorities kill me: "You were thinking about so-and-so when you wrote such-and-such a thing. . . ." and I'd never even heard of the person they were talking about.

Conversations: Do you always resent having anyone decide for you what you were supposed to have been thinking about when you write?

Oliver: Yeah. "What inspired you to write such-and-such a thing?" I'll tell you exactly what inspired me: the rehearsal was due at six o'clock and it was three o'clock in the afternoon and I had to get something ready in a hurry—that's what inspired me.

Conversations: And last, but not least, you were being paid for it.

Oliver: That's right.

Charlie Spivak isn't exactly sure of his birth date, but he's positive he was born in 1907, in Eastern Europe. He grew up in New Haven, Connecticut, one of ten children. He studied trumpet locally, and then began his career with the Dorsey Brothers before moving on to play with the big bands of Ben Pollack, Bob Crosby, Jack Teagarden, and Tommy Dorsey. He formed his own band in the early forties. At the age of seventy, Spivak continues to play, currently at Ye Olde Fireplace, a Greenville, South Carolina, steak house.

Charlie Spivak

*Charlie Spivak lives in the mountains bordering North and South
Carolina. For this conversation with Zane Knauss, he came down
from his Cleveland, South Carolina, retreat and took over a
condominium apartment he once owned in Greenville, South
Carolina. When Knauss called the present owner, he was told: "We
didn't know anything about your appointment here with Charlie,
but that's okay. Charlie does that sort of thing a lot. Come on over."
The conversation was recorded on Friday, 25 February 1977.*

Conversations: I'm fascinated with Ben Pollack. He had an
enormous capacity to recruit first-rate men, didn't he?

Spivak: He had a faculty of knowing a talent by just hearing him. I
became acquainted with him when he first came to New York.
He played at a place called the Little Club, and I hadn't heard of
the band except on recordings. He made a couple of Victor
records.

Conversations: Was he a good drummer?

Spivak: Excellent drummer for that type of Dixieland music that
they played. On the records that I heard he had Benny
Goodman.

Conversations: An enormous number of you went on to
become bandleaders. Glenn Miller was in the band too, wasn't
he?

Spivak: He was in the band; Jimmy McPartland was in the band;
Bud Freeman was in the band.

Conversations: Were you in it?

Charlie Spivak

Spivak: I wasn't in it at that time. I joined them later on. Jack Teagarden joined them later too, and so did Charlie Teagarden. Well, I joined Ben Pollack almost at the time he was working the Park Central Hotel. He was leaving the engagement to go off on the road. That's when Benny Goodman left him and started his own band—about 1936. Pollack had to replace Benny and he got a fellow by the name of Matty Matlock.

Conversations: He was a clarinetist who wound up with Crosby eventually, didn't he?

Spivak: Yes. I can get to that part of it too, because Bob Crosby was in the Dorsey brothers' band as a vocalist when I was with them.

Conversations: You were a member of the so-called "Pollack Orphans," weren't you?

Spivak: I don't know whether they called them the "Orphans" or not; maybe they acquired that name somewhere later on, but I was with Ben. Practically a new band started. Jack Teagarden stayed in it, but Eddie Miller came in—a fine tenor man, one of the best; Matty Matlock was in the band; Gil Rodin was sort of band manager.

Conversations: He really put together the Crosby band, didn't he?

Spivak: Right. We also had Ray Bauduc on the drums.

Conversations: "Big Noise from Winnetka."

Spivak: That's right. We were with the Bob Crosby band when that was written.

Conversations: Zurke was in it too.

Spivak: That's right. Excellent. "Little Rock Get Away" was one of his main features.

Conversations: He wound up with Crosby too, didn't he?

Spivak: Yes. He was in the band when I was in it. And it was a band composed of—I wouldn't say stars, because at the time we didn't consider ourselves as such. We were just a bunch of young, eager musicians wanting to play the best of jazz that we possibly could. And in the Bob Crosby band, which was mostly the nucleus of the Ben Pollack band, we had Bob Haggart playing bass, who was a fine arranger, still is. Deane Kincaide was in that band.

Conversations: Well, you played lead trumpet on one of the great recordings of all time, "South Rampart Street Parade," didn't you?

Spivak: Oh, do I ever take pride in that. That was one of the great things that happened to me in '37, '38. We also did one of the jazz tunes of that day, called "Dog Town Blues," "Yancy's Special," "Weary Blues," all the things that pertain to Dixieland bands. They were just so great. Now, what a pleasure it was to work alongside of Yank Lawson and Billy Butterfield, and then play in a band with a rhythm section like Bob Zurke on piano, Bob Haggart on bass, and Ray Bauduc on the drums.

Conversations: Jess Stacy wound up in that band too, didn't he?

Spivak: He came a little later on after I did. And we had some of the all-time great musicians in that band. I mentioned Eddie Miller, Matty Matlock. Eddie was so great on that tenor, and he also could play good New Orleans jazz clarinet.

Conversations: But, usually he had a counter melody on the tenor with the Crosby band, didn't he, or he had solos all the time?

Spivak: Most of his solos were on the tenor. It was done in such a tasteful manner; he knew what he was doing. He owned the horn.

Conversations: Before the Crosby band, even before the Pollack band, you were with the Dorsey brothers, weren't you?

Spivak: That's right. I was one of the members. I'll tell you how that all came about. When he organized the band he only had one trumpet, a fellow named George Thow. George is a fine trumpet player. I really don't know what has ever happened to him, whether he is still playing or not, but he might very well be out in California.

But Tommy wanted to add another trumpet. Just by chance I ran into him on Broadway one day and he said, "Charlie, what are you doing?" I said, "Nothing." He said, "Come on and join my band." That same night I was playing in the band with the Dorsey brothers.

Conversations: Is it true that Jimmy and Tommy were at each other's throat all the time?

Spivak: Constantly. But not in a manner that you'd think that they would want to do away with each other. It was just one of those things where brothers don't get along on the same bandstand. I'll give you an example. They used to rib each other, tease each other. We were working at a place called the Paradise Restaurant on Broadway in New York, and not only did we play for dancing, but we also had to play for quite a big show. Tommy used to direct the show and Jimmy used to snicker when Tommy would direct it. Tommy didn't appreciate that very much coming from his own brother.

Conversations: He had a temper, didn't he?

Spivak: Oh, very much so. And one night—I remember this just so plainly—he got aggravated at Jimmy for laughing at him while he was directing the show, and Tommy, just in the middle of the show, threw the baton right at him. He said, "If you can do better you go ahead," and with that walked off. We never saw Tommy anymore after that. As a result the band was given notice and we were through. That was the breakup; Tommy organized his own band and Jimmy did the same.

Conversations: Did you go with Tommy when he reorganized?

Spivak: I was with Tommy, yes.

Conversations: When they made "Marie" were you in the band?

Spivak: No, I wasn't there. I came in a little later on. Purtill was playing drums. We also had Jack Leonard and Edythe Wright as vocalists. We had Bud Freeman; Peewee Erwin, Lee Castle (Castaldo), and myself were the trumpet section. Other than Tommy we had Buddy Morrow—gracious, it's hard for me to remember all the different names. But, that was the Tommy Dorsey band.

Conversations: That was in the mid-thirties?

Spivak: That was around '38 or '39.

Conversations: Before that, then, you were involved with organizing the Noble band when he came over from England.

Spivak: That was in '35. He had just come over from England and was looking for somebody through the Rockwell-O'Keefe Office; they were the agents for him here. They were the reason for Ray Noble coming over here, and they contacted both Glenn Miller and myself to help him organize a band.

Conversations: How did that work? Did you two sign a contract with O'Keefe that said you were going to pick your musicians and organize the band for Noble? Or was it an informal thing?

Spivak: It was very informal. There wasn't any contract of any kind, because all Ray wanted was to get the best musicians available at the time. I think we got him a good bunch of guys who were really serious about their playing and the results they were getting from their playing.

Conversations: What kind of trumpet were you playing then?

Spivak: I was just playing the lead horn.

Conversations: But it was a big sound, wasn't it?

Spivak: Well, they always said I had a pretty sound and a big, fat sound, which they publicized me for. I like to think maybe I had a helping hand in doing that.

Conversations: How did you rate the other great trumpet players of the day?

Spivak: Randy Brooks was, I thought, one of the finest. Bunny Berigan was my idol. I worked alongside Bunny, and before, when I free-lanced in radio, he and I did some dates together. I used to marvel at the wonderful things he did on the horn. He was a very gifted trumpet player in that he did so many things that I thought were awfully hard to do. I used to try to mimic him in some of the things I did, but he sure had such an ungodly range for that time. He was just an exceptional talent.

Conversations: He was very accurate too, wasn't he?

Charlie Spivak

Spivak: Very much so.

Conversations: Of course, you were too. Your high notes were absolutely pure; you were there.

Spivak: I tried, along with the other boys, to do something that I thought would acquire an individual sound. My late good friend, Glenn Miller, thought he had something in the fact that I had a sound that was different from maybe another trumpet player. He thought I would be a good front man for a band.

He was at the Pennsylvania Hotel in New York City and had hit it big after a couple of records like "In the Mood" and "Tuxedo Junction." He was then also doing the Chesterfield radio program, and they needed a band at the Pennsylvania Hotel to replace him during the time he went from the hotel to the radio station to do his Chesterfield program, three nights a week. So he got me to do it. I had to organize a group to go in there and do that, and that was really the beginning. But it was a real tough beginning, because it was tough to follow a man like Glenn Miller.

Conversations: But you never played in his band, did you?

Spivak: The only actual playing I did with him was at the very outset. I rehearsed with the band, but because of circumstances beyond my control I could not join them and go out on the road. Otherwise I would have gone. I did make some of his early recordings before he went on the Bluebird label. I did some on, I think, Columbia, where he used men other than the ones that wound up in his regular band.

Conversations: Between 1934 and, let's say, 1940, you were with, if I have the order right, the Dorsey brothers, Pollack—

Spivak: I was with Pollack before I was with the Dorsey brothers.

Conversations: Then Noble, and then, in 1939, you joined up with Jack Teagarden to put together a band.

Spivak: It was right after my leaving Ray Noble that Jack Teagarden was looking for someone to help him organize his band, and he got in touch with me to ask if I wouldn't help him. I did and I became his partner. I was with him for about a year. There was a question at that time, just when Glenn Miller and

Teagarden were starting out, as to who was going to make it, because of the talent that Jack had as a trombone player. Of course, history proves that Glenn Miller made it. Jack had a very good chance, but he himself ruined it by some of the things he did.

Miller was a disciplinarian to a great extent, and I understood his reasons for it. His men didn't fear him in the sense of fearing a leader; they feared him and they also loved him, because they had a great deal of respect for his knowledge of music and his talent, too. When he disciplined that band he did it for a reason and he got the results. He didn't stand for any kind of nonsense. When he was on that bandstand, everything was business with him.

Conversations: What was the chemistry at that period that brought people together. You obviously came from all corners of the country. Where was the rallying point for all of you?

Spivak: I must say New York was at the time and, of course, I'm talking about from the late thirties on through the forties and even part of the fifties. New York City was the one point where everybody would meet.

Conversations: Was it a grapevine that told you when jobs were available, or did you just automatically keep in touch with different groups to see where the jobs were?

Spivak: It was like a grapevine. We used to meet at different places in New York. You've heard different musicians talking about jam sessions; well, we used to get together many, many times, and all of these fellows would be there: the Dorseys, Glenn Miller, everyone.

Conversations: Where did you jam in New York?

Spivak: There were rehearsal studios or we would go up to Harlem to catch a show.

Conversations: Were white musicians welcome there to sit in and jam?

Spivak: Very much so. Everybody, anybody that would come into these clubs.

Charlie Spivak

Conversations: Did white musicians copy what they heard from black musicians, or did they concede that swing was really some other definition of jazz?

Spivak: I think most of the fellows at that time had their own way of playing, their own styles of playing; they were all great jazz soloists. We used to go up just to get ideas from other fellows. Of course, the black musicians that we heard were fellows that we admired, and they admired us too, for what we did. There was something about going out and hearing these fellows and listening to their talent. We picked up a lot of knowledge from them, just like they did from us. I think it was a mixture of temperaments, a mixture of talents that possibly brought out better talents by hearing each other.

Conversations: At that time, I guess, Fletcher Henderson was working there.

Spivak: Oh, Fletcher Henderson was playing the Roseland Ballroom in New York City. We used to go and catch him. As a matter of fact, he wrote a little jazz tune that we recorded with my band; it was called "Let's Go Home." It was a cute little thing; the kids loved it.

Conversations: He was a good arranger, wasn't he?

Spivak: Excellent arranger. And I had with me a fellow at the time by the name of Sonny Burke.

Conversations: He helped you write your theme song, didn't he?

Spivak: That's right. He and I collaborated on it and up came "Star Dreams." We were just sitting around. He was writing for me, arranging for me at the time, and we needed a new theme song. The one I had at that time was an ASCAP song and we couldn't use it because ASCAP was having a feud with our musicians union.

Conversations: Petrillo?

Spivak: That's right. And we couldn't use any ASCAP music, so we had to use other music that belonged to BMI. We had to write a new theme and "Star Dreams" was the one Sonny Burke and I got together on. We were just noodling around one day at my home. I had my horn and he was playing something and I would play something. Pretty soon the both of us—just like the thing was already written out—played it and there it was: the melody of "Star Dreams."

Conversations: It has stayed with you.

Spivak: That's right; that's the same one we use today. It's been identified with me through all these years. The tag line that was handed to me was done by Glenn Miller: "The man who plays the sweetest trumpet in the world." I was a little against that at the beginning. How can you be the sweetest trumpet player or play the sweetest trumpet in the world when there were so many of them? But he said, "You keep that line and I'll bet you that catches on."

Conversations: Was that what prompted you to go behind the mute?

Spivak: Yes. But then I was criticized so much for using a mute. They'd say: "Here is a guy that gets such a beautiful sound with an open horn, and he puts that mute in and kills it."

Conversations: Did Miller really urge you to use a mute to develop this sound?

Spivak: He did. He did.

Conversations: Was this a condition of his helping to organize your band?

Spivak: Let's say it was one of the conditions. I don't think that was the entire condition, because I don't think he would have wanted me to continue if he had known it was a losing cause. He said that he thought I might have a more distinguishable sound by using a mute because everybody would want to play open horn. I disagreed with him on that, and I like to think that it came out right; of course, there are many that play open horn. I like to think there was something that could be identified with the sound I got, because it wasn't that harsh, metallic, brassy sound. It had a velvet sound, more of a velvet sound—a plush sound, you would call it, maybe.

Charlie Spivak

Conversations: How do you get those sounds? How does one trumpet player get, from roughly the same horn, what another trumpet player can't?

Spivak: It's a combination of the lip; it's a combination of your mind; it's a combination of your heart; it's so many combinations put together. And I worked very diligently on this, because I wanted to get a different sound from what someone else got. What I wanted the trumpet to sound like was a good voice—I'd like to think that I was successful, with all the work and effort that I put into it. I used to listen to records; I still do and try to play along with the records and have my vibrato sound just like the voice sounds. I used to play so many different recordings of different trumpet players, and I'd say, "Well, this sounds good, but I'm going to try and see if I can get something different from what he does."

Conversations: So you were very analytical in your playing?

Spivak: Very much so. I don't know that I've enhanced trumpet playing by having others try to play like me. There have been many who have come along that I thought have sounded even a lot better than I did when I was a younger man. But, I think, even today maybe I still get a little better sound than I did when I was a younger man because I have matured so much.

Conversations: But back in the days of the swing era you did some marvelous things: for example, the recording of "St. Louis Blues" where you played lead trumpet with the Ray Noble band; then on "South Rampart Street Parade"—there's an entirely different personality, really.

Spivak: I got a jazz sound for a lead trumpet player. And I think that was something that I took pride in.

Conversations: Let me ask you about the organization of a band. I think it's a matter of record that Goodman was instrumental in helping to finance Harry James's band. He put money up to get James on the road.

Spivak: I think he did. I don't know how much, but I think he did help.

Conversations: Now Glenn Miller was a great friend of yours. You've talked about your association in the Noble band and in the Pollack band; obviously, you were good friends. How did this work? Did you two sit down and did you say you wanted to lead a band, or did Miller say you ought to lead a band? What happened to get you in front of the bandstand?

Spivak: When Glenn became the tremendous hit that he was, he wanted to help some of his friends do the same thing. I had come back off the road and he was working the Paramount Theatre in New York City. I had called him and he said, "Come on over. I want to see you and talk to you. It's very important." I went up to see him backstage at the Paramount Theatre. He and I sat down and talked and he said, "Charlie, I would like for you to get your own band. I'll stake you to everything that you need and I'll help you get an arranger." In other words, he was the guardian angel. He put up all the money and everything.

Conversations: How much did it cost to organize a band in those days?

Spivak: To get the type of men needed. . . in round figures, union scale per man was fifty dollars, and if a fellow wouldn't want to come to work for that—if you wanted a good man, you'd have to give them, let's say, $100 a week. Well, when you got fourteen or fifteen people and you had to pay them fifty dollars a week more than what the scale was. . . Glenn paid that. Glenn also paid for the publicity; he also paid for the arranger or arrangers.

Conversations: How many did you have?

Spivak: I had four.

Conversations: Who were they?

Spivak: I had Dave Mann, Sonny Burke, Burt Ross, and Nelson Riddle. Then later on I had Sy Oliver.

Conversations: Before he went with Dorsey or after?

Spivak: After Dorsey, or he might have still been with Dorsey. He wrote quite a few things for me. I had Jimmy Mundy from California.

Charlie Spivak

Conversations: He did some things with Goodman for a while.

Spivak: Yes, I know that. And I had Manny Albam. I tried to keep abreast of the times by having all of the best arrangers. Miller paid for all of that.

Conversations: How about outfitting the band, the uniforms?

Spivak: Yeah, we had to buy those, too, for the boys.

Conversations: Did you have a road manager?

Spivak: Yes, I had a road manager and a personal manager. The same personal manager that handled Glenn handled my affairs. Glenn Miller had a stable of Claude Thornhill, Hal McIntyre, and myself.

Conversations: He staked all three of you then?

Spivak: That's right.

Conversations: What did he do, get a piece of the action?

Spivak: Yes, he did. He got a percentage of the net profits, which he received either on an annual basis or a semiannual basis. He had his own office with all kinds of bookings.

Conversations: Who handled the booking of the band?

Spivak: Well, Glenn Miller arranged for me to be taken over by the Rockwell-O'Keefe Agency.

Conversations: This is the one that brought Ray Noble to the United States?

Spivak: Yes, and they had the Miller band, too, at that time. I think they had a host of practically all the big-name bands, and they took us over and got us a recording contract. We then went with a subsidiary of Columbia, the OK label. We made a few recordings which weren't very popular, but at least the recordings made a little noise with the kids at the different colleges throughout the country.

Conversations: But before you got to that point, who had the say-so in terms of selecting your musicians? Was that your responsibility?

Spivak: Yes. I would have them come in and sit in and play. If they turned out to be what I wanted, we would keep them.

Conversations: *Then how long did it take you to really mold the band together, put it into a form that you could take out on the road? Did you have a certain period of time where you did nothing but rehearse?*

Spivak: We used to rehearse every day while we were at the Glen Island Casino. We rehearsed maybe from one in the afternoon till about four, then we would go out and get dressed and come back.

Conversations: *And play the show?*

Spivak: No. Before people would come in we would do a radio program, like around five-thirty until six, or six until six-thirty, a network shot on either NBC or CBS or Mutual.

Conversations: *Miller was influential in getting you in the Casino too, wasn't he?*

Spivak: That's right. He was very influential. That's where he had gotten his start too, Glen Island.

Conversations: *There were a couple of good rooms around the New York area like that: the Glen Island Casino. . .*

Spivak: Frank Daley's Meadowbrook, the Rustic Cabin. There were several of those places. But I think that the Glen Island Casino and Frank Daley's Meadowbrook were actually—well, Glen Island would be more the cradle spot. Frank Daley's was the place that they went to after they had gotten their apprenticeship.

Conversations: *With four arrangers how big of a book did you have to build for your band before you really took it out on the road?*

Spivak: At the very outset we really didn't have too much because we had to rehearse quite a bit. I'd say we had about twenty or twenty-five arrangements, and we would just keep repeating them during the night on an engagement. But, when we went into the Glen Island Casino we had a chance to rehearse

Charlie Spivak

every day. We used to rehearse in the daytime and we took special pains with rehearsing. We'd rehearse the sections, like the saxophone section.

Conversations: You were very meticulous, weren't you?

Spivak: Very much so, yes. We wanted our dynamics, in other words, our louds and our softs, to be just exact; that's the way we got it, by rehearsing and giving it all the time and having the fellows familiarize themselves with what I wanted. I didn't know them and they didn't know me and that was a way for us to become acquainted. We had to do it that way. They had to learn to know me and to know what I wanted. I got the results that way, and they respected me for it, because I would tell them what I wanted. If they didn't understand they would say so, and then we would go over it again. We would go over it any number of times until we got it the way we wanted it.

Conversations: What did a guy like Dave Tough add to the band?

Spivak: He added everything to it. Dave Tough was probably—and I say this with all the respect in the world to every other great drummer that there is around today—I think Dave Tough was one of the finest drummers to keep a band together. I never had to count one, two, three, four with him. All I did was give a downbeat and he knew the rhythm of every tune, whether it be a fast number, a jazz number, a slow number, a ballad, whatever.

Conversations: He was a little guy, wasn't he?

Spivak: Little bitty fellow, right, but a talent. If you didn't know him you'd think he was mad at the world; he had that kind of personality where his face looked like he was mad at you.

Conversations: He was with Dorsey too, wasn't he?

Spivak: He was with Tommy Dorsey, yes.

Conversations: How about Les Elgart? You had him in the band.

Spivak: Yes. Les and Larry both. Les was with me at the Glen Island Casino; so was Larry.

Conversations: Did they do any writing for the band?

Spivak: No, not at all. As a matter of fact, I don't know that Les ever did any writing. But they weren't with me too long.

Conversations: Nelson Riddle?

Spivak: Nelson came to me on a recommendation from Glenn Miller. Glenn called me one day and said, "I have a young man here that I think might be an asset to your band. He's a very good writer and he plays trombone; I don't know how much, but you can find out by listening to him." Well, he came over. Nelson was a very serious-minded young man about his writing. He'd bring in a score or an arrangement or a chart or whatever you want to call it, and if he didn't like the sound of it from the very beginning, after you played eight bars, he'd say, "Pass it in." He'd tear it up right in front of us. Then the next day he would bring in another one.

Conversations: Did you ever reject anything that your arrangers threw at you?

Spivak: Many times. If I thought it sounded too labored when it was played, I didn't like it. If it didn't sound like the fellows enjoyed playing it, then I didn't want it.

Conversations: At some point after Miller went into the Army, his trombone group came over to you.

Spivak: Yes. We had Frank D'Annolfo, Jimmy Priddy, and Tanner, Lightning Tanner—just three trombone players. We were supposed to have gotten some more of the boys. Johnny Best, on trumpet, was supposed to have come. We took the nucleus of the trombone section. When they came in we were doing a tour of theatres; the three trombone players sat right in and played the numbers like they had played them all their lives.

Conversations: Was Willie Smith the first black musician you had in one of your bands?

Spivak: When I hired him I didn't know he was black; he looks as white as you and I, but he was of the color.

Conversations: He was out of the Lunceford band, wasn't he?

Spivak: That's right. We took him from the Jimmie Lunceford

Charlie Spivak

band. He was a very close friend of Davey Tough's and we were looking for that type of saxophone player. Davey Tough said, "We can get Willie Smith." I said, "If you can get him, I'll pay him any amount of money." And we got him.

Conversations: He was your top man, then, for a while.

Spivak: He and, of course, Charlie Russo.

Conversations: What did he do, play lead alto? Or what?

Spivak: He played lead along with Charlie Russo. Charlie played lead too. Charlie was a fine lead alto man.

Conversations: He was one of your closest and dearest friends for years and years.

Spivak: Thirty-five years.

Conversations: And he was killed here in Greenville.

Spivak: That's right. Most senseless thing that ever happened. But he and Willie Smith were very dear friends and they both alternated on lead. Willie would play the lead on most of the jazz things, and then he was so cute about some of the vocals. He used to sing some of the jazz things. He was a most interesting musician to listen to.

Conversations: What prompted him to go to James, the money or what?

Spivak: Well, no. I don't think that was it at all. Willie went into the service with Artie Shaw; he went into the Navy.

Conversations: Then he played in Shaw's service band?

Spivak: That's right. When he came out of the service he called me first and asked me if he could come back. Well, I had a boy that was doing a good enough job for me; he stayed with me right through that bad part and I hated to let him go. So I told Willie that. Willie told me he had an offer from Harry, and he said if I didn't take him back he would go with Harry. Well, that's what happened. He did go with him.

Conversations: Wound up with a big hit in that "Kiss Me Once, Kiss Me Twice, It's Been a Long, Long Time." He did an alto solo that was just sensational.

Spivak: With Harry. And we did it, too.

Conversations: Well, that brings up a question. If a competing band came up with a tune that was a big hit, did your arrangers rush to get something similar on the stands so that you could play that kind of tune?

Spivak: Well, I'll give you an example of that. Glenn Miller did that movie, *Orchestra Wives.* In that movie they had a tune called "At Last," which he recorded and Ray Eberle sang. We recorded it too, and we had a group singing it, and our record of the same tune on another label outsold Glenn Miller's. We had a tremendous hit in that.

It was a business thing, you know. We had the tune and we wanted to do as good a job on it as we possibly could; and Glenn Miller had it too.

Conversations: It was sort of an interesting coincidence too, wasn't it? You would have to say that people like Harry James and Randy Brooks and other people were competitors of yours, even though they might be friendly competitors.

Spivak: Oh, yes, we were very friendly. We had our business to take care of, even though we were very, very friendly. I respected Harry as he did me. The same way with Randy.

Conversations: I thought it was an interesting coincidence that the big movie you made was with Betty Grable who was also Mrs. James.

Spivak: I got a lot of kidding about that because we made the movie, *Pin-Up Girl,* with Betty Grable just about the time Harry married her. On the set at Twentieth Century-Fox the people used to kid me about "How come Harry James got her and not you?" "Well," I said, "for one important reason: I'm already married."

Conversations: Did you make any other movies? You settled out there for a little while, didn't you?

195

Charlie Spivak

Spivak: We did some short subjects for Universal. We did one called *Follow the Boys*, which was actually a war movie. Donald O'Connor, George Raft, the late Sophie Tucker, and Joe E. Brown were in it. Oh, there was a cast. It was like a revue. Each personality did a segment for the Armed Forces.

Conversations: Were you the back-up band?

Spivak: No. We did our own portion. We did two or three numbers. I just don't remember, but it was part of the movie called *Follow the Boys*. It was a war movie as *Pin-Up Girl* was. We did many short subjects. You remember you used to go into a theatre and you would see a five-minute piece of Glenn Miller and his orchestra or Tommy Dorsey and his orchestra? Well, we did things similar to that.

Conversations: In order to sustain a group which had obviously a high overhead, you really had to stay on the road a lot, didn't you?

Spivak: Well, we did because the expenses were very, very high. And then, too, the one-nighters paid off, and so did the theatres. But when we would go into our location—this may seem very funny to you, but it actually is the truth—we used to lose money because the hotel would just pay the union scale for that engagement. Now my payroll might have been far above what the union scales were, so it would cost me. If I went into, let's say, the Pennsylvania Hotel for ten weeks, it would cost me money to work it. But I needed to sit down in one place at the time to get exposure on the radio, to advertise our recordings, and that's how we would be able to go out on one-nighters and demand the money that we asked for.

Conversations: When you were out on one-nighters I presume you traveled by bus.

Spivak: Right. Sometimes dates were carefully handled by the booking office, but then there were times, too, when it seemed that the booker got the map and used darts to figure out how we would play dates. But that didn't happen too often. We had some pretty bad jumps, but we were geared to take them. The fellows would gripe about making big jumps—they didn't get any sleep, didn't have even a hotel to check into many times, didn't have a place where they could shave or get their clothes cleaned or their suits pressed—but when we used to look back it was a lot of fun, because we'd make fun of those things.

Conversations: How did you maintain an enthusiasm for performing night after night after night after night? It would get rather tough to do, wouldn't it, particularly if you were playing through the same arrangements two or three times a night?

Spivak: It was a way of life, I think. That's the only way I can explain it. The fellows were geared to that type of life. They knew when they went out on one-nighters it was going to be rough— that they were going to have to make certain sacrifices as far as sleep and eating and all of those things were concerned—but once they got on that bandstand, it was all forgotten. There was a certain stimulation that hit us. I don't know exactly how to explain it, but once you got up there and projected properly, you forgot about the fact that you didn't sleep all night.

Conversations: You just played.

Spivak: And played.

Conversations: When did you begin to see the demise of the big band business? Did it hit you like a ton of bricks or was it gradual?

Spivak: No, it wasn't gradual. It hit us just like you said. We could see it; we could see it in the theatres; we could see it on the one-nighters. A lot of the different ballrooms throughout the country were starting to close because they weren't getting the crowds. The economy of our country was at a low ebb. We've gone through periods like that and probably will in the future again; I hope not.

But we knew it was coming and started cutting down the big bands. We had to cut from using eight brass to six, and then to five, and then we had to cut our saxophone section from five to four. Our rhythm section used to use guitar, and we had to cut out the guitar. We had to do everything and anything to cut down the payroll. There was only just that much that you could do to cut it down, and then there was no way. We had counted on working at least forty-five weeks during the year and that

Charlie Spivak

dropped down to forty, and then finally to thirty-five, and then pretty soon there were numbers of weeks off. You'd work maybe six or eight weeks, then you would have four to six weeks off, with maybe an isolated date in there. So it was hard to keep men together at that time.

Conversations: When did you throw in the towel?

Spivak: Around 1956. I really didn't throw in the towel. That's when we were starting to get dates down around Miami. We were working so much down South that I thought I'd move down to Florida.

Conversations: You had a smaller group, though.

Spivak: Yes. I used the five brass, four saxophones, three rhythm, and a boy and a girl vocalist. We did that and things started to get to a point where the bookings were isolated dates, where we would get three or four dates a week. I still had to keep up and pay the boys a weekly salary, and it got to the point where it was getting hard to meet those demands. So finally I decided that I would give up the big band and try to work out of Miami. Whenever we had a date to play, in Texas or wherever, we would take key men from Miami and arrange to pick up the different men in the different places that we played.

Conversations: I wonder if you could give me a description of some of the people that you were associated with. I gather you had absolutely no rancor in your soul. You seem to have enjoyed everybody that you worked with, and even if you didn't you wouldn't say so. How would you describe Ben Pollack?

Spivak: Wow. I am thankful the dear Lord led me in his direction, because Ben gave me the big break that I needed at the very outset of my career. He got me to rub shoulders with some of the all-time great musicians of our day.

He guided me and his helping hand showed me the correct way and the right way to handle myself as a musician and a gentleman. I think that he was one of the big factors in whatever success I have obtained in my life, thus far, as a musician.

I don't know of anyone else, with few exceptions, who has been as good to me as Ben was. I am so grateful that I had the chance to work for him and to know him. He was a man who was highly respected by musicians and people in show business.

Conversations: Glenn Miller.

Spivak: He was a great humanitarian and another man who helped people, not only me. Of course, I was fortunate that I was able to be helped by him, but he helped everyone. Not only that, but he left a trademark; his music will always be remembered. And rightfully so, because he had something. He had something to offer and he will always be remembered for the beautiful music, the great things that he left with the music world.

His trademark will be hard to beat. What we need in the business today is another Glenn Miller, someone who will give us a little shot in the arm, a hypo. This is what is sadly lacking in our business, speaking of big bands now.

Of course, there have been so many things that have come up since his time, but I don't think there has ever been another Glenn Miller. Maybe sometime in the near future there'll be another guy who will be able to come in and arouse the world with some more good music.

Conversations: How about Tommy Dorsey?

Spivak: Tommy Dorsey was the guy that I learned a lot from business-wise. I'd be a very unappreciative man if I didn't say I admired him for the things he did on a trombone. I learned a lot from him; I learned a lot from his mannerisms, although he had many mannerisms that I didn't like in the way he treated some of his musicians. He would have one fellow in the band that he would always pick on as a "goat." I'm glad I wasn't that man, but I used to feel sorry for the fellows and the men that he picked on.

Conversations: Did he treat you badly?

Spivak: No, I never had any difficult time with him—except one time when I tried to protect the fellow he was picking on because I thought Tommy was wrong. He was really on him and he didn't like my saying anything about it, and he fired me for it.

I accepted it, and then he came over to me when his temper had cooled down—he was very irate when he fired me—and said, "Charlie, why is it that the guys I love the best I can't get along

199

with?" I said, "That's all right, Tommy." He said, "Well, will you stay?" I said, "Nope." And I didn't. I left.

Conversations: Jimmy Dorsey.

Spivak: Jimmy was kind, just the opposite from his brother. There was a strong contrast between the two. Jimmy was a lovable man and a great player. I'm glad I had the chance to know him and play with him.

Conversations: How about Jack Teagarden?

Spivak: Oh, Jack was my buddy for many, many years. I roomed and lived with him. Jack had a very serious drinking problem—I must mention that and may the Lord forgive me for it. I certainly don't mean this to be derogatory because Jack was a great, great man. I loved him dearly and I loved to listen to him play.

I miss all these fellows. Now that you're talking to me I get very emotional about all these men because I knew them so well. I lived with them and worked with them and played with them— did everything with them.

Conversations: This was an emotional time, wasn't it? Unlike today, when music seems to be strictly business, in those days there seems to have been a lot of emotion connected with your relationships.

Spivak: Yes, I can't help but feel emotional because all of these people we have talked about have done so much and have asked so little in return.

Conversations: They just wanted to make music, didn't they?

Spivak: That's right.

Conversations: Do you think their kind will ever be around again, big bands with the same magnetism?

Spivak: I would like to think so. I think there might be. There's a lot of talent amongst our younger musicians today, and if they could only bring it out the way fellows like Glenn Miller, Tommy Dorsey, Jimmy Dorsey, and that type of musician . . . .

Conversations: Let me ask you just one more—a nonmusician, who yet in a way made his mark—Bob Crosby.

Spivak: Bob is a very close friend of mine. Bob knows good musicians when he hears them. You know, when I worked in the Bob Crosby band I used to think that because he was a vocalist he didn't understand musicians. But I know today I was wrong, because he does. I admire him for the fact that he respected and still does respect all those fellows that he stood in front of. He was just a vocalist, and he didn't play an instrument, but he knew in his heart that all those fellows that he was standing in front of were just great. Today when I talk to him he mentions incidents from the days we were together and we have a good cry and a good laugh about it. It's one wonderful thing. You know, this is a great business and a very emotional business. Most of those fellows that we have talked about were all good friends, and there wasn't any kind of intrigue where one fellow would try to do anything to damage the other fellow. We used to go to openings: if I had an off-night and Glenn Miller had an opening or Harry James had an opening or whoever it was, we used to go.

I remember many times when we had an opening at the Pennsylvania Hotel we'd have a bunch of bandleaders and vocalists down for the opening. This is the thing that stands out so vividly in my mind. The good fellowship we had was one thing, but the respect that we had for each other was something that is awfully hard to explain.

Conversations: It's obvious you haven't forgotten it.

Spivak: No, and I never will either. That's something I will remember for the rest of my life. And I'm glad and very, very happy to have had this life of mine. It's a delight for me to be able to review instances of my life with these great people that I was associated with who are no longer here with us. I'm one of the very few of that group who is still alive today and is still, in my opinion, able to perform on my instrument.

Billy Taylor was born in Greenville, North Carolina, and grew up in Washington, D.C. The product of a musical family, Taylor, now fifty-six, began his professional career forty-three years ago. He is one of the most active, and certainly one of the most articulate, spokesmen for jazz in America. With a Ph.D. in musicology, Taylor is a member of the National Council on the Arts for the National Endowment for the Arts, a frequent lecturer at colleges and universities, and an eager participant in jazz seminars and workshops throughout the country. His compositions are performed by symphony orchestras, and his piano artistry is in great demand in jazz clubs and concert halls.

Billy Taylor

Billy Taylor and Zane Knauss first met during an arts seminar sponsored by the West Virginia Arts and Humanities Council in Charleston, West Virginia. For this interview, they were to have met in Taylor's West 57th Street office. The now-famous New York blackout of July 1977 changed that—fifteen floors is a long climb. Next, the interview was set for Storyville, an Eastside club where Taylor and his trio were playing—but Storyville stayed closed the night after the blackout. Finally, when a battery-operated tape recorder refused to cooperate while they cruised the nearly deserted streets of Manhattan in Taylor's Mercedes, the pair retired to Knauss' hotel room, where power finally had been restored, for this conversation.

Conversations: What is academe doing with regard to jazz these days? You seem to be spending a lot of time in schools. Is there a renewed interest, or is it a brand new interest in jazz?

Taylor: No, I don't think it's a new interest. I think it's an interest that has been steadily growing, and the exciting thing about what's going on is that so many young people who are involved in the performance end of it are now involved in the instruction end—kind of sharing experiences and information with aspiring players and writers. I think this is healthy, because many of the people in former years, when I studied, were people who didn't necessarily perform. They were great in theory—they knew what to do and, in many cases, how to do it. But they, themselves, in some cases, did not do it.

Conversations: You're spending a lot of time in West Virginia and Texas doing residencies and concerts. You've been in the small towns, the big towns—what's the reaction there to jazz?

Billy Taylor

Taylor: Well, people respond to good music, if it's presented in a way that is relevant to them. I don't go in talking to someone who has not been introduced to jazz in the same way that I would talk to a group of musicians from North Texas State.

Conversations: What is an introduction to jazz?

Taylor: It would be an introduction to music, really. I mean, jazz just happens to be the music that I'm talking about. But what I'm saying, essentially, is that this is a medium through which I express myself. It has a tradition, and it has many aspects which are apropos to all American music. I think it is America's classical music, and, therefore, I think everyone who is of this culture should be aware of it and relate to it in one way or another. You can reject it, but, at least, you should know what you're rejecting. You should say, "Well, I don't like that because—" or "I do like that because—" The problem is that so many people who understand the improvisational aspect of jazz, for instance, make such a fetish out of their belief that only the annointed can understand what's going on in the minds of improvising musicians.

Conversations: Sort of a copy of the attitude toward classical music, isn't it?

Taylor: Yeah, yeah. Unfortunately, all the worst aspects of it. I don't think it's necessary, and I think the people who are really creative in the field and who really are the doers don't hold to that either—at least the ones that I know. They do what they do, and the music speaks for itself; and those who are articulate, in terms of sharing their techniques and devices and so forth, do so willingly and frequently.

Conversations: Zoltan Kodaly, a Hungarian composer and teacher, had the theory that you could teach kids music in a very meaningful way if you use music from their own origin. Is that what you're talking about: using American folk music, which is to say jazz, to teach music?

Taylor: Exactly. And I think that many young people have come into jazz through the back door, if you will. A lot of kids who were weaned on rock and who felt that all of the other kinds of music had no meaning for them reached a plateau in playing or listening to rock and decided, "Well, let me just check around and see if there's anything else that appeals to me," and found jazz.

Conversations: There's a tendency to put the blame on media for exposing the young exclusively to rock. Yet, I suspect the educational machinery doesn't give them an alternative.

Taylor: Well, it's a combination of the two things. I mean, we are the most vulnerable people in the world because we have been programmed to accept programming, if you will. The media is what we look to to kind of help us make our decisions: to tell us what to do, what to wear, what to think. And it's not just television or radio or newspapers or magazines, but the whole media—using the term in the broader sense. We look there, not just to get our guidance, but to be told what's what. And I think this is an unfortunate attitude to take, because it keeps people from making up their own minds. I used to do a radio show in which I would read reviews of jazz musicians' records, and then play the record—a famous music magazine rated records—five stars, four stars, and so forth. What prompted me to do this was a guy who called me one day and said in all seriousness, "I only buy the five star records, because, you know, I have a limited budget, and I figure if I'm going to buy anything, I'm only going to buy the very best." It was logical from his point of view. I said, "Well, that's unfortunate, because you're going to miss a lot of good music that you'd like. Listen to the program and I'll show you what I mean." So I read several reviews and I played the records. I read the review without editorial comment, just what the writer said, and then played the record. And so the guy called me back, as did several other people, and said,"Hey, those guys—what were they listening to! That's ridiculous!" So I said that was my point. I feel that a writer may be absolutely honest in expressing his opinion. That may be exactly where he's coming from, but that doesn't necessarily mean that his opinion is correct as it applies to this particular record. And so I incorporated the idea as a regular feature on my radio show, because I felt that having started it, it was a good way of getting to the point that I reached in another way when I came up with the idea of Jazzmobile: that is, to get the music right straight to people, with no editorial interference, no middle man at all. I mean, a musician, if he's a good performer, creates something and communicates that to you. Now, if anywhere along the line that communication breaks down, then you turn on your heel and walk away. He doesn't have an audience. It's that simple. So the burden is where it should be—on the performer.

Conversations: Are performers in jazz equipped to handle the burden?

Taylor: Oh, yeah, sure. As a matter of fact, I think that many people who have been bolstered up by records and by what I consider a false sense of security need to get out and perform in the Jazzmobile context to really find who they are and what they do best. I have nothing against multi-tracking, or any of the things that can only be done in a studio, but that's only one side of creativity. There are many other sides.

Conversations: One is audience participation.

Taylor: Absolutely.

Conversations: You're an educator, but you're also into things like the Jazzmobile; you're concertizing; you're doing things with symphony orchestras: you're a conglomerate. Are you one of a new type of jazz person who's into the mainstream now—not a saloon player?

Taylor: I think so. I think so. And actually, I think this came about not only through jazz musicians, but certainly through rock musicians and through people in other fields of music who wanted artistic control of what they were doing. A creative musician says, "I want artistic control of my records; I want artistic control when I play in a concert; I want artistic control of whatever I'm offering to people who are coming to hear me."

Conversations: The only way you can do that is to do it yourself.

Taylor: That's right. So more people are producing their own records; they're producing their own concerts; they're booking themselves; they're doing a lot of things that in the past someone else did for them.

Conversations: Are you up front in this regard?

Taylor: Oh, I've been doing it for a long time. I've been doing it for about twenty years. I did it as a survival mechanism. I had a manager once who told me quite frankly, "You know, the same dime that I spend to make a phone call, I could keep in my pocket. Somebody is going to call me for Buddy Rich, or Dizzy Gillespie, or guys with names."

Conversations: Was it pretty hard for you to take at that time?

Taylor: Damn right it was! I said, "Well, you know, I'm not trying to compete with them, but I think I have an audience." At that time I played around in New York quite a lot, and people seemed to come and listen, and they seemed to like what I did. So I honestly felt that somebody out there among 8,000,000 people or so wanted to hear what I did. The manager didn't buy it though. He said, "Well, I don't have to work so hard to book these others. The money is bigger, and the jobs fall right in my lap. So when you get it together, then you come back to see me."

Conversations: He forced your hand?

Taylor: Yeah, he was kind of cold, but then I went out and tried to get it together.

Conversations: Before you got into that you obviously were associated with a number of the names. You played with Gillespie at one time, didn't you?

Taylor: Right.

Conversations: Were you a bop pianist then?

Taylor: Not exactly. I'm what I refer to as a prebop player.

Conversations: What does that mean?

Taylor: That's the term that I invented. Many people don't realize that there was a transition period between swing and bebop. Many people think that bebop just suddenly appeared. The fact of the matter is that it was emerging in the Earl Hines band and the seeds were there in many of the early bands—Basie's band and a lot of other smaller groups, like Nat Cole's trio, and in jam sessions in New York and Kansas City. And yet it did spring into full flower at one particular time in New York, but it had been growing for quite a long time.

Billy Taylor

Conversations: And you were a part of that?

Taylor: I was a part of the later development. I wasn't one of the originators of bop; I was too much under the influence of Art Tatum at first. I was intrigued by Art, Fats Waller, and European classical composers, such as Debussy and Ravel. So I was trying to fashion a piano style out of all of those elements. On the other hand, people like Bud Powell and other contemporaries of mine were saying, "Hey, I want to sound just like Charlie Parker and Dizzy Gillespie on the piano," and really achieving that, you know. One interesting bebop device was the use of a kind of countermelody in the bass. That concept came into the bebop vocabulary with Bud Powell. To show my students where Bud's roots were, I show that Earl Hines developed a personal way of playing a countermelody with his left hand, which had a great influence on Nat Cole and Billy Kyle, both of whom influenced Bud. But Bud also absorbed Charlie Parker so well that his right-hand lines could have come straight out of the Parker-Gillespie songbook.

Conversations: Jazz, then, literally has a family tree you can explain to the students.

Taylor: Oh, sure.

Conversations: Earl Hines was an enormous influence on Jazz, and he's relatively unsung, too.

Taylor: That's true. You know, one of the terrible things about living as long as Earl Hines has lived is that he is now in that period where too many people feel: "Well, I know what there is to know about Earl Hines."

Conversations: Until you start digging around a little and find out his contribution.

Taylor: That's part of not recognizing jazz for what it is and not really being able to relate to homegrown talents and homegrown products. We, for many reasons, go for Japanese cars and German cars and other kinds of things from other places. Foreign products, in the view of some people, are made better or perform better or whatever. But the fact of the matter is, when it comes to jazz, there's no one who makes it better or performs it better than the homegrown geniuses that do it.

Conversations: Phil Woods suggested that American universities and colleges ought to think about having people such as the late Ben Webster, and now Earl Hines, as jazz-musicians-in-residence.

Taylor: Absolutely, and I can see someone like Jo Jones, the old Count Basie drummer, and Sonny Greer, who used to be with Duke Ellington and Lucky Thompson, Phil, himself, and other people who are tremendously well organized in the context of what they do. I mean, Phil is well trained and can teach as well as he can play. But some of the others that I spoke of—Jo Jones and Sonny Greer—are of another generation and have experiences that younger musicians like Phil have only read about. I mean, these guys were there when certain things happened, and can set the record straight on what the music was really about in its formative stages.

Conversations: Greer goes back to 1919.

Taylor: Yeah. He brought Duke Ellington to New York and was quite a pacesetter in many ways. So it's remarkable to have a person like this alive, where you can sit and rap with him and learn firsthand what Jelly Roll Morton was like, what James P. Johnson really did around the time he wrote "Charleston." These guys know; they were there.

Conversations: Do you still have an affection for this kind of history?

Taylor: Oh, very much, very much. As a matter of fact, when I was doing the dissertation for my doctorate, I found that I've lived through a lot of jazz history—52nd Street, The Royal Roost, Bop City, Birdland, The Downbeat, The Hickory House, and much more. And like Jo Jones and some of the other people that I was talking about, I met many legendary figures—Jelly Roll Morton, for instance. He bought an interest in a nightclub in Washington when I was a kid. I met him, and I met many other legendary pianists over the years. I found that I could talk about every aspect of jazz piano in the first person—from ragtime right up to the present—by quoting Eubie Blake, Willie "The Lion"

Billy Taylor

Smith, many of the legendary people, who a lot of friends of mine, who are my age, have never heard. Steven Henderson, James P. Johnson, Donald Lambert, Cliff Jackson, Willie "The Lion" Smith, and people like that. Because I was Tatum's protege, I got to hang out with his friends. They were older than he was, and he really loved and respected them.

Conversations: In what sense were you Tatum's protege?

Taylor: We were very good friends, and he allowed me to take him around to various places, to come to his home and listen to him practice and play. He never taught me, in the sense of formal music teachers that I've studied with that say, you know, "Now here's something that I want you to work on. Go home and practice it and look into this"—not that kind of teacher. But if I asked him any theoretical question, he would not only answer it, he would demonstrate. And when I asked him about the reasons he did certain things, he'd tell me. This was invaluable.

Conversations: What kind of personality was he?

Taylor: He was both strong and sensitive. He was extremely sensitive and independent, even though he was blind and could hardly make his way around by himself. What freedom he did have, he guarded jealously. He liked to play cards—he'd hold the card right up to his face and he could make out just barely what the card was, in one eye. And he would like, for instance, to have me to take him to a track meet. I would describe what was going on, and he would visualize it. When we came back, he could tell what happened better than I could, because I didn't remember half of what I had seen.

Conversations: How long was this association?

Taylor: Well, until his death, but the closest part of it was, I'd say, from about 1944 until maybe 1952, '53, something like that. A couple of years before he died he lived on the Coast much more, and I was really scuffling in New York, so I didn't get to see him very much.

Conversations: I've been listening to the seven or eight albums of Tatum's that Norman Granz has put out now, and his left hand comes down like a sledgehammer. How did he get so much power?

Tatum: He really wanted to have equal facility in either hand, and many of the things that he did with his right hand, he did also with his left. He practiced seriously, and he developed a tremendous facility for playing. Intellectually, Art had a tremendously broad concept of what jazz piano was about. He took all of the elements that he had heard in pianists with other points of view and molded them into one super-pianistic style.

Conversations: Where did you learn? Was your whole philosophy of piano playing extended from the experience?

Taylor: Much of it, and much of my philosophy of jazz, as it applies to the piano, came from the things that he did. Number one, his touch was just remarkable. It was a very personal touch; it was a very beautiful touch, very sensitive. He could express, even on an instrument which was not particularly good, just really lovely thoughts. And he could scream and holler and play funky and do all kinds of things with the instrument.

Conversations: Was he a happy man?

Taylor: Yeah, he was. Though he was obviously limited by his handicap, he had a lot of fun. He loved to hang out and party. He was a handicapped person who resented, in many cases, the fact that it limited his mobility and limited his ability to do things that he wanted to do. But he didn't mope about. He was a relatively happy guy. We went to a lot of places and had a lot of fun, and he was a joy to be with. Tremendous sense of humor.

Conversations: In the jazz family tree how did piano players evolve? Who came before Tatum who might have influenced him, for example?

Taylor: Fats Waller. By his own admission, Art was highly influenced by Fats, but I also hear Earl Hines in him. I heard the older pianists like James P. Johnson, whom he loved. I heard even older pianists, whose names I don't know, but I also heard the Midwestern boogie-woogie kind of thing. And though I can't identify the people by name, the style was a combination of a Kansas City, Chicago, Mississippi, Texas, and many other elements from mid-America that found their way into jazz. He heard that stuff, I guess, in the Midwest, and it became just a part of his vocabulary, as things that I heard in my childhood in the Baptist church became a part of mine. It's not something that's necessarily obvious, but it's always there, and I can call on it anytime I want.

Conversations: Well, you're from North Carolina, originally, are you not?

Taylor: I was born in North Carolina, yes, but I lived in Washington.

Conversations: Did you have a musical family?

Taylor: Yes. Everybody played and sang. Most of the people in my family played European classical music and church music. There were only two uncles on my father's side that played jazz, and they were obviously the two that I liked the best. But everybody played Mozart and Bach, et cetera. My father was the choir director—he was a dentist, professionally, but his father was a minister, so he directed the choir in his father's church. At Easter and Christmas they always put on special programs—oratorios and stuff like that. So there was always a lot of really beautiful music going on all the time.

Conversations: You have this Jazzmobile in New York. Obviously, it has been a tremendous success, endowed by NEA and others. How did it come about?

Taylor: About fourteen years ago, I was a board member of the Harlem Cultural Council, and they needed a program that would give them visibility as a concerned, grass-roots arts organization. The first program that we came up with was a mobile music program, which happened to be the Jazzmobile. What I did was to organize a group that would go out on the street and perform, the theory being just take quality music to people who normally could not afford to come to Carnegie Hall or Town Hall or the major jazz festivals. The tickets, even though they were less expensive then than they are now, were still out of the reach of many of the people in whose community jazz was born. They couldn't hear the best artists—Duke Ellington and people like that, so it seemed to be the thing to do to bring that music back to the community and help them re-establish the kind of interaction that had been so important in the early days of jazz.

Conversations: And did the top people respond?

Taylor: They certainly did. Our biggest supporters have been people like Dizzy, Horace Silver, Art Blakey, and Ellington, when he was alive.

Conversations: Ellington participated?

Taylor: Oh, yeah. As a matter of fact, he played on the street where he lived for a long time in Harlem—126th Street. I remember when we put the sign up that said Ellington was going to come; people said, "Well, maybe the band will come, or Mercer or something, but Duke is not going to show, not here on the streets. Are you kidding?" But he did! They loved him.

Conversations: Were you close to Ellington?

Taylor: Yes. Once again, I guess when you truly admire somebody, then there are a lot of words that have to be said. He knew the kind of respect that I had for him and what he meant to me as a larger-than-life figure in American music. Ellington influenced me in ways that had to do with the way I present my music, and also in the music that I play.

Conversations: He was a great presenter of music, wasn't he?

Taylor: Yeah. I think it had to do with his view of who he was and what the music that he was trying to play was about.

Conversations: But nobody mistook that for ego, did they?

Taylor: No. Well, that's what I meant when I said that there's a difference between buttering up a person to get next to him and someone that you truly admire. You would just feel honored to be close to him—a friend, in the best sense of friendship. And that was the difference in his presentation of his own music. He was speaking musically in a very eloquent way to friends, no matter where he played. I remember his birthday party that was given at the White House.

Conversations: You played for that, didn't you?

Taylor: Yeah, along with a lot of other musicians. And after the formal program the President thanked everyone and said, "You're free to stay and dance and so forth; it's a party"—you

Billy Taylor

know, "Happy Birthday to the Duke" and so forth. So then, as it would be impossible to get that many musicians together and not have some kind of a jam session, Duke was kind of the orchestrator of the jam session.

Conversations: Ringmaster.

Taylor: Ringmaster, indeed. Really, just "Okay. Why don't you play." He had this guy join that one. It was really nice.

Conversations: I also recall the line that he gave when he was given the medal: that the only other place that he would rather be was in the arms of his mother. It was quite a moving thing. The tributes that came to Duke were rather belated, though, were they not?

Taylor: Absolutely. This is, in my opinion, the most influential figure in contemporary American music, and, in an overall sense, his compositions and the approaches, the innovations that he made have become a permanent part of the American lexicon. It really is just amazing that people have waited so long to say that this man was really very, very special and should be honored as such.

Conversations: Might a lot of the things he wrote, because he wrote for specific musicians, just wind up on a shelf forever because they really can't be copied?

Taylor: He felt that way, but I don't feel that way, and I don't think Mercer does. Much of the music, though it was written for Johnny Hodges and Ben Webster and Cootie Williams and Harry Carney and people like that, takes on another kind of character when played by someone else. But it's playable, eminently playable. I play a medley of Ellington pieces, which keeps getting longer and longer, and I certainly make no attempt to play like Ellington on the piano. But there are certain things that he did that I liked, and I'm sure that comes out. There are certain things that Garner did in Ellington's music that come out in my playing of "Satin Doll," and other pieces like that. So I think that his music will not only be around for a long time, but it's going to be played by a wide range of musicians.

Conversations: Mercer Ellington took the band out on the road the day after Ellington's funeral. Is this sort of a copy of the Glenn Miller syndrome and the Tommy Dorsey syndrome?

Taylor: No. As a matter of fact, before he died Duke had asked me if I would lead the band on this particular occasion.

Conversations: Really?

Taylor: And I did. We went to Bermuda. It was for IBM. I accompanied Ella Fitzgerald, who sang at the Ellington funeral. Then we flew down the next day and joined the band. The engagement was "Ella and the Duke"—that was the original idea—but he was too sick, and he knew he was going to be too sick to make it. So several weeks before his death, he had called me and said, "I don't think I'm going to be well enough. I don't think they're going to let me out of the hospital to play this job. It's a very important job, and I'd appreciate it if you would go along and, you know, present the band and play in your own inimitable style"—you know how he was. But what he essentially was asking me to do was the thing that I had obviously gotten from him, which was the presentation of the music. It was one of those jobs where he especially wanted that kind of thing. It wasn't that he didn't think Mercer could do it; it was just that he knew I did it all the time and he felt I would add something special to the occasion.

Conversations: How did you feel about that?

Taylor: Well, number one, I was delighted that he asked me, because when someone that you admire asks you to do something like that, it's really a chance to do something for a friend which you don't often get. So, you know, I was honored to be asked. It was a very difficult thing to do, in point of fact—right after the funeral, you know. But it was something I felt was a responsibility. It came off very well, and I was delighted that it worked as he planned.

Billy Taylor

Conversations: You're writing for larger groups now, with strings and so forth.

Taylor: Yeah.

Conversations: Where is this taking you to?

Taylor: Well, it's taking me in a lot of different directions. I did the "Suite for Jazz Piano and Orchestra."

Conversations: With the Utah Symphony.

Taylor: Yeah. Since then I haven't done anything for a large orchestra, but I did a score for an off-Broadway show, which is called *The Lion and the Jewel.* And I also did some dance music which was not used on the Broadway production, but which was used in the original production of *Arms Too Short To Box With God.* So I've been kind of dabbling a little bit in Broadway and getting some things done.

Conversations: That show opened in Washington and it's been doing well in New York.

Taylor: It's been doing very well. One of the kids won a Tony out of the show—Delores Hall. I went to the Ford Theatre in Washington and worked with the show as musical director. I did the arrangements for the small combo that accompanied the singers and dancers. There are many of the things that they still use in the show now based on the arrangements that I originally did for them.

Conversations: Are you going to pursue assiduously writing for symphony orchestras?

Taylor: I don't know. I like it and, you know, if asked I'll do it. But I really don't have a tremendous amount of experience and friends like Manny Albam and Howard Roberts have been very helpful. It's a different area—it's one that I enjoy, but I'm not sure how deeply I'll get involved in it.

Conversations: Can jazz and symphony orchestras live together in the same hall?

Taylor: They both can very comfortably be performed together. A symphony orchestra should play jazz. Jazz is American music, and for an American symphony orchestra to fulfill what I think is its real role as a cultural instrument in this country, the instrument should be utilized to play American music—and play it well. Many of the attempts to play jazz are half-hearted—they'll have a jazz group standing out in front, and the strings will play half-notes and simple phrases behind them, you know. I don't think that serves any purpose.

Conversations: Who is really writing, though, to make them play well at this point?

Taylor: There are any number of people. David Baker has some very fine works available; there are things by Quincy Jones, Oliver Nelson, John Lewis, Stephen Chambers, Fred Tillis, and William Fisher for large orchestras; and many jazz players, such as Jimmy Heath, Ernie Wilkins, Phil Woods, and Jimmy Owens have also created works which are jazz, and scored for symphony orchestras.

Conversations: Are they getting played?

Taylor: No, not to the extent that they should. Hale Smith has also written works of this type.

Conversations: Are these commissioned materials?

Taylor: Many of them are. And what happens too often is you get a commission; it's played once, then put on the shelf and then, you know, it just lays there for a while.

Conversations: Yeah, you can't take it into a saloon, can you?

Taylor: No. Not every work is adaptable to other types of instrumentation. New spaces may be one answer—outdoor locations, malls, parks, museums, places other than the symphony hall that are attractive to audiences. And I think that a lot of audiences are looking to go to places other than Carnegie Hall or Lincoln Center.

Conversations: What do you have to do with the symphonies' personnel—wash out the European influence? A lot of musicians can't adjust to playing jazz.

Billy Taylor

Taylor: Well, I don't think it's that they can't adjust, I think it's that they won't adjust. I think some musicians have decided that it's beneath them, or that they don't want to do it. I find that there are many musicians who are tremendously well trained and can learn things which are very atonal and contemporary. But they will not learn music of a very contemporary nature unless they are motivated. It is comfortable to stick to Mendelssohn.

Conversations: What could motivate them?

Taylor: The reasons may be different for different people. It may be money; it may be survival on a job; it may be a musical challenge; it may be any number of things.

Conversations: Who do you have to infect with this fever—the conductors, the presidents of symphony societies, or who?

Taylor: Well, I think it's an overall job. I don't think you can do just one or two people. It has to start with the existing audience that wants to hear this; it has to start with the many musicians who want to play the music; it has to start with conductors who want to study the scores in order that they may really understand and properly interpret the music; it has to start with creative people who are as serious about this music as they are about Mozart and Mahler. The jazz vocabulary has to be worked through so that symphony players are familiar with it, in the same way that if you're going to learn a foreign language, you just can't get the phrase book and pick it up every time you want to order breakfast or something. I mean, you've got to really be convincing to say what you want to say—to use the language properly, you've got to learn it.

Conversations: You're in a position to exert a little bit of clout here—you're a member of the National Council on the Arts. What kind of reaction do you get from those folks about this notion?

Taylor: I get, surprisingly, an interesting amount of support. I get, of course, some resistance, also, because there are people who are very traditionally oriented. But some of the support I have gotten obviously has been from artists like Maestro Maurice Abravanel, conductor of the Utah Symphony, who is not on the council now, but who certainly is a firm believer in the tradition of the symphony orchestra, as well as utilizing the orchestra in other creative ways to reach a wider audience. He is very traditional in his thinking, but because he also wants the instrument to survive, he's willing to listen and experiment.

Conversations: You're talking about the symphony orchestra now?

Tayor: Yeah. He's willing to listen to other points of view and to experiment with them.

Conversations: You talked recently to the American Symphony Orchestra League at their convention in New Orleans. What was their reaction?

Taylor: The jury is still out. They were very receptive—at least outwardly receptive—to what I had to say. Many people came up and spoke with me privately and said that they thought that what I had to say was something that they were interested in acting upon, and I was really delighted. We'll find out in the next couple of years whether they are able to follow any of my suggestions. But I really seriously believe that the possibility of a symphony orchestra extending its season and extending its ability to be meaningful to the community it's serving, may be greatly affected by whether it's playing the music of this culture or not.

Conversations: It's suggested that an alternative might be an attempt to establish, supported by private funds, the so-called jazz band or orchestra. Does that make sense?

Taylor: It makes a lot of sense, but it's very difficult to do. It's difficult. We tried to start a New York Jazz Repertory Company, and it's eminently workable in New York. I don't know about other places, but it could work here because we have a large reservoir of individuals and organizations who could be called upon to do all kinds of things, you know—musicians who can play any kind of music and who could do justice to the jazz repertory, plus the kinds of corporate support that one needs to get something like this off the ground. George Wein, whose idea it was to try and who tried to make it work, tied it too closely to the Newport Jazz Festival and tried to run the repertory

219

company as he runs the festival; and that, in this particular case, just wasn't workable. The company, as originally conceived, could have worked, but it was never given a chance. It was underfunded, mismanaged, and, in some cases, over-produced. George really tried, I think, but, in my opinion, his efforts were misdirected.

Conversations: He was a commercial animal?

Taylor: I suppose so, but he would be away making money with festivals, and the repertory company would be losing money because of decisions he had made.

Conversations: How can a union influence these movements? Hal Davis, the musicians' union international president, has a background of being a business agent in a market where most of the local's members belong to a symphony orchestra. Do the top echelons of the International have empathy for jazz musicians?

Taylor: I haven't seen a lot of activity in that regard. Most people give lip service to jazz in the union. However, they do not present as many jazz groups on the trust fund concerts as, perhaps, they should. In the statements that I read in the union papers·about where they're ostensibly spending their money, it seems to me that a lot of other kinds of music are presented, and that may be as it should be, I don't know. But I see a lot less jazz than I, for one, would like to see. The music could be presented to show the kinds of things that the union says it wants to do—stimulating live music and/or live performance, having all kinds of people come to see and hear and relate to live music.

Conversations: The last part of that triangle, I suppose, is the record industry. It seems now that they have a sort of new format where individual artists are controlling their material, putting it through individual producers, who, in turn, seem to be turning it over to major labels. It gets quite complicated. Is this the way it should be done? Does this get more jazz on the market?

Taylor: Well, there's a whole resurgence of jazz on records now, so it's coming from both ends. You're getting the big guys who are doing it themselves; and you're getting it from people who see that with a little promotion and astute public relations, they

220

can get something going on a very meaningful business level with record companies—with catalogues and with other things.

Conversations: You're saying that jazz now is a saleable commodity?

Taylor: Absolutely. It always has been, but music business types are just beginning to realize that.

Conversations: Well, what's that going to do for jazz in its purest sense?

Taylor: It's going to water some of it down, to some extent, and it's going to make the true, unwatered-down jazz, I think, a lot more saleable also. It's both going to help, and it's going to hurt. It's going to help in that people are going to say, "Hey, jazz is saleable"; and then it's going to hurt in that someone is going to be, as George Wein is doing, taking packages out on the road, billing them as jazz festivals, when they are really something else—the Kool Jazz Festival, with Al Green and other soul acts. Al Green is a fine performer, but he's not a jazz performer.

Conversations: So separate music gets flattened out by the commercial necessities?

Taylor: It's difficult not to do that, and the record companies insist that you do the crossover thing.

Conversations: Even for you?

Taylor: Everybody. That's one of the reasons I haven't recorded for quite a long time. But one other is because everyone who has asked me to record has had their own idea of what I should do, most of which I wasn't interested in doing.

Conversations: Can't you go to them with what you want to do?

Taylor: I have. I've gone to people and said, "I want to do this." At the time I did, they said, "That's not saleable. People are not buying that. They're buying Keith Jarrett, Herbie Hancock, and Chick Corea. Can't you do something like that?" It took me a long time to develop what I do musically, and since for twenty-five years I have made a comfortable living doing it, it's inconceivable to me that it won't sell on records. The record business mentality—you're dealing with someone who says, "Give me

221

another Erroll Garner, or give me another whoever." George Benson's problem was that his record producer was trying to make another Wes Montgomery out of him for a long time. But look what happened when they let him do his best. The same thing happened with Aretha Franklin: Columbia Records would not let her be herself. So what happened when she went to Atlantic?—Zap! Straight through the roof doing her own thing.

Conversations: Is there any chance of having your "Suite" published and, perhaps, recorded?

Taylor: I hope so. I haven't really followed through on that. But I want to record now before I change it too much.

Conversations: What's next?

Taylor: Well, I'm really trying to get back to playing and doing some meaningful teaching. I was trained as a teacher in my early days, and never really did any of it until recent years. Now, I think I'd like to do more teaching—master classes, workshops, clinics, and so on. I'd like to really work—spend a lot of time performing with different types of groups.

Conversations: Is a Ph.D. a big advantage in selling jazz to academe?

Taylor: It cuts across a lot of problems that I used to have before I got it. Now I don't have to go through the facade of convincing someone that it's worth taking the time to study jazz. On the other hand, they don't dangle their degrees in front of me as though that's going to frighten me off. It never did, but now they don't even try. In academia I have a lot of things going for me. I have the fact that when you say, "Dr. Taylor" then that is equivalent to "Dr. Jones." You know, we're through that hurdle; we're on an equal footing in that regard, so we don't have to bother with that. Now when we begin to talk about jazz, as opposed to another kind of music, there's nothing that this doctor is going to say that is going to cancel out what the other doctor is going to say, or vice versa. So, you know, it really puts me on another kind of footing, just for fencing purposes. And I hate the fact that one has to go through that, but that seems to be a game most people in academe enjoy playing. It's a waste of time.

Much of my time is spent, when I go in to do a workshop or clinic, convincing the music teacher or people in the music department that I'm not there to do them in, and that there's nothing that I'm going to say that they don't say to their students all the time—How do you play better? You practice. How do you learn more about music? You study it. How do you advance faster? You get a good teacher. That's purely and basically the way you have to go. So, you know, it really is frustrating to me to have people who resist what I'm trying to do in the context of education, when I know, and they know, that they're ineffective. I mean, they don't know why they're ineffective, but they know they're not really doing the job. Too many seem afraid to try to change.

Conversations: Do you know why they're ineffective?

Taylor: Sure. Because in some cases they have concentrated on too small an area of music to be functional. I mean, no one can say: "I'm going to be a Scarlatti specialist" and survive in today's concert world. Every year you've got just hundreds, thousands, coming from music schools all over the country. They don't get into the orchestra; they don't get into a lot of places. Many of them are wise enough to end up in Hollywood, or they end up writing for TV or commercials, or in some other way they use the talent and the knowledge that they have acquired in a practical way for the betterment of their careers. As a matter of fact, I did a tribute to Stanley Adams, the president of ASCAP, the other night, and one of the other people who was performing was a composer, Charlie Strouse—he wrote the score for the Broadway show *Annie* and has had many other popular hits, lot of hits. And his teacher was Aaron Copland. Aaron Copland was on the dais, and so when Strouse got ready to play, he said, "Mr. Copland, I haven't seen you in a long time, but this is what I've been doing." Then he played a string of hits, things that he has written, which—you know the kind—he sings a couple of lines and everybody applauds.

Conversations: Well, then, the answer seems to be the amalgamation of American jazz, American folk music, and everything else that we can put together.

Billy Taylor

Taylor: That's one answer. I don't think we have exhausted the cultural outpouring of what American music is about. And I think it's high time we got into that. Jazz, like other types of American music, is unique and is constantly growing. It's exciting and very much a reflection of who we are and what we're about.

Phil Woods was born in 1931 in Springfield, Massachusetts. He became interested in music at fourteen, when he inherited an alto saxophone from a deceased uncle. Woods spent a year at the Manhattan School of Music and four years at Juilliard, where he majored in clarinet. After graduation, he became one of the most respected alto saxophonists in the world. He played with Charlie Barnet's band, toured Europe with Dizzy Gillespie, and traveled to Russia with Benny Goodman. He currently has his own jazz group, but also records as a soloist and as a conductor. He is now writing material for his group and other ensembles, and has recently recorded with Lena Horne and Mel Torme.

Phil Woods

Phil Woods and Zane Knauss met briefly in July 1977 at the South Carolina Ports Authority Building, hard by the Cooper River in Charleston. Woods had just finished a rehearsal and had only minutes to change clothes and get something to eat before appearing as the featured performer at a Spoleto Festival concert. However, in those few moments, Woods gave Knauss his telephone number, and, within a week, the two were recording this conversation in Woods's comfortable home in the Poconos.

Conversations: You live in the Poconos in Pennsylvania. That's difficult to understand because your action is in major cities—it has to be for the type of music you play. Jazz isn't being played on mountaintops, is it?

Woods: I've been a commuter for twenty years now. I moved out of the City in '57. I originally lived in Bucks County—New Hope, Pennsylvania. I used to commute to New York quite a bit.

Conversations: You were involved in a school there, weren't you?

Woods: Yeah. Ramblerny Performing Arts Camp. But I just can't live in the City, per se. I love the action of working in the City. But in those days I was raising a family—family is all grown now—and I just refused to put my kids through the dues. I thought it was better if I paid the dues driving through the tunnel than to have them do it. We couldn't afford private schools, and I just didn't want to subject them to that kind of living. I knew that kind of life, because I used to live in Brooklyn with my first wife when I was a young student. I knew about city life, and it's tough, you know. There's nothing better than going into town, doing a gig—you know, really doing a good job—and then slipping through that tunnel. Once you're through that tunnel, you're home. Plus, at one time, it was the only time I was alone. I was either in the studios, or running in the streets of New York or whatever, or I'd be home with my houseful of kids. That commuting gave me time to listen to the radio, catch up on the news, music, pop tunes, whatever, and just be by myself. So I kind of used the cocoon of the car—which I'm against entirely—but it can be used.

Conversations: What was the school at New Hope that you were involved in? Were you teaching there?

Woods: Well, it originally began, if memory serves, about '62, '63. It began as The Maynard Ferguson School of Jazz. Maynard got hung up on the road. I was living in the area and the local—the cat was from New York, I can't remember his name—but he knew of my reputation. I was visiting the camp in the early days and started doing some classes and volunteered my services. I've always worked with kids. I always liked to teach; to this day, I still teach and do a lot of college and high school things. That year the place went up on sheriff's auction. The people that had the school when it was The Maynard Ferguson School of Jazz went bankrupt or something. By that time, I was in charge of the jazz band. We'd given a couple of concerts, and the people that bought the school the following season liked what I was doing with the kids, so I was hired the following season to manage the whole music department.

Conversations: So it was seasonal, then?

Woods: It was a summer camp. It ran about eight weeks. It was a performing arts camp—it had modern dance; it had ballet—people like Joyce Tristler and Jose Limon used to come and do master classes. Well, it was great to have the jazz kids there because so many of the schools—the jazz schools—had about them a certain eliteness, snobbishness: "I'm into jazz." If you're in a performing arts camp—I mean, these young hippies, these young men are kind of cocky about their hobby, or whatever it may be. You'd see a young girl working out at the ballet bar, and she's just as serious about her act as you pretend to be about yours. So, you know, let's get a little more serious thought into this creative process without snapping your fingers, hanging out in the cafeteria. I want to see you practicing. So it was good. I think the kids got a lot out of realizing that the arts make up a big field, and just because they play a little bit of jazz doesn't mean that they shouldn't pay attention to all of the other things.

Conversations: You're not isolated, then, in your art?

Woods: Isolated—here? No.

Conversations: I mean, you haven't isolated yourself from the bigger field of the arts?

Woods: Not at all. Not at all.

Conversations: But some people have. You have suggested that there are some snobs in the business.

Woods: Well, I went to Juilliard. I don't agree with the music establishment at all. I don't understand the whole music business. I'll tell you: I don't understand how we can graduate 13,000 music majors a year. We don't have 13,000 gigs. It used to amaze me when I was in Juilliard that I would see, like, 80% of the cats were—we used to call them "lounge lizards." Maybe a high 80%. But I know that out of the student body there weren't too many—of what I considered—really serious musicians. And a lot of them were going to Columbia to pick up their education points, because Juilliard didn't give academics at that time. I always thought that was hedging your bet—either you were going to be a teacher and be dedicated to the profession of teaching. . . . You don't just pick up. This was S.O.P. at that time— pick up your education points; in case you don't make it, man, you can always teach it. This country seems to be built upon that premise. I mean, if we have anything wrong, it's our education system. Right now jazz is supposedly flourishing under the guys at the universities and the stage-band movement.

Conversations: Is it?

Woods: I say it's good, because it puts the instruments in the kids' hands, and maybe they'll turn to listening to records and all that. I mean, I don't think that the schools have anything to do with nurturing artists. If you're going to play, you're going to play—damn the torpedos, no matter what! I think that that's the way it is. I was dedicated to being a jazz saxophone player at the age of fourteen. I think that's probably the way it goes in a lot of cases. So we've got the built-in thing about becoming teachers if you can't make it as an artist. The stage-band thing really shows that in its worst light, because you've got these cats graduating from Berkeley and North Texas State and all these places. There are not enough gigs; there are only four bands for all of these saxophone players, and they only use two altos in each band. What do they do? Well, a lot of times they go back and teach: they teach more kids how to graduate and not find any gigs. So we're getting, maybe, a more educated audience. I see more young people checking out my music, and I think that's directly related, maybe, to the media and to the education thing. But we need a broader base of financial support. We need more jobs for quality musicians.

Conversations: Do you think that jazz bands can become like regional theatres or community theatres, where they generate local support instead of depending on the commercial wheel?

Woods: Well, it's not only that, but—take the National Endowment for the Arts. Poor Chuck Israels has been trying to keep the National Jazz Ensemble together for three, four, five years, and it's a scuffle all the way. He gets a grant for a pittance from the National Endowment for the Arts. George Wein got something like $50,000 from the Endowment for the Arts to maintain his repertory—he doesn't need it. I'm not knocking the fact that he got it. But there's something like $90,000,000 dispersed through the National Endowment for the Arts. As I understand it, half a million dollars is given to folk, ethnic, and jazz. Now that's wrong! All of these millions of dollars to support all of these regional symphony orchestras, who play Mahler for blue-haired old ladies—you know, they have some young conductor from some exotic country. It's all European horseshit, man, until we start to get to the grassroots of American music—and that includes every form of American music. My hero is Charles Ives. He immediately said, "Europe? We don't need Europe." Emerson said, "We don't need Europe."

We're still proliferating this image of a symphony orchestra in this country, and we can't get a jazz repertory orchestra—can't get anybody to do it in Washington at the Kennedy Center for the Performing Arts. There should be a jazz orchestra there. There should be two or three in New York; there should be one in every major city—paid for by, I would hope, a combination of the government and big business. Big business will only do it if there's a buck in it, right? There's money in good music; I'm convinced of it. I don't ask them to go into the red to support the arts. I'm saying that if you have a healthy state of arts, you have people coming to see them and you charge them money. It's called good show business.

Conversations: I think industry is becoming more and more aware that the people they want to hire are going to demand cultural amenities in any city in which they're going to work.

Woods: That's a hard struggle.

Conversations: Therefore, industry is putting their money down on symphony orchestras and this sort of thing.

Woods: I know, but the symphony orchestra. . . . The whole thing about jazz is that imagery we have of, you know, "from the brothels, and it came up the Odessa"—or some river, I forget what. The Russians will tell you it was the Odessa. But, actually, most of the young jazz musicians and the older jazz musicians— the ones that can really play—are fairly bright, articulate human beings, and extremely disciplined. You must be disciplined to do your job and travel.

Conversations: Well, I recently watched you in Charleston come in off a bumpy light plane ride. . .

Woods: Oh, and I love to fly!

Conversations: And you weren't in that hall more than ten minutes before you had your horn out and you were ready to go to work.

Woods: That's what I'm there for.

Conversations: But that is not the stereotypical image of the jazz performer.

Woods: No. No, it isn't. I could have used a cup of coffee. But rehearsal was called for four o'clock and it was then 4:20. Considering where I came from, I thought I was on time—and extremely shook-up. I detest flying; it's only been in the past three years and I've been flying for twenty years. My first trip was with Dizzy to the Mideast—you know, going from Charlie's Tavern to Abadan, Iran, never bothered me, but I don't know. Maybe probability or whatever. I have this weird fear.... But that image of jazz is a drag.

Conversations: A lot of people have it.

Woods: Well, until big business, until the government starts disseminating more information about its people.... I keep mentioning the government, but it's only because I've done three State Department tours. Seems when America wants to present a nice image, it sends a jazz band. It sent Benny Goodman to Russia—I was part of that tour. It sent Dizzy Gillespie to the Mideast and South America—two separate tours. It sent Ellington to Russia. So that made three out of, maybe, the five or six tours that they have done. Just recently the first tour boat in sixteen years called on Havana.

Conversations: With Earl Hines and Dizzy Gillespie.

Woods: Who do they put up there in case they start shooting? The jazz cats. Now The Voice of America is the most listened to radio station in the world, only because of Willis Conover and its jazz. I know this for a fact. And why cannot the government do something internally about what it loves to export? It seems to me that we need a council for the arts—we're getting there, I suppose. We do have The National Endowment for the Arts. I did receive a grant from them. It really helped me; I'm not knocking them. I'm just saying let's do more. Let's get the quality of life better, then the quality of the arts will improve. I think it just means a certain awareness, and jazz has been ignored too long. Yet it's recognized as a very strong art form. There's a contradiction in the image and in the reality, and until we get more solid support from the media, more jazz on TV—there is no jazz on TV, and it's never presented properly when it is on TV. But then you should improve the sound of TV. Don't tell me they can't get good-sounding TV sets. I mean, all of these little, basic things. I know these are not all original thoughts, but it seems to me they're so realizable. And we just keep putting it off and putting it off and putting it off.

Conversations: Are you in a position to proselytize what you're saying?

Woods: I talk about it all the time—I mean, when I visit universities. If I taught at a school, I would charter a bus and after I picked out my A-lab band. . . . Lab band—don't you love that sound? Next time I do a clinic, I've sworn I'm going to appear in a green surgeon's costume, wheel out the drummer, and say, "All right. Send in the patients." No, I would get this bus and I'd get all the kids and I'd have them get their libraries together and their music stands. I'd get uniforms for them. Have them get all their crap together, pack, get on the bus, close all the blinds, and just drive around the campus for about eight hours—don't go anywhere, no visual delights to intrigue them, just whatever they want to do. Get off the bus, set up, pick out a set, tune up, put their uniforms on. That's it; they're not going to play any music. Pack up, back on the bus another eight hours, circle some more, and then have a talk with them: "All right, now. Who wants to do this? Because this is what it is." It's an exaggeration. I admit it doesn't have to be that way, but it's just an exaggerated reality, because they're not getting any reality from the people that are teaching them in school. Most of the teachers have never been on the road. They're the cats that couldn't make it; so, they went back to teach it. Some of them are qualified, dedicated men— don't get me wrong; I'm not rapping them. I'm just saying the colleges, the powers that be, have got to take advantage of people like me and all the pros—have us visit them and tell them.

Why don't we have a jazzman-in-residence in universities? Why did Ben Webster die in Europe alone? Why wasn't he given a post? Jazzman-in-residence—give him all the beer he wants and a room. "Ben, you don't have to do nothing. Just stop by the jazz department if you feel like rapping with the kids." Now you know human nature, and so do I. You'd make that man so proud he'd probably cool his drinking. He'd live longer. He'd contribute to the kids. We don't think of these things. They're afraid to take a chance: "Maybe Ben would go ape." Well, we've had poets go ape on campus before; that's very chic for a poet to go ape on campus.

Conversations: Do you think any of this is going to come about? You've got some strong notions; do you see any light anywhere?

Woods: I guess I'm just not satisfied. The improvement I see as I travel more is that clubs are a little better. I'm still working in saloons, man. I've been playing music for thirty years professionally—or longer—I'm still working saloons, but the saloons are getting nicer. There are some nice music rooms. Pianos are better; sound systems are a bit better; the bosses that are into it love the music.

Conversations: How about the people who listen to you?

Woods: The audiences, I find, are fine—maybe a bit noisy, but that's a saloon attitude. They're noisy in Europe, too. This propaganda about Europe understanding culture more than we do—well, maybe they are a little older, but they are not necessarily better. You know, I think American audiences are fine. Perhaps some of the rudest audiences I've seen have been in Paris, Berlin, Bologna. That always intrigues me: Europe has never produced one jazz musician. I'm leaving out Stephane Grappelly and Django Reinhardt; they are exceptions. I'm talking about out of all the players, not many major figures.

Europe is very good at accepting our discards and nurturing them, saying: "Ah, America doesn't understand you." Now this is not sour grapes on my part, because Europe did give me my identity as an artist when I left in '68. America didn't give me that. But I'd just like to put it into the proper perspective. There is a reality about the European jazz community which is very small. I mean, there's a whole lot of them that think if you're white, you can't play at all. There's a lot of ignorance there, too.

I get a lot of young jazz musicians who say, "Man, you went to Europe and you spent five years there, and it really seemed to solidify your career. Should I do that?" And I always recommend against it. I say, "First, you've got to make your mark here some kind of way, even if you're just mentioned in *Down Beat* some way, somewhere in the jazz press, or make a record, or something." Then it's easy, because then Europe says, "Ah, he did okay in America. He must be able to play." This is still, to them, the final arbiter of who can play and who can't play. They don't know.

Conversations: I sat down last night and listened to a couple of albums I didn't know I had until I started rooting around: Birdland One *and* Two.

Woods: Oh, goodness. That was before Vaseline.

Conversations: 1956.

Woods: Yeah, the really early stuff.

Conversations: It was interesting. . .

Woods: It was a hype. I think four tunes were recorded live.

Conversations: Most of them were Ernie Wilkins's songs.

Woods: Yeah, but there were twelve tunes. Now, you know, on a Birdland tour we didn't get that much time. Not with people like Al Hibbler, Sarah Vaughan, Count Basie, Bud Powell, Lester Young. They were all on that tour.

Conversations: Everything you did sounded like it was written.

Woods: It was. We only did, I think, three or four charts on the road, which we got together and memorized real quick, because you couldn't use music out there at the Birdland all-star gig. It was a nice group: Al Cohn, myself, and Conte Candoli, with Sarah Vaughan's rhythm section—very nice. That was my first biggie.

I had been doing Monday nights at Birdland, and I had appeared there, I think, with Neal Hefti's band. And so I got on that tour. They needed a small group, as I say. But getting on that bus, man. There's Basie's band to start. They got the front; they got their seats; they're cool. There's Bud Powell and Lester Young sitting together. I'm reeling! There's Al Hibbler, seeing everything, you know, and Joe Williams—dear friends.

Conversations: This was the show?

Woods: This was the package.

Conversations: You were a young kid, then.

Phil Woods

Woods: And I had just got on the bus, and I didn't know what was happening. Al Cohn saw my befuddled-looking face and motioned to me. We got a seat in the back over the wheel where all the action was, man. Basie and Pres would be shooting dice; Bud Powell would just be sitting, staring out the window.

Conversations: What was it—a coast-to-coast tour?

Woods: We went as far as Chicago. We didn't go any farther west, and we went down south. It was my first experience with segregation. You know, all over the country we stayed together, but in the South at that time. . . . It was my first exposure to that kind of thing, you know, which, I'm happy to say, has now passed. Quincy Jones heard me on that tour, and he asked me to join Dizzy's band. Quincy was forming the band in New York.

Conversations: This was Gillespie's big band?

Woods: Yeah. The band was getting ready for the State Department tour, and I know exactly why I was called.

Conversations: Why?

Woods: Well, I know they had to have a certain ratio of white people to blacks. I think I was called because I was a pretty hot player. But I don't think Dizzy would have that ratio in his band. I'm not implying anything by it; I'm just saying that one of the reasons I was on there was that my government felt you couldn't send an all-black band, because that would be the way it is. I've never understood the tokenism or any of that crap, but I know it is a reality. It gave me a gig, man; that's the main thing.

Conversations: Did you enjoy yourself in the Gillespie band? Do they have good stuff?

Woods: As I say, we never met Dizzy. We used to rehearse. . . . Melba Liston was in that band, Charlie Persip—great band, great band. Ernie Wilkins, Quincy.

Conversations: Did Wilkins write for it?

Woods: Oh, yeah. Melba wrote; Quincy wrote; Ernie wrote; I tried to write—never did finish a chart at that time.

Conversations: But you never saw Gillespie?

Woods: Well, we picked up Gillespie in Rome. So we get the band together, and we leave, and we go from Charlie's Tavern to Dublin, Ireland, where I proceeded to get some very good whiskey. And then on to Rome. I'll never forget Lorraine, Dizzy's wife, was on the plane, and here comes Dizzy out on the tarmac playing "Sweet Lorraine." This is my first introduction to the leader—here he comes walking and playing, the door just opened and Dizzy got on; nobody else got on, just Dizzy playing his trumpet. He said, "Oh, my God, I'm home."

The next thing I remember was Abadan, Iran, where we had some problem about nobody having any Iranian money. For what, I don't know. I just remember it was very silly. We were just exhausted. There were seventeen hours of flying time, not counting touchdown time—refueling and all that—it was all flight.

The next thing I remember was being in an opium den. What can I tell you? I mean, from Charlie's Tavern to an opium den. As I say, Dizzy's band at that time was a mixed band: it had six alcoholics, six junkies, and six potheads.

Conversations: And you still made music?

Woods: Well, it was a great band, but, I mean, we were intrigued with the delights of the East, as any healthy young men of the bebop era would be.

Conversations: On the Russian tour with Goodman—your style was not exactly Goodman's style, was it?

Woods: Well, the band was not Goodman's style, I suppose.

Conversations: It didn't sound like one of his bands. Zoot Sims was in it; you were in it—

Woods: Mel Lewis, Bill Crow, Jerry Dodgion, Willie Dennis, and Jimmy Knepper, Jimmy Maxwell, Joe Wilder, Joe Newman: it was a dynamite band—I guess it would qualify as a first-class studio band. All of those cats were more or less active in the studios at the time. It was just a very high-salaried band, you know. He knew they were the best players. And he commissioned a lot of new stuff from Bob Prince, John Carisi, and Tadd Dameron, which we didn't play at first. We didn't get to that until later, until the Russian fans started to get tired of "Milenberg Joys." Well, Benny is a hard man to work for, what can I tell you?

Conversations: Is he?

Woods: Yeah, I found him difficult. I don't mind a demanding leader; I mean, my first bandleader was Charlie Barnet. That was when I was still in Juilliard and I was playing fourth tenor with Charlie Barnet. That was a demanding leader—"the Mad Mab"— but, boy, I mean, he made music, and that was the thing that I understood. You can do almost anything to me if it's in the name of music. That, I can relate to, but if you pick on me as a human being, then I resent it; then it interferes with my work and I can't do my job properly. I think the most insecure period I ever had was when Benny Goodman told me I was starting to sound good.

Conversations: Did the Russian people dig what you were doing with a horn?

Woods: The people were into the music. As I say, through The Voice of America, they had tapes and stuff. They would yell during concerts: "Zoot, Pheel! Zoot, Pheel!"—until we played a solo. Benny had to let us play. Even Benny Goodman couldn't stop us from playing in Russia.

Conversations: So your name was in Russia in the sixties?

Woods: Yeah, '62. Yeah, they knew about me. I met a young alto player from Leningrad. I remember sneaking into the university to have a jam session—I had to sneak.

Conversations: You did?

Woods: Yep. At that time, it was still kind of tight. I mean, I remember being in Yugoslavia with Dizzy's band in '57, and I've played there many times since, and I've seen it loosen up. I mean, I've seen the government change. I remember not being able to speak to students.

Conversations: Where? In a place like Zagreb?

Woods: Yeah, yeah. And Belgrade, also. Belgrade, I suppose, is a little more liberal. Ljubljana is loose. So in '62, anyway, you'd be walking through the park, and from the bushes you'd hear, "Psst. Thelonious Monk. Dizzy Gillespie. Charlie Parker." You'd think, "These bushes are talking to me," but it was just that fraternization was kept secret. The Russians didn't want to be seen. I wanted to give a bathrobe to this alto player who visited my room. And he said, "I can't take it." And I said, "Why?" He said, "If I leave with a package, the KGB will stop me and ask me what the package is, and they'll take it from me." Maybe he was just too proud, I don't know.

But seeing jazz impresses these people. I mean, the concerts were packed. They did know the music. But not all of the Russians—Moscow I found very dour. Muscovites are kind of weird. Leningrad I really loved; it reminded me of Paris—sidewalk cafes. People were lovely there and very hip. I guess it's like the cultural capital of Russia. Tashkent—they didn't know too much, but the rhythm, I think, intrigued them. I mean, playing "Brusbeckes," you can't expect them to be too hip, you know. But that's always killed me. I can go anywhere in the world and play for my supper. You know, after five years in Europe and many, many tours, I've been just about everywhere. The next logical challenge for me as a human being and a musician is to see if I can survive in my own country.

Conversations: Is this what drove you to Europe in the first place—you couldn't survive here?

Woods: No. I could survive financially, but I was doing jingles. Everybody kept saying, "Get a flute! Get a flute; then you can double. You'll pick up more jobs." The flute didn't lead me to music; the alto saxophone led me to music. I love the alto saxophone. I don't have any affinity for the flute. I was damned if I was going to be another reed man contributing to the abuse of this lovely instrument. There are people that take it, too. Me, I just got dizzy.

Conversations: What prompted you to give up the clarinet? You don't play that much anymore.

Woods: Well, I played a lot of clarinet in the sixties—bass clarinet, too, on many dates. A lot of sound tracks.

Phil Woods

Conversations: Well, you won a Down Beat *award, for heaven's sake.*

Woods: But those were my doubles. If I was hired in the studios—in those days, you see, there were a lot of arrangers in New York still. They hadn't all gone to California. Quincy was about; Billy Byers; Oliver Nelson; Kenyon Hopkins was doing a lot of film work, TV work. We did *Twelve Angry Men, The Hustler;* I did *Blow-Up,* did *The Eastside, Westside* TV series. I did *The Reporter*—all dynamite stuff. I mean, all first-class material that used good music. So there was this thing about good music then, which is kind of weird. I never quite understood what happened to that. I mean, the writers went to California and it stopped happening.

Conversations: In New York?

Woods: No. The writers stopped happening. They went to California and were stilled as voices, to my way of thinking, or died.

Conversations: Did the industry eat them up?

Woods: America has a great thing with its composers, you know. I'm fascinated with the idea of jazz composition. The whole tradition of Ellington intrigues me; and it's being totally ignored. It bugs me when I see a stage band—they're all playing Don Sebesky or Thad and Mel charts. Fine charts, but why don't they play something by a kid in the band? "But it won't sound as good, and it won't win at the festivals"—you know, like a winning football team. We don't nurture the composition of jazz in this country. If we do get a young composer. . . I know in New York, you give them a jingle; you give them $1000 to write some pap, and then you get them hooked. They've got to live this way, and they've got to write pap, and they can't write good music—they haven't got time.

Conversations: You have Ellington's picture on your wall. Did you work with Ellington?

Woods: No, my son worked with Ellington.

Conversations: Really?

Woods: My son, Garth, who left for Paris a few days ago. He's in his first year at Rutgers majoring in—I don't know; he's going to save the planet with ecology, and he's studying Chinese and French. He's doing a film class in French. Fascinating boy. This would be '72, '71—something like that. Duke was touring in France doing a sacred concert series, and he needed a little boy to recite something about Adam and Eve. So my son got the gig because Simone Ginibre, who was managing me, knew my son would be perfect for the gig, because he could do it in French and in English. So he got a chance to tour with the band. No, I never played with Mr. Ellington. I was only in his presence once.

Conversations: You obviously admire him, though.

Woods: Well, it's funny you should ask me that—I've never been a big Ellington fan.

Conversations: You haven't?

Woods: Only in later years. I mean, I was always into Johnny Hodges—I shouldn't say I'm not an Ellington fan. How can you be a jazz man and not be an Ellington fan? I've always loved the band, but I mean when I was a young cat I was interested more in the further out kinds of bands, I guess.

But back to composition. There's no contact anymore between classical and jazz composers. If we start teaching jazz composition, I just say, you know, "Jazz is a people's thing; it's a street art." Of course, it can be taught in the classroom. I teach; I have many, many young students.

Conversations: You teach jazz composition?

Woods: I teach improvisation; I teach writing. I can teach jazz voicings, but it's really just orchestration in voicing. I'm in the process of writing for a string quartet and a woodwind quintet. Now, to me, I did learn something at Juilliard about that. I studied with Peter Mennin, who was probably a very important influence on me. But I figure my first two years of Juilliard were a total waste of time. I learned how to get high at the Hotel Claremont—I was bebop alto player. I was fourteenth in line to play with the training orchestra.

Conversations: At Juilliard?

Phil Woods

Woods: I could outplay any of those turkeys, but I was too jazzy, I guess. I don't know. I've always thought that, anyway. I've always felt a slight frost from there. I could do their thing very easily, but they couldn't do my thing at all, and I think this bugs musicians. For my keyboard placement exam I played Bud Powell bebop. But that was much more piano than the violinist could play, who could barely chalk out something from her childhood lessons, you know, or whatever. It took two years to get to fifth species counterpoint. I mean, what is that horseshit? You could only write whole notes—I mean. . . .

Conversations: You've put some stuff on stage at Town Hall. Are you taking the alto into classical music?

Woods: Well, playing in Town Hall has got nothing to do with classical music.

Conversations: But you've written "The Rites of Swing" and other very impressive stuff.

Woods: Yeah, I've always composed. I've always written if it's just a song or—I've done a children's suite. I took Now We Are Six—A. A. Milne— and wrote a series of seventeen songs. I finished the songs and they told me I couldn't use any of them.

Conversations: Why?

Woods: Well, the A. A. Milne Estate had some stodgy lawyer in England who didn't want to know anything about jazz. I didn't mention jazz in my letter, and they never even offered to hear them. And then, I understand the rights were bought by Walt Disney. I can't fight Walt Disney. They're just some songs that I— you know, that's like leaving something to your children. That's kind of nice that nobody will ever hear them but my kids, who can sing them.

So composing and writing, I've always done that. I remember always writing. I minored in composition at Juilliard, if there is such a thing—I don't know. I just took a lot of classes and monitored the Columbia composers, contemporary composers, forums, and have always been interested in people like Henry Brandt and Edgard Varese. And I listened to Charles Ives when I was in Juilliard. I was exposed to Ives's "Concord

242

Sonata." They didn't tell me about that in class; one of the jazz musicians told me about that. I was led to Schoenberg through Charlie Parker. I read in *Down Beat* magazine that one of the pieces Parker liked was "Pierrot Lunaire." I went to my local library—I was still in high school—and I got this music and I put it on. My parents thought that I was really bonkers. I must say, I didn't quite get it either, but I listened to it. I don't know. I seem to be rapping establishments, but I've always liked to do that. Nothing wrong with that. It's the complacency of the establishment that annoys me.

Conversations: Earlier you mentioned that you liked Johnny Hodges.

Woods: He was the first alto player I ever saw live with a big band. You see, I was lucky as a young man; I had a great teacher. I think that's all. I was fortunate in that way and also in having parents that said do whatever you want—just take your best shot at it. There was never any onus on my being a jazz musician. That was fine—just be a good one. This is common knowledge—I think it's in *The Encyclopedia of Jazz*; I don't know. My uncle died and left me my alto and I went for my lesson. I didn't want to, but they said, "The man died. The least you can do is take a lesson." And I met this teacher; his name is Harvey LaRose, and he's still teaching to this day up in Chelaro's Music Store in Springfield, Massachusetts. He gave a lesson and, okay, I'd put the horn away and I wouldn't see it all week. I'd go back the next week and I'd play the lesson. Now after a couple of weeks, this cat dug immediately that I was faking it, but that I must have a great sense of retention and a pretty damned good ear. So instead of yelling at me and saying, "You're faking! You've got to do it this way!" he nurtured my ear and my talent. Gradually, he got into playing the piano. He would give me Johnny Hodges solos, and he would accompany me. I studied Coleman Hawkins solos.

Conversations: So he didn't force you into classical stuff?

Woods: He taught me chords; he taught me the basis of improvisation. I've been with many, many teachers. I've met many teachers, but never a better one, you know. Not a great instrumentalist, but a marvelous teacher, you know. That was truly fortunate.

243

Phil Woods

Conversations: He had you at heart rather than what he was trying to tell you?

Woods: Exactly, exactly. I had a student refused admission to Eastman because he didn't fit their needs. I thought they were to accommodate his need. But he didn't fit into the slot they had open for him. All too often you get that. Music is a very sacred thing to me and I hate the. . . .

Conversations: A very personal thing, too, isn't it?

Woods: Yeah, but it's not that deep. I mean, we have so many highfalutin—you get kids going up to Berkeley School of Music to learn jazz, and they end up carrying around more books than I ever carried at Juilliard. They have books of scales and when to use them, and here's Lester Young's solo on this. Now this is all valuable on the printed page and all that, but it's much more valuable if you do it yourself—if you listen to the music and then transcribe it. Now, all too often, it's all done for you. You can buy records and things. It's easy. The accessibility—a lot of times you get kids into it who maybe shouldn't be into it, but the accessibility makes it a little easier for them to go a little further until the reality hits them: "Hey, I can't play jazz. What am I doing?" I mean, everybody wants to play jazz today, you see. All the kids want to get into jazz. This is good. But as a living art, man, it's not that accessible to everybody—to perform it, I should say. I mean, you could make a pretty good pass at being a Maynard Ferguson-styled band on the university level; but as soon as the soloist stands up, you know that you are not. There's nothing happening. Ensemble-wise, it's good.

Conversations: I've watched you perform with the North Texas State lab band. I've talked with Leon Breeden, and I said this to him, too: the thing that impressed me about the band was its ability to read, but the thing that depressed me about the band was its mechanical exterior.

Woods: Well, any big band can give you this. I think the kids were tired; I think the kids were fatigued. I don't think they were ready for that bus journey and a week of rehearsals and performances. They looked like a typical band that had been on the road for about six weeks to me. As young kids, they shouldn't have been that tired, but they haven't learned, maybe, how to time their partying and stuff, you know. They were having a ball, and I thought they had exceptionally good soloists, but that's one of our outstanding bands. Leon has done a fabulous job in getting really fine soloists.

Conversations: They sure read your stuff pretty fast.

Woods: Yeah, no problem. They're good musicians.

Conversations: Is the type of thing that you are writing—that I heard with the band—in truth, jazz, as such? It's so cerebral; it's so complex. It's beautiful to hear, when it is well played.

Woods: I don't know. It's the way I feel about music. It has to be. All I listen to is jazz. The bottom row is classical. I guess it's about half and half. It's music. It's all music to me. I hate to label jazz. I hate the factionalism that goes on within jazz.

Conversations: What do you mean by factionalism?

Woods: We're less than 100 years old. How many periods have we gone through? I mean the Dixielanders, the trad cats, didn't like the beboppers, didn't like the swing cats, didn't like the avant-garde, didn't like the Coltrane. . . . Now we have loft jazz. How can we represent a unified, strong art if we have this divisiveness? I trace it directly, sometimes, to the black-white thing. That's been the whole thing about "You stole my music."

Conversations: Is that feeling still strong?

Woods: Well, whatever it is, that's horseshit, too. It's the music that counts, and you can't steal a gift, for God's sake. Bird didn't play for blacks only, neither did Art Tatum or Louis Armstrong.

Conversations: What did you think about Bird's alto playing versus Hodges's? You said Hodges was the first player that you saw.

Woods: Well, Bird was the virtuoso. Nobody played more saxophone than Bird. Hodges would have told you that and Mr. Carter will certainly tell you that. Mr. Carter has never even considered himself a great technician. I don't think you have to be a great technician to play beautifully, but as a young saxophone player his technique, I guess, was his ability to create with just basically the same scale, the same chords that everybody else had had for years. He made such incredible personal statements; I mean, it was unmistakably Mr. Parker's music. Even when it was emulated you'd say, "Ah, that's Bird."

Conversations: What gives a man's music that distinction? The horns are the same; the pads are the same; the mouthpiece is the same. What is it that creates the difference?

Woods: For me, it's sound; it's the quality. It's, like, all music should represent the human voice. The best opera singers—you can always tell who they are. I'm not a big opera fan; I don't mean to impress anybody.

Conversations: Well, how do you get this sound?

Woods: That I don't know. I could say either you've got it or you don't, and it can be worked on and developed, I believe. I just never had that thing out of my mouth once I finally got hooked. Once I had been with this teacher for a while, then I got a kid band. I had a cat who was a couple of years older who lived up the street playing piano. He's still around; he was Julie London's musical director—of all names, Hal Serra. But we had a whole musical community up in Springfield. Sal Salvador is from there; Teddy Charles the vibes player; Joe Morello was our drummer; Chuck Andress who was our bass player—now with Woody Herman. We were jamming together, and I heard Charlie Parker and I said, "That's it!" As I say, when I was about fourteen I knew what I was going to be. How lucky, huh, to have that kind of direction at such an early age? I've often thought about that. I've often been swayed a little bit, but I've never changed my direction. And I've never had to do very many unpleasant things to exist. It's been lean sometimes, but I haven't really had to prostitute myself. I dug postholes once, but I think that's more honest than playing disco music.

Conversations: William Steinberg once said a good musician or conductor doesn't have an ego as much as he has self-assurance.

Woods: I would say self-assurance is very important. I've always known I could play. At one period I didn't know whether I could make it as a jazz player—that was in '68 when I went to Europe.

246

Conversations: When was the first big shot that you had, when you had to really cut it? Do you remember?

Woods: I guess, the first Monday night at Birdland with Neal Hefti's band when I had to play "Repetition," which was always associated with Charlie Parker. Opening night, you know. I had worked a few Monday nights with a few small groups, but every time I play I feel that way.

Conversations: Do you?

Woods: Well, I'm going to go to work tonight for a few hours, and I haven't played. I just did two weeks at Hopper's in a club. I find it hard to divide myself into the performer and the writer. I love to write. I'm a very good saxophone player; I'm learning how to write, but I find it difficult juggling the two. Now in the past few days, I've been on a schedule that—I don't even know what the schedule is. Today is the first day I've gotten dressed. I've been chained to that piano for about three days. I just work until exhaustion and then lie down. It's got to be done; it's a job I've got to have done, and I'm excited about it. It's good stuff. It's part of a *Seven Deadly Sins* album which we were doing. We recorded the seven sins—we did that last January. I got seven young arranger-composer cats nobody had heard of—famous names like Joe Roccisano, Chris Swansen, Pete Robinson, Chris Gunning—people might know he did *Floresta Canto*—Mike Abene they might know, Barry Miles, of course, people will know, and Gary Anderson from Woody's band. I gave each of them a sin.

Conversations: This is the record you're going to do in England?

Woods: Well, that's been done. The major pieces have been done—sixty-piece orchestra. I'm the alto soloist; Gordon Beck is piano soloist; Barry Miles is on synthesizer, Terry Silverlight plays drums. I gave out these sins: I'm giving lust, gluttony—I felt like the Pope. It was incredible. So we have those pieces, now we want to put some words in between. We want some chamber music in between the big blocks of the seven deadly sins. It's like the one major theme that should occur and be interrupted by these stumbling blocks, as it were. It's a concept we haven't really homed in on yet. We're doing research.

Phil Woods

Conversations: Who is doing these bridges?

Woods: I'm writing the music. We have quite a few people in England and the States doing research on the seven deadly sins—dates, on the number seven, on the Bible.

Conversations: Put a text to it?

Woods: It's not program music, although we're trying to make a statement. When you say gluttony, that can mean many things; that can be pollution, abuse of the planet. You can say about what you want under these big headings, so we're trying to say something that will reach people today—not in the classical sense of the Seven Deadly Sins, which has been done by a few other people. So I'm in the process of writing that. Now when I have to play my saxophone, that's another thing, you see. I've got to forget that for the moment. And I'm right into it, too; I'm right into the seventh section. I've got the woodwind quintet swinging—a lot of flat fifths—and I've got to leave it and go play with my band. But that's okay; I just have to shift my head.

Conversations: You can?

Woods: I can. With my band, I can. Not if I go out and do a single with a local rhythm section, say, "Okay, what are we going to play? What do you know?"

Conversations: Well, do you have a group that is yours?

Woods: I have a group that is my band, yes. We've been together three years now—quintet.

Conversations: And they stay working all the time?

Woods: We all live in the Poconos, you see. We all live up here—Al Cohn lives up here; Urbie Green lives up here. So, in what you might mistake for total isolation, down here at the Deerhead Inn on Friday and Saturday nights either Barry Miles is playing, or Johnny Coates—the legendary Johnny Coates.

Conversations: I've heard about him.

Woods: We're going to record him, hopefully, this summer. My producer, Norman Schwartz, is very interested in having him on RCA. So there's a lot of activity up here. There are a lot of young people. There's a leather shop, and people are making clothes, and there's a co-op for food. It's nice here, very pleasant.

Conversations: And you're making music here.

Woods: Yeah. I haven't been outside to enjoy it, but that's all right.

Conversations: You're going to record with Mel Torme, too. Are you writing music for him?

Woods: I'm doing an arrangement for him, yeah, on an old song called "That's It."

Conversations: That's another shifting of gears, isn't it?

Woods: Yeah. That's going to be a kind of fun thing, though. That's big-band stuff. That will take me about a day. I can do that in London. I'm having a piano, an electric piano of some kind, in the flat in London, so I'll have a few days to work.

Conversations: Torme handles his voice really like an instrument. Does this pose an interesting problem for the composer, for the arranger?

Woods: No, because what we want to do is get Annie Ross, who lives in London—a great jazz singer—and do a thing with Annie, Mel, and the alto saxophone as a sound. I think it would be nice if it's recorded properly.

Conversations: In harmony, or the alto has an obbligato, or what?

Woods: I thought about it three ways, but maybe two ways would be best—with an octave split or something. I haven't gotten into that yet. That we can work out. I want to just get the notes down. That will really be jazz composition, in that it will be up to the players and the performers to bring something to it. I mean, there will be a sketch—the band will come in here—but, essentially, it will be the parlay between the three voices, and that we're going to just do in the studio. That will be fun.

Conversations: And Torme says yes?

Woods: Mel says, "Hit it." Mel is always ready for music. I've never worked with him before; I'm looking forward to it.

Phil Woods

Conversations: Have you worked with any other singers where you've had to construct material to accompany them?

Woods: Well, I played behind Billie Holiday for quite awhile out at the Cork 'n Bib in Westbury, Long Island. They had a band that she was singing with, but they wanted to bring in a saxophone player to just play behind her set.

Conversations: You didn't tour with her, did you?

Woods: No. I recorded with Sarah Vaughan, a lady who is a good friend, Al Hibbler, Dinah Washington, God rest her soul—that was a marvelous talent. No. I've had to, maybe, not write for them, but make music with them. You have to pay attention to the words.

Conversations: Have you ever gotten into the classical literature for the alto sax?

Woods: Well, if you listen to "Cheek-to-Cheek" on the new album, I do quote Ibert—and I do it tongue-in-cheek, if it's "Cheek-to-Cheek." The whole legitimate saxophone world is really asleep. They haven't recognized any contributions made by jazz saxophone players. I'm talking about the various timbres and sounds that you can get technically on the saxophone, of the overtone series that Coltrane developed, the Ben Webster growl. All of these things that are really part of the saxophone technique. I had a student call me—he is going to Eastman—and he said, "I've got to change my mouthpiece." I said, "Why?" He said, "I don't get that legitimate sound, and they're going to scream at me." I said, "Screw 'em."

Conversations: What's the legitimate sound?

Woods: It's when you sound like you got a mouth full of codfish and a pole up your ass at the same time. These cats all sit and look constipated. Come on, man. I know about that. I've written the music, the whole thing in the tuxedo image. It's the blue-haired ladies again.

Conversations: Is the alto sax really meant to be "legit"?

Woods: Sure. It's an instrument. It's more legitimate, certainly, than the bassoon.

Conversations: Is it meant to have starch in its back, or is it meant to have warmth?

Woods: Any instrument is meant to have starch in its back.

Conversations: But isn't some of the warmth of the instrument inhibited in a symphony orchestra, where no vibrato is permitted of the reed players?

Woods: Well, I'm talking about the saxophone player. So you have a man like Gompers on oboe. Man, that man swings. Yeah, so does Julius Baker on flute.

Conversations: Basically speaking, it's straight up and down. Is this what an alto is supposed to do?

Woods: No, an alto is supposed to sing. It's like a cello. Marcel Mule was a cellist who brought a certain legitimacy to the saxophone, I suppose, with the French quartet—with a certain French sound, you know. If you listen to the jazz greats like Frankie Trumbauer, Rudy Weedoff, Jimmy Dorsey, they didn't all have great sounds, but they certainly had unique individual sounds.

Well, in the legit world everybody has got to sound exactly the same as a way of fitting in. Sure, if you're doing the *New World* Symphony, the saxophone part must go like this. Well, if the composer has really meant—I don't believe it. I think Bach would have loved the way Glenn Gould plays his music, because he plays it. "It's supposed to go this way." Music doesn't know anything about "supposed to go"; music is just supposed to be, you know. A great composer, I think, would love the idea of taking liberties and bringing something to the music, which is the jazz tradition. I mean, you put up a bunch of chord changes to a legit cat, or give them a tone row, they don't know what do to with it. If you tell them what to do with a tone row—that's technique as old as Dada. It's not even being taught in school. I don't know if they talk about improvisation. I was never taught improvisation at Juilliard, and my life is improvisation—make do with little.

Talk about conservation. There's a whole message that jazz has for people, I mean philosophically—any kind of way you want to take it. There's something there that I think is valuable to other people, and it doesn't seem to be getting through. But the artists, maybe, are not getting through. We don't listen to artists in this country—we're afraid of them.

In Europe they're not afraid of the artist, I'll say that for them. They know he's an important part of their society, maybe a little weird, but they expect an artist to be a little weird. That's okay—they're not afraid of that. If you go really bananas, there's a certain fear of you, you know. We have to be more healthfully integrated into the society. We're not an elite. It's our fault, too—jazz musicians, especially. Turning your back on the audiences was fashionable at one time. We've made a lot of mistakes; we're still making them.

Conversations: You mentioned improvisation and the fact that you've had the ability all the time. Is there such a thing as practicing improvisation? Can you sit at home and take a given melody or something and then begin to weave and—

Woods: My teacher taught me how to do that. Well, I was instinctively doing it anyway. I was fooling around with a melody; that's all it is—you fool around; you decorate. I used mordants and all those classical terms, if you like—there's a whole literature to describe it, which I've fortunately forgotten. There's a very fashionable term now in jazz circles—Lydian mode.

Conversations: What does that mean?

Woods: Lydian mode—it means that you put an F-sharp in the key of C. Big deal, that's what the overtone gives you anyway. That's what you get when you play a major seventh. Kids are talking about "Oh, you mean Lydian mode?" I say, "What are you talking about—a term that's talking about music of ars nova or whatever and applying it to an art form that is not a hundred years old yet?" Is that the most imagination that we have in this field? We have to even borrow these dumb words? It's convenient and all that, I guess. It's a small annoyance.

Conversations: When you improvise something that you really like, that's pleasing to you and maybe even to other people, do you make an attempt to write it down?

Woods: No, but I used to study other people's solos. I used to take down other solos and analyze them myself. I played along with the record and wrote it down and played along some more. It was easier with 78s—you could find your place. Hard with LPs, but it's getting easier with LPs, because everybody has got all these pieces of equipment now. Going to be the death of us yet, man. You put it on tape and play it at half speed and you have the same key, but it's half as slow. You can really do it easy.

Conversations: *Don't you have an urge to preserve what you are creating as an improvisor?*

Woods: Oh, kids send me my solos written down all the time. I have a whole collection of my solos written down. They don't interest me; I can't play them; I can't read them; they only appeal to me at the moment, and then that's it. I mean, we're putting out too many records as it is.

Conversations: *I guess what I'm getting at is the preservation of a culture.*

Woods: It's on record, though. If it's on record, man, it should be listened to, not looked at. You don't listen to music with your eyes. It's good for the student, but I mean, it's a very small—it would only interest a small group of people, and I think that the small group of people that are interested are already involved in doing it. There is a man who has put out a book of saxophone solos. He's taken off different solos from all different periods, so it's done. One of my solos is included. But that doesn't interest me. If I'm going to sit down and write, I'll be damned if I'm going to write what I played twenty years ago. Because if I did, I would have to change it, and then it wouldn't fit the record; then it would really blow the historians' minds.

Conversations: *How about electronics and the alto saxophone?*

Woods: I had my fling with the ring modulator and a wah-wah pedal when I first left Europe, I guess, in '72. I first went to Los Angeles, under some misguided reason that I wanted a home with a pool—I don't know what that was.

Conversations: *All the way to L.A. for that?*

253

Phil Woods

Woods: Jesus Christ. And I got a band together with Pete Robinson. Anyway, out of that ten months in Los Angeles, I worked four nights at playing music that I wanted to play. And that was a very experimental group—synthesizers and all of that. Leonard Feather came the first night and he said, "Oh, my God, you're not going to use a wah-wah pedal, are you?" I said, "You're damned right I am, Leonard." Before he listened to it, I knew that that review was going to be terrible. Welcome back to the United States! It's equipment. It's there. I tried it. I explored it. I recorded with it. I made an album which nobody will ever find.

Conversations: Did you drop it?

Woods: Yeah. With my present group, we're going strictly acoustic. It doesn't interest me anymore with the kind of music that we are playing. Besides, it's a bother.

Conversations: Does the kind of horn that you play really need anything but what you give it?

Woods: Well, it was just something that I wanted to do. Something I've been working on all my life is to destroy the sound of the alto saxophone. With one flick of the switch I could totally destroy it, and that intrigued me. Just to see the shocked look on the people in the audience who wanted me to sound like I sounded in the fifties—so I could put them on their nostalgia trip and play some bebop for them. I liked that part. Even among musicians in L.A., which really surprised me—you wouldn't get this in New York, I'm sure, but L.A . . . .I think once musicians accept the L.A. way of life, it necessitates that when they see you they want to remember you from the fifties, when they were swinging, too. I refused. I didn't want to meet those needs. If I stop growing, I'm dead, man. It is just getting interesting now; I'm starting to figure out what music is all about. I think I'm on to something. I'm going to get more into writing. Eventually, I'd really like to write a work for alto saxophone and symphony orchestra. I'd like to take a stab at it.

Conversations: Every musician wants to, doesn't he?

Woods: I hope, by then, that they are extinct, however.

254

Conversations: What—symphony orchestras or altos?

Woods: Altos gonna persevere, man; symphony orchestras, I'm not so sure. No, I mean, I don't need all those strings. I want to do a piece that's not just performed, but it's mixed media, the multi-media thing, you know. I want to improvise a sound track to a movie with my group sometime. I'd love to try that. When I say improvise, improvising is a responsibility. I think aimless improvisation is a one-way street. I think avant-garde has finally found that out after pursuing what they thought was something new. It's old hat, what the avant-garde is doing. It always is; it's always a derriere-garde. I mean, they're using Dada techniques which were done in the 1920s. That's just ignorance in the arts.

We have a lot of ignorance on the jazz levels. Cats don't do their homework. You've got to do your homework, man. Otherwise you're going to make a fool out of yourself. You're going to come up with something: "Ah, I've got something new!" and you point to a record that's made in 1907, and somebody says, "Oh, really?"

Conversations: What's it like to play The Newport Jazz Festival or any of these festivals? Is it a mechanical exercise for you, or are you so professional that you can really give everything you've got all the time?

Woods: I've done Newport a couple of times, and I always remember being very nervous.

Conversations: Really?

Woods: Yeah, well, I'm always nervous when I play Carnegie Hall, no matter what it is. I was part of an Al Hirt show there once, and I remember saying, "This is still Carnegie Hall, man." That's just conditioning, I suppose. We'll need a good audience, that's for sure. I don't think programming us with Maynard Ferguson is too hip, I really don't. But nevertheless, I assume they are there to hear music, and we're going to get very hot. Thank God, we open. I wouldn't want to follow a big band. But it's not routine; it's never routine. We're playing in Gulliver's tonight in West Paterson, New Jersey, for a man named Amos Cahn. Now I've been knowing Amos since he had the Clifton Tap Room back in the sixties—and his wife Pat. They've always had a jazz joint, you know. Always in New Jersey, you know, that part. But they're lovely people and they make you feel real at home. People that come, come to listen, so that's always a treat. It's very comfortable. Won't be like playing Carnegie Hall, you know.

Conversations: So you're not jaded after thirty years?

Woods: God, no. I get more excited now than I ever did. That's why I talk so much.

Conversations: I know you're excited about your composition, but how about playing?

Woods: Well, the new record, *Live at the Showboat*, is getting some good reactions—more reaction than I've ever gotten. That's a direct result of the quintet. It's the people who like the sound of the band, because we're a very cohesive, well-knit organization. We play everything from Stevie Wonder to Johann Sebastian Bach. We do cover a lot of ground. We have a lot of experience on the band. Bill Goodwin on drums has been around for quite awhile—with Gary Burton's group, worked with Stan Getz, Mulligan, you name it. Mike Melillo I've known since the Clifton Tap Room days; he used to be the house pianist there. Steve Gilmore is a dynamite bass player, has been around with Thad and Mel; Harry Leahey, an undiscovered, overnight success. Harry is about forty-one years old and this is his first record. He's been doing just club dates and things. So I'm excited for the cats in the band, because I know the band is good. And, as a jazz musician, I know how important it is to have the right cats behind you. I've done enough singles to go out. I've been to many towns where I've played with just rhythm sections. I've had many, many bands, and I've never had a better one than this one.

Conversations: Are you taking them to England?

Woods: Well, not to England to record, because actually that's Barry Miles's record so he's bringing his rhythm section. I'll be bringing my band to London in September to record, and then we tour Europe.

Conversations: Are you big over there in Scandinavian countries?

Woods: I haven't been there since I left, but I used to be pretty good.

Conversations: How about Japan?

Woods: Oh, I'm hot as a two-dollar pistol in Japan. Japan is extremely avid for jazz. It's the second biggest record market, period. Per capita, it's the most literate country in the world: they read more books than anybody. I love touring in Japan. It's difficult—you do a lot of one-nighters, but their audiences are something else, man, and the people who take care of you, who present you. . . . You don't have to scuffle. First class all the way, man. Always first class. Makes you feel like a million dollars. We'll be doing some concerts in Tokyo with some music we are writing now. Mike Melillo did a thing on the Bach piece. He's taken a French partita and made a beautiful ballad out of it. He's orchestrating it now for strings and chamber orchestra. I'm going to try to write something new. I'm trying to get a repertoire for the quintet that permits us not only to play colleges, but also concert halls, with anyone, any size, any formation. I'm rapping the symphony orchestras, but I'm not above using them.

Conversations: You'll play, if invited?

Woods: To me, they are just a group of musicians. It's not the musicians, it's just the term "symphony orchestra" that bothers me. We've all got to be playing music somewhere; we've just got to call it by something else—that's all. I mean, you cats can't be the the "legit cats" and I'm the "jazz cat." We're American musicians trying to survive. Let's get it together. Music can unify us, if we just listen with our hearts and our ears instead of always with our pocketbooks.

Conversations: When you go to a college campus, what do you tell the music students who gang up on you?

Woods: Just about what I'm telling you.

Conversations: Do you have a message for them?

Woods: Just what I'm been telling you. I tell them about all the horseshit they're going to be told. I try to tell them the way it is from my perspective, having been out there since I was fourteen years old.

Phil Woods

Conversations: Do they want to hear the way it is, or do they want something else?

Woods: Well, the real ones do. The real ones will always listen to you. I gave up judging people a long time ago. I once told this student he would never make it; he should give it up. But a year later, I heard him playing—boy, did I want to eat those words! So, I never write anybody off, but I can kind of tell the serious ones and the guys who can really play. The first time they put it in their mouths, I can tell where they're at. After I talk with them for a minute and, say, play a chorus, I know about where they're at, you know. They can fool me sometimes, but not too much. So I just try to tell them what I think it is. I don't know what music is. I have no idea what music is. It's a great mystery to me, music. And the more I study it—I still don't understand it. I know there are a lot of people that claim they understand it, and write books about it, and say, "Well, here is the principal theme and the subsidiary. . . ." That has nothing to do with the music, to me. All that knowledge did not help me love and learn the music. If anything, it got in the way of it, because I wasn't told the reality of what the listening experience is and about the spirituality of music. The strength of music, the importance of it—these things are not being told.

Conversations: You can't teach those things, can you?

Woods: You can tell them the truth. Just don't lie to the kids, that's all. Just don't deceive them, you know. It's not necessarily deceit if you don't know what to tell them. I just don't understand the whole process of music education. I know if playing music makes you feel good, and you're prepared to suffer a bit, and that's what you want—do it. I have never recommended it as a life—only if the music gives you pleasure. If it's an ego trip and you want to be a star, man, forget it. That's out. See, when I was a young musician, the most I could hope for financially would be a couple hundred dollars a week on a big band. That was my dream. Since the Beatles—I hate to pick them, but it's a convenient historical period—found out that by playing three chords. . . . I'm not rapping their musicianship, but a lot of kids got this idea that if you pick up three chords on a guitar, you can, maybe, make a half a million dollars a night. I mean, all of a sudden you've got a difference in these figures that—

Conversations: What does that do to your efforts?

Woods: That doesn't matter. I mean, I've given up the idea of making half a million dollars a night a long time ago. Doesn't even interest me. That would be a pain in the ass, I'm sure. It's got to be, if you're dealing in those figures. I don't mind making more money, and I think that as you evolve through life your income should grow. I'm happy to say mine is: I'm doing better now than I've ever done in my life. But in cold practical terms, it's not a whole bunch of bread, man—you don't need that much bread—it's just complications. But I can see how it could turn a kid's head around. He says, "Man, if I get a fusion band, and I play a little rock, and a little jazz, and a little loft, and a little. . . that should do it!" It's tempting, I suppose. How can you sell out for $200 a week? But if you're talking about $10,000 a week, I might have thought about it more.

Conversations: Are you saying that the music you are talking about is contrived?

Woods: The way music is handled by record companies, by most talent agencies, by all of the TV people, it is just a commodity. The handling has nothing to do with the music.

Conversations: You're recording; you're dealing with agents.

Woods: Well, I'm very fortunate to have a producer who feels very strongly about the music, and he fights for me. Thank God, I don't have to handle that. He's got to put the budgets through. We discuss the projects, but he—that's the hard part. Norman Schwartz has got the hard part, as a producer who believes in the artist and in the music. He's got to deal with these idiots who couldn't care less. It's the bottom line, of course.

Conversations: They don't even know you?

Woods: Some of them do. They're starting to know me. Well, there's been. . . . You know, we did get a couple of Grammys— Michel Legrand and I won Grammys for *Images*. The new record is making a lot of noise. Now I think, sometimes, that on the top level, the bottom line is not always the only priority. I mean,

Phil Woods

RCA, as an old company, is not ignorant of the fact that having the honor of two Grammys and a record that is making some noise is good for the company. Even if they lose bread on it, it's good for the company. So there's even hope that way. But if it's always the bottom line, then the music is going to lose—that I know about.

Conversations: Tell me about Chris Gunning. He seems to be a favorite of yours, somebody that you go back to when you record.

Woods: Well, I only discovered him after *Images. Floresta Canto* was the first thing that we'd done together. No. Actually he was a discovery of Keith Grant, who is our engineer. He recommended him to Norman Schwartz to do the string writing for the *Floresta Canto*, and I did the brass writing. I just thought he was magnificent—some of the best writing I'd heard in a long time. And I love the man so. We do work in London twice a year. On the *Seven Deadly Sins*, although he wrote one of the sins, he conducted all of them. We make a good team. That's what we're building: we're building a team. Not just a team, it's a family. People like Norman Schwartz, Keith Grant, Barry Miles, myself, we just recently signed Tom Harrell—he's a young, fantastic trumpet player—Mel Torme, hopefully, Lena Horne is part of the family. Woody Herman, Buddy Rich. These are all quality acts, like—artists.

Conversations: How about this piano player, Gordon Beck, from England?

Woods: Well, he's coming to the States, I think, in the fall. He hasn't been doing too well in London. I know that. He was part of my European Rhythm Machine and is just a fantastic pianist, but he doesn't want to end up in the studios. He doesn't want to do London session work; it's not very rewarding. RCA London does not make one record on their own. They do not do any recording in London. I don't understand that. They take things from Europe—they take finished products and then issue them in the U.K. But they do not make new music in the U.K. by using the talent they have, not RCA anyway. England is weird.

Conversations: So their talent goes begging, then?

260

Woods: Well, it's people like Gordon Beck having trouble getting a record out. I don't understand it. He appears on Lena Horne albums; he's on my albums, which are issued by RCA America and which go all over the world. We can't get RCA in London to get off their buns. But that's just part of the little corporate fight that goes on.

Conversations: One last element of your music making. You're doing some conducting, too. You did some conducting for Barry Miles—you described it as being a traffic cop. Is that another thing that you are into?

Woods: I conducted Tom Harrell's session—he wrote some music. I've always conducted when I had the music camp Ramblerny. I had to conduct the kids. It doesn't matter who you conduct, you've got to conduct the same way. So I can get by with it. If it's a particularly difficult score, I'll have to study it a bit, but I can conduct pretty well. I can get them through the music, and that's really all that counts. The nuances—hopefully, you're dealing with fine players. They bring so much to the music that you're just a timekeeper, essentially; you just keep them together. I mean, all this expressive motion—the players have got to feel it. You can be waving your arms, but if they don't feel it, it doesn't matter.

Conversations: But if they're not looking up, they're not going to see anything?

Woods: They're looking up. I told these cats: "Don't look at me, and we'll get along fine."

At fifty-five, Sol Yaged continues to be the number one fan of Benny Goodman. His clarinet tone suggests Goodman; his style is, for the most part, Goodman. Sometimes, when he puts on a pair of glasses and picks up the clarinet, he looks like Benny Goodman. But Yaged also is a polished musician with a classical background. He has played with Phil Napoleon's Memphis Five and dozens of other jazz greats during the past nineteen years. He has also fronted his own groups at the Metropole and the Gaslight Club, both in New York City.

Sol Yaged

On 15 July 1977, Zane Knauss interviewed Sol Yaged in Yaged's
fourth floor apartment on West 56th Street in New York. Typically,
Yaged had played the night before in an Eastside jazz club, had
spent the noon hours listening to another clarinetist, Johnny Mince, at
The Drake and, between Knauss' questions, was warming up for a
big-band job that night in the Bronx. When the interview was over,
Yaged startled passersby on 56th Street by leaning out his apartment
window and blowing a clarinet farewell to the interviewer.

*Conversations: Everybody who's into music in New York tells me
you're about the busiest musician around. You constantly find
places to play with your group in clubs around the city. How do
you stay so busy?*

Yaged: I just happen to be fortunate to be working in New York
City most of my life. We try to play things to make people happy,
and we enjoy what we're playing. We just happen to be hitting it
right. We go from one club to another club—like one time we
were at the Metropole for nine years. The only interruption I had
was when I went out to the West Coast to make the Benny
Goodman picture with Steve Allen. We left for about three
months at that time. But for nine years we were like the house
band at the Metropole on Seventh Avenue and 48th Street. We
played opposite some of the greatest bands—Henry "Red"
Allen, Charlie Shavers, Lionel Hampton, Buddy Rich, Red Norvo,
Woody Herman's band.

Conversations: You had Ray Nance in your group, didn't you?

Yaged: Right, I had Ray Nance. Well, that came later. I had Ray
Nance with me at the New York Gaslight Club where I was for ten
years. That's another story: we went in there for two weeks; we
stayed there ten years—unbelievable. And I was always doing

other jazz concerts. In fact, there was a time when I was working seven nights a week and five or six afternoons in various places in and around New York.

Conversations: At the Metropole, the music started at noon. When did you come on?

Yaged: I would start at night with the big bands; I would come out about eight o'clock. In the afternoon, they would have a couple of trios, like Louis Metcalf, trumpet player, and Tony Parenti. Then we'd come on in the evening with my band. Then we'd have either Henry "Red" Allen, or Charlie Shavers, or Roy Eldridge, or they'd bring in a big band for a week or two, like Lionel Hampton or Woody Herman. In fact, they even had Stan Kenton playing there one time. Unbelievable. Yes, they had them all.

Conversations: When Jimmy Ryan's and all the other jazz clubs—Downbeat and everything else—were on 52nd Street in the forties, what was the climate? Was it an exciting place to play?

Yaged: Oh, yes, quite, to me. I was very young at that time. I was very thrilled to get up on a bandstand with people like Sidney Bechet.

Conversations: Did you play with Bechet?

Yaged: Oh, yes. I played on the same stage with Sidney Bechet, Edmond Hall, and Pee Wee Russell. And, let me see, also we had Kansas Fields on drums.

Conversations: What was it like at Nick's and Eddie Condon's during the forties? What kind of a guy was Condon?

Yaged: Well, I don't know too much about him. He had his own little clique. In fact, those who worked at Nick's very seldom worked at Eddie Condon's, believe it or not, and those that worked at Eddie Condon's didn't work that often at Nick's. They were like different camps. Phil Napoleon was at Nick's for a long time and he never worked Eddie Condon's.

Conversations: Well, what was this—bad blood or feuding?

Yaged: No. They were just like different camps, you know—like

264

the Republican Party and Democratic Party—two different camps.

Conversations: And you played with Phil Napoleon, didn't you?

Yaged: Oh, yes. I worked with Phil Napoleon for years. In fact, I went out of town a couple of times with Phil. We went for a couple of weeks to Boston and we played a beautiful place out there called the Savoy, on Massachusetts Avenue. And we had a hell of a band—we had Marty Napoleon on piano; we had Tony Spargo on drums; we had Andy Russo on trombone, a great jazz trombonist. And then I went out of town a few times with Max Kaminsky and Jimmy McPartland.

Conversations: How did you break into jazz? Can you remember the first time that you were ever on a stage?

Yaged: The first time I ever sat in, I had my Army uniform on. A very dear friend of mine, Hot Lips Page, invited me up on the bandstand at Jimmy Ryan's. I'll never forget that. He didn't even know who I was, but he saw a young kid with a clarinet, and I had my uniform on. He asked me if I'd like to sit in. And I said yes. He was very kind to me for many years, Lips Page, and that's how I actually got the job playing there with Danny Alvin and Hank Duncan as a member of a trio.

Conversations: Through Page?

Yaged: Right. I took Mezz Mezzrow's place.

Conversations: And this was your big break, then?

Yaged: Right, in 1945. Mezz Mezzrow had been at Jimmy Ryan's for quite a length of time. They wanted to make a switch, and they asked me to come in for a couple of weeks as a sideman with Danny Alvin's trio. Hank Duncan and myself came in for two weeks, and we stayed one year. I sure learned a lot playing at that time. Then I went to the Village around 1948, '49. I played the Village Vanguard, the Little Casino, and a place called the Swing Rendezvous.

Conversations: How did you end up with Napoleon?

Yaged: Well, I think I sat in one night with Phil Napoleon, and he needed a clarinet player to go out of town with him one time. In

265

Sol Yaged

fact, we did a weekend at Cherry Point—that's a Marine base. He asked me if I wanted to do a weekend with him, which consisted of a Friday and a Saturday night. So I traveled with his band, and that's how I got the job playing with Phil Napoleon and His Memphis Five.

Conversations: How did you happen to get Ray Nance in your group?

Yaged: Oh, that's a good story. Ray Nance came up to see me one night at the Gaslight Club, and he happened to have had his violin with him, not his trumpet. He asked me if he could sit in with us. I said, "I'll be more than honored"; I was very flattered. I knew Ray Nance for many years with Duke Ellington's band. And he sat in with us and the manager happened to be in the room when he sat in. He asked me if I would like to make an addition to the group. Now at that time, when Ray sat in with me, I only had a trio. Then we added Ray Nance and we made a quartet. He stayed with me for about five years. He played cornet and violin; he sang and danced. In fact, on one of my albums he sang a song called "Nagasaki"—and "Hot Ginger and Dynamite."

Conversations: Your only instrument is clarinet, isn't it?

Yaged: Clarinet, right.

Conversations: Did you begin studying the clarinet to become a classical musician?

Yaged: Right. I was supposed to go once with the Buffalo Philharmonic Orchestra, conducted by William Steinberg. In order for me to work with them, I'd have had to move to Buffalo, and we didn't want to move out of New York at that time.

Conversations: Did you study clarinet in Manhattan?

Yaged: I studied clarinet in New York City with a teacher named Simeon Bellison. Simeon Bellison was the first clarinetist of the New York Philharmonic for over thirty years. When I was studying with him, around 1947, Benny Goodman was taking lessons with him at the same time. We both traveled to Walton Avenue in the Bronx to take our lessons. I was living in Brooklyn then—it took me two hours to go up there by subway and trolley car.

Sol Yaged

Conversations: I studied a little clarinet, and my teacher, who was the principal clarinetist of the Pittsburgh Symphony, simply wouldn't tolerate jazz. How did you get away with jazz in your studies?

Yaged: Right. How did you know about that? My teacher was the same way: if he knew you played saxophone, he wouldn't teach you. The only reason he taught Benny Goodman was that he knew that Benny Goodman was studying to do some concerts with various classical groups. He was also studying with Bellison, my teacher, to do a couple of records with the Budapest String Quartet at that time.

In any case, he didn't know too much about me. At that time, I had just gotten out of the Army. He didn't know if I was going to play with the Buffalo Philharmonic or be playing at Jimmy Ryan's—a jazz concert.

Conversations: You sound very much like Goodman. Is that deliberate?

Yaged: No, just the way I felt—everybody asks me that. I'm not trying to copy anybody. I mean, I idolized him and I still do—as I said, he's the world's greatest; there will never be another Benny Goodman. I just happened to like his style and the way he swings. He has an exceptional vibrato—he's always had that. His was, I thought, the correct way. I mean, when he played, he played the clarinet the way a clarinet should sound. He never played too high; he always played in the middle register, and he made it sound perfect.

He's been my idol all these years—he still is. My favorite story is that if it were not for Benny Goodman, I'd be a juvenile delinquent. I'm being very serious about that. No one could play like him. Nobody will ever come close to any of the things he has ever done musically—with jazz, with big bands, with classical music. I mean, when Benny Goodman recorded *Constrasts* for clarinet by Bela Bartok in 1939, Benny Goodman was also playing at the Paramount Theatre, and things like that. This was unbelievable: Benny Goodman, the King of Swing, playing with the Budapest String Quartet and playing Bela Bartok with Joseph Szigeti. I mean, it was just something phenomenal. When I first heard him was in 1935, and that's when I first started to play

Sol Yaged

clarinet—I was about twelve years old. When I first heard his clarinet, it sounded like electricity.

Conversations: Where did you hear it?

Yaged: It was on a radio program. I think it was NBC, one of those National Biscuit Company shows.

Conversations: And you were living in Brooklyn then?

Yaged: Yes. I was living in Brooklyn—on Coney Island at that time. My dad bought me a clarinet and I started studying with a local teacher, who was actually a student of Simeon Bellison. After going to him about a year or two, he suggested that I go to the master. And Simeon Bellison was like another chapter; it was unbelievable. He taught people such as clarinet players with the Los Angeles Philharmonic, the Louisville Symphony Orchestra, and the Dallas Symphony Orchestra—he taught a phenomenal number of clarinet players who themselves were soloists and teachers. He was a specialist. The man was playing clarinet up till about eighty years old—this was unbelievable. He was from Russia, from the old school. He played a half Boehm and a half Albert system clarinet—a very unusual thing. Some clarinet players still play Albert system today.

Conversations: What do you play?

Yaged: I play the Boehm system.

Conversations: Goodman switched, didn't he?

Yaged: Right. Benny, I assume, originally when he was a young man, was playing the Albert system, too.

Conversations: As I understand it, Goodman even had to shave off the calluses on his fingers when he was changing systems.

Yaged: Well, there are little stories about that—he had to get rid of the calluses on his fingers, and he had a couple of calluses on his thumb. You know, you always hear those different stories.

Conversations: The tone you get is very big. Is that a product of the teaching, or is it something that any clarinetist could cultivate?

Yaged: It just takes a lot of practice. It's something you have to give a lot of time to—practice and practice, you know.

Conversations: Has your reputation as a Goodman sound-alike been an impediment to your career?

Yaged: Well, some people say that it has been. They say I've been living in Benny Goodman's shadow too long, and that's why, actually, I am the way I am, or where I am. But I don't know— who knows? It's just something I've had since I was first learning how to play clarinet, and I'm very much inspired by him. I have records of him I first heard thirty-five, forty years ago, and I still enjoy them today.

Conversations: Did you have any personal association with him?

Yaged: Well, every once in awhile, you know, we see each other. You know, he speaks to me—he says hello.

Conversations: Never comes to hear you play?

Yaged: Well, he came once. He came to the Gaslight Club. I got scared to death. I was playing on the stage and he walked in by himself. I couldn't believe it. As he walked in, I was playing a song called "Stompin' at the Savoy." He was very nice.

Conversations: Did you have a quartet?

Yaged: Well, nobody ever had his kind of quartet, but I had a pretty good quartet. They were swinging. At that time, I only had a rhythm section: I had drums, piano, bass, and clarinet. When I have the vibes, that becomes a quintet.

Conversations: When you're improvising or when you're playing things which essentially belong to the Goodman era, are you tempted to play the same type of solo—even the same solo note-for-note as Goodman plays? Or do you try to come up with some things of your own?

Yaged: I try to play my own solos. A lot of people have said, "Sol, you know, you've still got your own style." This is fine, you know, whatever it is. The main thing is I like to get a good tone; I like to get a good sound; I like to swing; I love to play the melody. Like Benny Goodman once said—I'll always remember that—"That's the most difficult thing to play, a melody."

Conversations: Is it?

Yaged: Oh, yes. We try to play a correct melody and make it swing and make it sound. That's why Benny was so great on ballads. He could play a melody like "Smoke Gets In Your Eyes" or "The Man I Love" and make it really sound musical. I enjoy it; it's like a challenge. Anybody could play loud and fast, believe me. You know the old saying: When in doubt, play chromatic. You've got to hit a right note coming down or going up. But to play melody, or ballads, that's difficult—to play the right notes and, you know, just get the phrasing.

Conversations: It must be more difficult to embellish on a ballad?

Yaged: Oh, yes. Right. And that's why I love Benny. I mean, everybody knew Benny was a swing man, but I got a big kick out of hearing him play a song like "On the Alamo," or "Embraceable You," or "If I Had You." I mean, here's an ordinary melody in a ballad, and he knew how to just play around it and make that thing swing. He was something else, and I heard them all. I was next to every clarinet player that was ever alive; you mention them.

Conversations: The clarinet is basically the same instrument in the hands of every musician. So how do you account for the wide variety of sounds that different musicians get?

Yaged: Probably the reed—and the feeling. Everybody has his own feeling, you know. I mean, a man like, for example, Artie Shaw, whom I've always respected and admired, would play "Moon Glow" one way, and Benny Goodman would play it another way. Benny Goodman may play ten notes, while Artie Shaw may play thirty notes. And a guy like Buddy De Franco may play fifty notes. But it's what a person feels, you know.

Conversations: Do you have to practice during the day?

Yaged: I play every day; I really do. I actually cannot let one day go by. I mean, it's like being an athlete: you have to keep in shape all the time.

Conversations: So what do you do?

Yaged: I play scales; I play exercises; I just play certain things to limber up. I mean, if a man like Vladimir Horowitz, or Artur Rubinstein, or Jascha Heifetz, or any classical musician who's been playing fifty, sixty years or more could still get to a concert hall a couple of hours before the concert time and warm up and rehearse and practice and get themselves together, there's no reason why a jazz musician shouldn't do that also. I know that some of the greatest legitimate musicians still practice and get together.

Conversations: What's the maintenance on a clarinet with the workout that you give it?

Yaged: Once a week I take it in just to get an adjustment of the clarinet; to check it out; see if I need any pads or any corks; if there are any leaks. And sometimes all the man has to do is adjust the key. But he checks it out for me thoroughly, knowing that I give the clarinet a good workout.

Conversations: What was your role in The Benny Goodman Story?

Yaged: Well, they gave me sort of a fancy title—they called me a technical adviser. I had a great relationship with Steve Allen. In fact, before I went out with Steve to the Coast, I taught him for three months in New York City.

Conversations: To play the clarinet?

Yaged: Yes. I taught him for three months in New York. I went up to his apartment once a week on Park Avenue. And he had to learn exactly, right from the beginning. I even had to teach him how to open up the clarinet case without the clarinet falling out—little things like that are important.

Conversations: You mean he had never played a clarinet?

Yaged: No. If you open up a clarinet case the wrong way, the clarinet is going to fall out. He did that a couple of times—it even

271

happens to me today. Then I had to teach him how to put the instrument together, and show him where the reed fits into the mouthpiece. In a matter of two or three months, he picked up a tremendous amount. In fact, we made quite a few things together with two clarinets. He wrote a song called "Blues for Two Clarinets," which I played on his television show many a time.

Conversations: But you didn't cut the sound track, did you?

Yaged: No. Benny Goodman cut his own sound track.

Conversations: But that's the only time you've ever been out of New York?

Yaged: No. I may have gone out to Philadelphia for a week; I may have gone out to Pittsburgh for a couple of days; I may have gone to Florida for a weekend; but I've never gone on the road, as some of the other people have. I've been pretty fortunate in that respect.

Conversations: Is there a reason for this?

Yaged: Well, I've just been, as I said, pretty fortunate to be working in New York City all this time.

Conversations: You don't like to go out on the road?

Yaged: No, it isn't necessary. You ask any good entertainer: they say there's nothing like working in New York—the Big Apple they call it. I'm talking about people that work in Las Vegas, New Orleans, California, and Chicago. They say it's something about working for people in New York City or in New York clubs and hotels. They call it being cosmopolitan. Just like me working at the Gaslight Club for ten years and the Metropole for nine: you meet people from all over the world—it's unbelievable. Who comes to New York but people from Europe, people from the West Coast, and people from the Far East? I have a lot of fans, if you don't mind me saying, from Japan.

Conversations: Really?

Yaged: Oh, yes. They're the big lovers of jazz music.

Conversations: Do you think you'll ever go to Japan?

Yaged: I'd like to go there someday very much. They love music.

Conversations: Did you do any studio work in New York?

Yaged: Yes. I did studio work for a while. Like I did work for ABC and CBS. They used me on special shows, and I've done quite a few television shows. We once did an April Fool's TV show: it was supposed to be the Benny Goodman trio, but they had me on clarinet with a pair of glasses, and they made a blackface out of Joe Bushkin, the piano player. We had Buddy Rich on drums, and they put a wig on him to look like Gene Krupa. That was a great show.

I've also worked with Lionel Hampton. In fact, I just did a show about a year ago called "CBS Cavalcade" where we had Lionel Hampton on the show, Count Basie's band, Gerry Mulligan, Stan Getz, Dizzy Gillespie, and Joe Williams. We had like twenty or twenty-five—Dave Brubeck was on the show. It was a tremendous jazz show on TV. I've done a lot of radio shows, too.

Conversations: Where do you find the musicians for your bands?

Yaged: Well, I'm always looking for new musicians. It's always good to hear a new singer or a new instrumentalist. Sometimes I go to different places like Jazz at Noon, Jimmy Ryan's, or different clubs; I'll hear somebody singing or playing an instrument, and I'll ask him to come in and join me.

Conversations: You're your own contractor, then, too?

Yaged: Right. Surely. Definitely.

Conversations: Do you have to have agents to get all of this work that you have around town?

Yaged: I have some agents working for me, but a lot of my jobs are booked directly. People call my home. I have a mailing list of over 20,000 names accumulated in all the years I've been playing—people that like music, and people that enjoy my music and like jazz, Dixieland, and swing. In all the years I've been playing, since 1945, I've been saving these names.

Conversations: Then in order to stay in business the way you do, you have to build your own company and do your own promotions?

Sol Yaged

Yaged: Oh, definitely. That's what they say—I'm my own PR man. I have a mailing list; I write to people constantly; I correspond with people. And I let people know where I'm playing and what I'm doing. I'm always writing to people, contacting people.

Conversations: *And this pays off?*

Yaged: Well, yes, in the long run. Most people do come down to see me and people want to know where I'm performing.

Conversations: *Is this a selling item to the clubs that book you?*

Yaged: Well, it is a good selling point. In other words, people ask about me, and I say, "We also have a mailing list of thousands of people." They usually have some cards printed up with some publicity, like we did at the Steak Row.

Conversations: *But you do that yourself?*

Yaged: No. Usually the clubs do that. And they print up all these different cards, like the Pan American made up 5000 cards. All we do is just put down the name and address and shoot them right out to the people. This is definitely a business to me. I'm not kidding around; I'm very serious about this.

Conversations: *You're also rather gregarious at your jobs; you go and shake hands with people at the tables; you pass out cards—*

Yaged: I'm very serious about this. We always play as if we had a full house. I mean, I play every job like it's an important job to me.

Conversations: *When you play in a small group, do you have to adjust your style depending on the leader?*

Yaged: No. Not quite, no. I mean, everybody will have their own arrangement of the "Muskrat Ramble" or a song like "That's a Plenty." They'll want a certain thing. Now, for example, getting back to Phil Napoleon, whom I enjoyed working with—he was a very, very disciplined leader, and every note had to be a certain way.

Conversations: *Did you rehearse?*

274

Yaged: Oh, yeah, we rehearsed. In fact, I'll never forget one song called "The Clarinet Marmalade." He made me play the break in the clarinet like a guy named Larry Shields from New Orleans. I had to just play the clarinet break note-for-note, the way it was originally done about fifty years ago.

Conversations: What did you have to do, listen to it on record?

Yaged: Well, Phil sang it to me or he gave me an idea, but I had a good idea of what Shields sounded like. And Phil wanted that clarinet break like "da-da-da-da-da," you know, one of those old-time breaks. He was that sort of man to work for, Phil Napoleon; he wanted every note to be just right.

Conversations: Let's take, for example, "Muskrat Ramble"; you're with Napoleon. Now what happens? Do you get together before a job and decide how it's going to be played?

Yaged: No, no, we get together on a job. But for "Muskrat Ramble" every band will have a different tempo. I don't know if you've ever heard Louis Armstrong play that. He plays it so slow it sounds like a blues. But that was his style: "bump-ba-dump bump-ba-dump do da ba ba." And then other bands would play it like they were playing "I Got Rhythm."

Conversations: What's the role, then, of the clarinetist?

Yaged: You mean when I'm working for another leader?

Conversations: Yeah.

Yaged: Well, my role is to support him and play good, to back him up and make his band sound good. I usually play the harmony.

Conversations: How much latitude does a clarinetist have in a Dixieland band?

Yaged: Well, you have to stay pretty close, because you have a trombone player, too, and you both can't be playing the same notes. I tell musicians when they join my band that the two most important things in playing music are to listen and to pay attention. That is very important: to listen and pay attention to what's going on. Now, if you're listening, you can hear if the band is playing loud or soft. Now, if they're going to be playing a figure that's soft, and you're going to play loud, you're going to stick out like a sore thumb—you're in a trouble. If the leader is going to point to you to play a solo, but you're looking at a couple dancing on the floor and don't pick up the cue, you're in trouble.

You've got to be very attentive; that's important. It's like a manager of a ball team telling the fellows on the ball team what to do and what not do to. You've got to be prepared for any eventuality. If a man's playing center field with a baseball team, and he knows the fellow up there is not a good hitter, that doesn't mean he's not going to be attentive. This guy could just be lucky today and hit that ball. If the fielder isn't ready for it, he's going to be in trouble.

Conversations: Does a leader sense when a musician is up and give him solos?

Yaged: I think so; I think so. For instance, Jimmy McPartland always likes to hear somebody play well. If he's doing a good job for his band and the audience likes him, there's a good reaction and Jimmy lets him go. Oh, he never holds anybody back—not Jimmy. Jimmy McPartland is one of the greatest.

Conversations: Have you run into other leaders who stomped on you?

Yaged: Oh, yes. I've worked with bandleaders who, as soon as you got a hand, would cut you down from two choruses to one chorus. And if you got too much of a hand, they would cut you down to half a chorus. Oh, yeah, I've seen that happen.

Conversations: How much of a repertory do you have to have to work as frequently as you do?

Yaged: We have about 500 arrangements. All head arrangements, believe it or not. I think my group could play an evening of four, five, or six hours without repeating a song. We've gone through a whole evening—we've gone through a week without repeating a song. I'd say we're good for close to 800 songs.

Conversations: What is your forte? Is it basically nostalgia for the Goodman sound?

Yaged: Yes. Swing music, right. The music that came up in the early thirties, late thirties, and early forties.

Conversations: Are you forced to explore modern develop-ments? For example, have you thought about wiring up your clarinet?

Yaged: Never did, no. I don't like anything with electronics. I don't like anything regarding rock 'n' roll or anything that's too loud. In fact, I enjoy a band better without any microphones. You get a natural sound, sure. Some of the greatest singers, Enrico Caruso, for example, used to sing in concert halls without microphones. A great performer doesn't actually need a microphone.

Conversations: Have you ever done big-band work as a section man—not as a soloist?

Yaged: No, I never did, because I didn't play saxophones.

Conversations: You don't double at all?

Yaged: No, I don't double.

Conversations: Did you ever think about it?

Yaged: Never did, no. I just devote all of my time to clarinet, knowing that there's a lot of work entailed in a clarinet.

Conversations: Do you regret that you haven't been able to front a big band?

Yaged: Yes. That's one of my ambitions someday.

Conversations: Occasionally you put together a big band, don't you?

Yaged: Well, actually I don't put it together. Somebody puts it together for me. They'll have their own band, and I'll just be a guest with their big bands. Like, for example, I'm doing a concert this evening at the Marina Del Ray, and we do two concerts a year with them. I'll be playing with Hal Hoffman's big band—I'm a guest with them.

Conversations: Will you work from charts?

Sol Yaged

Yaged: Right. They have arrangements of "The Jersey Bounce" and "Undecided" and "One O'Clock Jump" and "Don't Be That Way." And we have "Begin the Beguine," and a couple of things by Glenn Miller. And I just about know where to come in with a clarinet solo. A lot of solos that were given originally to a piano player or a trombone, they delete, and insert the clarinet in that part. We'll do "String of Pearls" tonight. All the solos, I assume, I'll take.

Conversations: Do you enjoy that work?

Yaged: Oh, yes. I enjoy it because it's a very, very easy feeling, playing with a big band. It's like floating on air, if the band is right. Because when you're playing with a small group, you'll have to fill in all the empty spots yourself. While the big bands are playing all the different figures in the background, all you have to do is just play a little blip and blop and blip here, little notes here and there. You don't have to play too much. I don't like to play too many notes as a start.

Conversations: Is the time gone when you'll be able to put together your own band?

Yaged: No, nothing has gone. No, no, no. Nothing is ever gone. It may happen tomorrow; it may happen next week; it may happen next month. But there will be a time when I will get a call to get my own band.

Conversations: Do you do any composing at all?

Yaged: No, no, no. I may do some head arrangements, which I've done for my band all these years. Maybe someday I'll have somebody put them down on paper for me.

Conversations: What would you recommend to someone who is interested in jazz? Should they follow the way you've gone, or would you recommend a different direction?

Yaged: Well, I'd recommend that they go the way they want to go, you know. To be an entertainer, or a dancer, or a singer, or any kind of an artist—I don't think anyone could be forced into it. I mean, a person has to have it in them. You know, in the old school, they said the mother used to make the child practice and stay home. You shouldn't force anybody to practice against their

278

will. If they want to play four, five, six, seven, eight hours a day, and enjoy playing, or dancing, or singing, or doing art—that's a different thing.

Conversations: Have you done any teaching?

Yaged: Well, I used to teach clarinet years ago—oh, I'm going back about fifteen years ago, twenty years ago. I used to have quite a few students. But then I got to the point where I felt, "Gee, I need to practice myself; I need a teacher myself," and I discontinued teaching, and I just began devoting all that time to myself.

Conversations: Can you teach jazz at all?

Yaged: That, I've never taught anybody.

Conversations: What did you teach?

Yaged: Just how to play the scale. I always try to teach the other students like I taught Steve Allen. That's how I got my reputation. When people found out that I taught Steve Allen the clarinet for *The Benny Goodman Story*, I got phone calls: "Teach my son"; "Teach my daughter." I taught people in their fifties that wanted to take up the clarinet, and I would teach them. I had politicians as students; I had writers of *The New York Times* and *Variety*, and people who are connected with the police department, fire department. I had everybody learning how to play clarinet at one time. Everybody wanted to play it.

Conversations: Over the years, jazz has been associated somewhat with black people. Some say that's not accurate, that jazz is sort of a potpourri of the whole American experience. What's your notion about this? Your roots are Polish.

Yaged: Well, my parents are from Poland, but I'm from Brooklyn, New York. There are some good musicians and bad musicians of every sort. I mean, I assume in Count Basie's band and Duke Ellington's band there were some fine musicians, and, I assume, a lot of musicians who weren't that good, but were covered up by a twenty-piece band. When you're playing with five saxophones and seven brass, there's a lot of covering up. When you play with a trio, or a quartet, you have to be a little more outstanding. But when you're playing with a big band, you could

279

be a mediocre bass player or a mediocre guitar player and still get covered up by the rest of the band which is carrying you.

Conversations: How would you rate the clarinetists of your day?

Yaged: I can't do a thing like that, because they were all great in their own right, believe me. I mean, I worked alongside of people like Buster Bailey and Edmond Hall.

Conversations: What did Hall bring to the clarinet?

Yaged: Edmond Hall was one of the clarinet players whom Benny admired for many years. Benny Goodman always spoke about Edmond Hall. He thought of him as a very exciting clarinet player, and he enjoyed his style. Benny Goodman enjoyed Pee Wee Russell, just like I do—they all had their own styles.

And there was another bandleader called Tommy Reynolds. Then there was another bandleader, "Rudy Bundy and His Sizzling Clarinet." He had a hotel band that worked out of Florida and the band sounded like Benny Goodman's band. He had, like, three saxes, four brass, and he had a very, very distinct style playing the clarinet. He used to triple tongue a clarinet, which was unbelievable.

Conversations: You've been around for quite a few years. Who were the strongest sidemen that you worked with?

Yaged: My biggest inspiration was working and sitting in and being allowed to play with Lionel Hampton. He has always been very kind to me. He always invites me up to sit in with his band. I've also played many times with Harry James's big band, but Lionel Hampton is something else. Very inspiring.

Conversations: Where did you meet him?

Yaged: Well, he knew me from being connected with Benny Goodman. I go back with Lionel for many years—we've known each other over twenty-five years. Great, great musician. Whenever he's in town, I go to see him. He's been up to see me many times. He sat in with me—even if I didn't have vibraphones; he played drums. One night Lionel Hampton came into the Gaslight Club, the same night that Cab Calloway happened to come in with a party of people, and Cab came up on the stage and sang "St. James Infirmary Blues." We had a hell of a show.

Conversations: Was Hampton on drums or vibes?

Yaged: No, no. We didn't have any vibes then. We had drums, bass, and piano. He sat in on drums. Oh, it was a hell of a session. We were up there for nearly two hours.

Conversations: How old are you now?

Yaged: Gee, that's a good question. I was born in December 1922; what would that make me?—fifty-five next December.

Conversations: How long are you going to play?

Yaged: Oh, I'm going to go on until I can't play anymore. And if I can't stand, I'll be sitting down—still playing, I hope.